Finding the Muse explores of the lives of a group of aspiring fine artists from the mid-1960s, when they completed art school, to the mid-1980s, focusing especially on problems of artistic creativity as they relate to such issues as the mystique of the artist, the challenge of establishing community among artists, the place of the art market in the construction of artistic identity, and the limits and possibilities of modern and postmodern art itself. By identifying salient problems of contemporary artistic activity, Mark Freeman seeks both to reconstruct more optimal conditions of creativity and to provide direction for how these conditions might be achieved.

Finding the muse

Finding the muse

A sociopsychological inquiry
into the conditions of artistic creativity

MARK FREEMAN

College of the Holy Cross
Worcester, Massachusetts

CAMBRIDGE
UNIVERSITY PRESS

Published by the Press Syndicate of the University of Cambridge
The Pitt Building, Trumpington Street, Cambridge CB2 1RP
40 West 20th Street, New York, NY 10011–4211, USA
10 Stamford Road, Oakleigh, Melbourne 3166, Australia

First published 1993

Printed in the United States of America

Library of Congress Cataloging-in-Publication Data
Freeman, Mark Philip, 1955–
Finding the muse : a sociopsychological inquiry into the
conditions of artistic creativity / Mark Freeman.
p.   cm.
Includes bibliographical references and index.
ISBN 0-521-39218-7
1. Artists – United States – Psychology. 2. Creativity in art.
3. Art and society – United States. I. Title.
N71.f655   1993
709′.73′90946 – dc20   93-3468
CIP

A catalog record for this book is available from the British Library.

ISBN 0-521-39218-7 HARDBACK

Contents

Acknowledgments

This book, which began as a doctoral dissertation at the University of Chicago (all too long ago), is the product of many influences. First and foremost among these are Mihaly Csikszentmihalyi and Jacob W. Getzels, who, as mentors, colleagues, and friends, provided exactly that sort of guidance and care one hopes for. I am extremely grateful for all they have been and done through the years. I also wish to thank a number of others at the University of Chicago without whom this work would not have been possible. Among the faculty, this includes Bert Cohler, Ray Fogelson, Peter Homans, Paul Ricoeur, and Marvin Zonis. Among my fellow graduate students, each of whom were participants in the research project from which the present work emerged, I wish to thank Steve Kahn especially, whose leadership kept the project going, along with Pat Lorek, Jeanne Nakamura, Rick Robinson, Daniel Schouela, and the many others with whom I had the pleasure of working.

At Holy Cross, where I presently teach, I wish to thank the members of the Psychology Department, particularly Chick Weiss, whom I frequently subjected to my latest ideas; Stephen Ainlay and Vicki Swigert, friends from the Sociology Department; the Philosophy Reading Group; and those members of the Visual Arts Department with whom I have had useful discussions regarding the trials and tribulations of contemporary art and artists. Last but certainly not least, I want to acknowledge my students at Holy Cross, particularly those in the First Year Program, who have stimulated my thinking about the issues addressed in this book more than they probably know.

Acknowledgments

As concerns scholars in the area of art and creativity, special thanks are to be given to Margery Franklin and Bernard Kaplan, whose support of my work has been of great value; Suzi Gablik, whom I've never met but who has become an important influence on my thinking about the limits and possibilities of modern art; Louis Sass, who is something of a fellow traveler in this arena of ideas; and the many researchers and theorists of art and creativity whose ideas have found their way into this work.

As concerns those without whom this book literally could not have been written, I wish to thank the Spencer and Mac-Arthur Foundations, who supported the Artists Project; the School of the Art Institute of Chicago; my editor at Cambridge, Julia Hough, who has been wonderfully patient and supportive during the past few years; the various reviewers for Cambridge, whose incisive critical comments helped me immeasurably in my efforts; and, perhaps most importantly, the many artists who were kind enough to speak with us about their lives and work. Indeed, I wish not only to thank these people but to dedicate the book to them, in the hope that what has been said here is of value to them and to those other artists who will follow in their footsteps.

Finally, I want to thank my family. To all of you, immediate and otherwise, please know the depth of my gratitude and love.

Chapter 1

Social reality and the space of creativity

INTRODUCTION

This book grows out of an abiding fascination with three distinct, yet interrelated, spheres of human experience. The first and broadest of these spheres has to do with the interpretive study of lives, specifically the narratives people tell about who they have been, who they are, and what they have done across the course of time. This is not to say that my interest here is purely retrospective, in the sense of focusing on the "storied" dimension of experience alone, for the stories people tell about themselves often contain revealing information about their own courses of development as well and how these have variously been enhanced or impeded by the social worlds through which they have moved. In this respect, inquiring into life histories can be of service in exploring not only the psychological realm but, in addition, the social, the cultural, and the historical. Indeed, a primary contention of this work is that there is no separating these realms from one another, except perhaps for analytic purposes: A human life, insofar as it exists *in* society, culture, and history, cannot help but tell us about the mode of its construction, about the complex interplay of influences responsible in significant part for its very shape.

The second sphere of interest is the psychology of art and creativity. In certain important respects, this second sphere grows directly out of the first, particularly if creativity, broadly conceptualized, is seen as a subspecies of the developmental process more generally. Framed another way, the study of

1

creativity, to the extent that it is situated in the concrete lives of individual creators rather than the artificial setting of the laboratory, is at the same time about the study of development; it is about how human beings move forward to what can arguably be considered more ideal modes of experiencing the world, thinking about it, and acting in it. From this connection, it follows that the study of creativity is of necessity every bit as much *about* society, culture, and history as the study of development is. As such, even though some might speak about creativity as if it were a strictly individual affair, taking place in the so-called cognitive apparatus of the sovereign thinker, there will be ample reason offered in the pages to come to show that doing so is insufficient.

The third sphere of interest concerns "social reality" – this dynamic interrelationship of society, culture, and history itself, as it pertains to both human development in general and creativity in particular. In my own attempt to make sense of what artists have told me and my colleagues about their own art and creativity, I have found that one must inquire deeply into the social reality they have inhabited in the course of becoming who and what they are, including especially the specific art worlds of which they have been a part. Indeed, one cannot possibly understand artistic creativity – again, in its real life manifestations, at this point in historical time – without knowing something about extant myths and images of art and artists, about the market, the art community, critics, dealers, collectors, and, last but not least, the domain of contemporary art itself.

My aim in this book, I hasten to emphasize, is not merely to assert *that* creativity is socioculturally constituted, which by this time is obvious enough to many, but to show, as concretely as possible, *how* it is – that is, to begin to articulate the *conditions* of creativity and, by extension, the conditions of artistic development. As Feldman (1988, p. 282) has noted, "Asserting that natural talents and personal qualities are not sufficient to account for development, prodigious or not, is of value only if something new about these forces and their manner of interacting is discovered." Without this something new, assertions of

2

this sort will not only be empty, giving way to the usual abstract models; they will more than likely serve to advance ideological convictions of one sort or another as well.

Two qualifications are in order. As Hennessey and Amabile (1988) note in their own experimental work on the conditions of creativity, there is no denying that "personal qualities of ability and personality" often exert a considerable influence on creativity. Any model of creativity that aspires to be complete will therefore have to take into account both internal and external factors. I nonetheless want to make it clear that my own treatment of internal factors will be tied not so much to those qualities, abilities, traits, and so on often assumed to be "natural" – including, for instance, innate (predispositions to) talent – but to those aspects of social reality that have become *internalized*, woven into the very fabric of subjectivity. Thus, even though essentially individual conditions of creativity must enter into any complete equation, they will not be the primary focus of the present study.

The second qualification is that my discussion of the conditions of creativity is limited mainly to how they have applied in recent years. Clearly, the conditions of creativity, like creativity itself, *change* over the course of time, in line with how human subjectivity is constituted and understood, how development is, how art is, and so on. Far from seeking to articulate the conditions of creativity for all time, therefore – which would in turn require a constant human subject, a constant conception of development, and a constant conception of both art and creativity – the aim of the present work is the much more modest one of outlining these conditions here, in this society and this culture, and now, at this moment in history. If the significance of these conditions turns out to extend beyond the here and now, all the better.

FROM THE PSYCHOLOGY OF CREATIVITY TO THE SOCIOLOGY OF CULTURE

With regard to the basic methodological framework by which I attempt to carry out this study, it is perhaps most succinctly (if somewhat academically) considered to be one of "negative re-construction." By this I mean that I will be focusing on prob-lems or *pathologies* of creation and then working my way backward, to the more optimal conditions within which artistic activities might take place. In speaking of pathologies, I do not refer to creative blocks and the like or to the vast array of intra-psychic conflicts that prevent many artists from creating as freely as they might wish. Rather, pathologies of artistic cre-ation, as they are to be treated here, refer to the various ways in which individuals' actual or desired artistic activities may be thwarted, corrupted, or deformed as a function of the specific spheres of social reality in which they live and work, from the marketplace all the way to those forms of discourse and prac-tice associated with what has come to be known as "postmod-ernity." In sum, I am inquiring into the relationship between social reality and what I call the "space" of creativity, my fore-most aim being to determine how this space might become en-larged in line with certain transformations of social reality itself.

My rationale for adopting this methodological framework is twofold. For one – and I realize that in the wake of Freud this has become something of a methodological truism – there are some definite advantages to beginning an inquiry of this sort with pathologies and working backward. To take the example of Freud himself, he was surely not the sort of thinker who was given to making sweeping claims about the fundamental pur-pose of human existence; outside of the drive for pleasure (and, later on, the drive to die), there were few grand pronounce-ments about the ends of human development to be made. At the same time, he knew a good pathology when he saw one: However difficult it was to define precisely what psychological health was, what it was not was often painfully clear.

The second and more substantial reason for my adopting this methodological framework has to do with the fact that ac-tivities in the visual arts especially, as they have taken place over the course of the preceding 20 to 30 years, have abounded with pathologies. This, admittedly, came as something of a sur-prise to me, which is testimony to my own naïveté and igno-

4

rance, more than anything else, at the time of commencing this inquiry. My project then, which I was fortunate enough to undertake alongside Professor Csikszentmihalyi and Professor Getzels of the University of Chicago, was to study the developmental profiles of a group of aspiring painters and sculptors who began their careers in the mid-1960s after having attended the School of the Art Institute of Chicago. I was particularly interested in the ways in which artists perceived themselves to have "progressed" in their work during the time in question, whether there were any common patterns, and, if so, how they might be accounted for. An unusually rich store of life history information gathered during the early 1980s provided a wealth of material from which to draw.

Judging from much of what I had read about the particular period of time in question (the mid-1960s to the early 1980s), I also thought myself to be in the fortunate position of being able to witness the salutary effects of what some writers were claiming was a virtual renaissance in the making, the specifics of which will be addressed in greater detail later on. For the time being, suffice it to say that what had *appeared* to happen – and this is still the story told by some – was that sometime during the late 1950s and early 1960s, particularly with the advent of Abstract Expressionism, the situation of art had changed in such a way as to allow for a measure of artistic freedom and spontaneity that had been all but unknown in epochs past. In place of the countless fetters that had existed in years gone by, from the demands of bourgeois patrons all the way to primacy conferred upon representational art, there was now pluralism and difference, the ostensible result being that artists would be able to soar off in entirely new directions.

In addition to this pluralization of the art world and the expressive freedom that allegedly accrued from it, artists were seen to become more and more a part of "official" culture (Adler, 1979). As Calvin Tomkins (1976, p. 3) argued a number of years ago, somewhat tongue-in-cheek, "Artists were no longer isolated creatures forging private myths; they inherited and dominated an 'art world' – visible stars in a gaudy million dollar production with a supporting cast of . . . well, hundreds

5

anyway." The implication here is that the art world was not really as big or as grand as the images people had of it; in fact, it was ultimately quite small. Images aside, however, there were some very real changes going on. To present only a hint at the economic side of the rosy picture many seemed to want to paint, government support for the arts went from some 21 million dollars in 1965 to some 282 million dollars by 1975; and much of this support could be traced, it appeared, to the public's interest in the arts, which, "by every index," suggested a 1973 National Endowment for the Arts report, was growing in "spectacular terms." As the National Committee for Cultural Resources put the matter a couple of years later, in 1975, the arts were unquestionably a "growth industry," changing in new and exciting ways. "All of the evidence," they wrote, "points in one direction. There is no need to argue the case for the arts in this country. The people themselves are making that case" (p. 11). By all indications, the committee continued, "The individual creative and performing artist is the backbone of the culture of our time" (p. 19).

Perhaps in light of these kinds of sentiments, we can begin to understand some of the reasons why the population of actively working painters and sculptors went from some 130,000 in 1971 to nearly 200,000 in 1980 (National Endowment for the Arts, 1982); why, by 1982, there were some 14,000 artists with gallery affiliations in New York City alone; and why the art market in New York had by that time soared to a whopping total of approximately 2 billion dollars per year (1982 Summer Gallery Guide; cited in Gablik, 1984). Whether the art world was as grand as some imagined it to be or not, something was indeed happening. As Toffler was able to write in 1965, the initial steps toward the "democratization" of the arts were finally being taken. Standing "in antithesis to the standardization of contemporary life" (p. 63; see also Simpson [1981] for the idea of the arts being a "sacred profession in a secular society," an "antidote to rationalization," etc.), the "cultural explosion" in operation during the mid-1960s was best seen – contra skeptics and pessimists – as "the beginning . . . of something profound, colorful, and exciting" (p. 68). Offering a prediction that would seem to have been confirmed by some of the statistics just described, Toffler's contention was that the position of the arts would move "from the edge to the nucleus of national life" (p. 68). Of course, a danger was present in all this, he acknowledged: Capital and democratization went hand in hand. But lest we suppose that economic concerns could only serve as contaminants to the creation of art, a la Marx, Toffler insisted that "it would be a mistake to underestimate the importance of the genuinely interested individual in propelling business toward its increasing involvement with the arts" (p. 115). "Art," he concluded, "is more resilient than most of us imagine. And so is the artist. What is good for General Motors may conceivably be good for art" (p. 123). Toffler's main argument, therefore, was that capital, rather than automatically leading to alienation, as many on the left assumed, might be exactly what was needed to turn the fabled isolation of the artist into little more than a bad memory. Or, put another way, the main problem facing the artist was not capital per se; the problem was not *enough* capital. And there was some reason to believe that this problem, like a good many others, was in the midst of being solved.

It wasn't for nothing, then, that I had bought into the renaissance-in-the-making idea: With a newfound freedom, a hungry and receptive climate, and a progressively greater influx of capital, it appeared that many artists would have a field day creating new and exciting works. Well, to make a long story short, rather than hearing stories of development and progress on the part of the aspiring artists with whom we spoke, it proved much more likely that they would tell about their own artistic stagnation, about creative dead ends, even about their "regression" from the projects they had initially sought to undertake. And the main reasons, ironically enough, were bound up with just those allegedly salutary conditions to which I have referred. Despite the manifest pluralization of the art world, freedom was something of an illusion. Despite the manifest receptivity of the viewing public, many had become alienated from what they perceived to be the esoteric, private musings of people who were being supported in part by them. Despite the

7

influx of capital – or indeed because of it – the art world, the products in it, and the processes leading to these products were increasingly becoming commodified, as were artists themselves. The list goes on. The main thrust of the project I had planned to undertake therefore had to change: I would still study artistic development but by exploring its inverse – hence the present framework.

A recent comment made by Howard Gardner (1988) is appropriate in this context. Of special interest to socioculturally minded researchers and theorists of creativity, he notes, "will be those rare communities, institutions, or situations in which creativity seems to flower – which may range from a period of several generations in Florence to the ambit of a particular high school in Budapest or the Bronx. And by the same token," he adds, "it will be of interest to carry out studies of communities or schools in which high creativity might have been anticipated, but where, for reasons as yet undetermined, there were few, if any, creative individuals or creative products" (p. 315). Now, it would be stretching things severely to claim that "there were few, if any, creative individuals or creative products" over the span of time in question; it would be insulting and wrong. Moreover, I am not about to assert that every artist we studied had an awful time trying to create meaningful works of art; there were Sunday painters, people who were content creating work outside the market, others who were content confining themselves to their own local art scenes, and so on. Nevertheless, it seems fair to suggest that the efflorescence of creative activity that some had anticipated did not quite come to pass; many artists themselves, some of whom will be represented here, have said as much. Indeed, given that our interviews were not explicitly problem-oriented, it was that much more striking to learn just how difficult things had been for many of the people concerned. What we have before us, in any case, is something of a natural experiment, a dynamic concatenation of social, cultural, and historical factors that can allow us a measure of access into the conditions of creativity that might otherwise not have been possible.

I shall try my hardest not to be whiny about the perils of

8

modernity. Because I have chosen to deal mainly with negative rather than positive conditions of creativity, it would be unfair for me to offer a blanket indictment of some sort. Moreover, because recent works about the underside of modern life have been plentiful enough, adding another to the list would serve little purpose. Serious problems *do* exist and we know what many of them are. Rather than whining, then, I try to be constructively critical, a goal that is implicit in the project of negative reconstruction itself insofar as it aims toward imagining how the conditions of creativity might conceivably change for the better.

On the basis of what has been said thus far, it should be clear that this work is at the intersection of the psychology of art and creativity and the sociology of culture, as I believe it must be. Indeed, not only will psychology and sociology be included in the pages to follow, but, to some degree, the disciplines of history, art history, aesthetics, and philosophy as well. The task will not be an easy one. But as many contemporary theorists of creativity (e.g., Csikszentmihalyi, 1988; Csikszentmihalyi & Robinson, 1986; Feldman, 1986, 1988; Freeman, 1986, 1990, 1993a; Gedo, 1983; Getzels & Csikszentmihalyi, 1976; Gruber, 1986, 1989; Gruber & Davis, 1988) have either testified or demonstrated, there is no other way to proceed.

CONTEMPORARY THEORIZING ON CREATIVITY AND ITS CONDITIONS

To situate the present work in relation to the state of contemporary research on creativity and its conditions, it may be useful to briefly survey the field, with particular emphasis on a number of the root assumptions presently being made. First and perhaps foremost, as Csikszentmihalyi, Feldman, Gruber and Davis, Perkins, and Weisberg have recently argued (in Sternberg's [1988] "state of the art" edited volume), the so-called genius view of creativity must be cast into question; we must abandon the longstanding "Ptolemaic" view of creativity and move instead in a more "Copernican" direction, "in which

9

the person is part of a system of mutual influences and information" (Csikszentmihalyi, 1988, p. 336). This does not mean that there is no such thing as inherent creativity or genius or that every able-bodied person has an equal chance at excelling in any given domain, for it is clear that different individuals, given roughly the same training, yield different outcomes, some great, some not so great. What is being claimed instead is that inherent traits, abilities, or personal qualities, while perhaps *necessary* for the attainment of genius or excellence in a given domain, are not *sufficient*; what is also needed is both an attribution of some sort – that such and such a person, process, or product is indeed worthy of being deemed creative – as well as a sociocultural environment that allows for inherent creative potential to be actualized.

An extreme version of this thesis might go so far as to claim that what is deemed creative is, fundamentally, a matter of (mere) consensus and, in that sense, a social construction, a decision made on behalf of the powers that be. The reason for this, it might be argued, is that the idea of creativity is essentially normative – just as there is no empiric, transhistorical, transcultural way of saying what *art* is (see, e.g., Danto, 1981; Dickie, 1974; Goodman, 1976), so too with creativity. Be that as it may, it must also be recognized that creativity, far from being a matter of mere compliance with consensually established standards of value, involves precisely the meaningful transformation of these standards, as they pertain to a given domain of expertise. That which is deemed creative, in other words, ordinarily effects a change in the structure of consensus itself – a change, we might note, that becomes that much more difficult to effect when there is not much consensus to begin with, as is the case with much of contemporary art. The main point, in any case, is that genius, prodigious talent, and creativity, rather than occurring prior to or outside the fabric of social relations, are thoroughly enmeshed within it.

The second reason for regarding the idea of inherent creativity cautiously is, again, that creativity is most appropriately understood to be the product of a multiplicity of factors, both intra- and extraindividual, rather than of the former

10

alone. It exists in a "system" of influences, requiring the complex coordination and "coincidence" of these influences (see especially Feldman, 1988) in order to be brought to fruition. It is only recently that this idea has been taken into consideration in creativity research (see Getzels & Csikszentmihalyi [1976] for a notable exception). Rothenberg, for instance, was able to write in *The emerging goddess* (1979) that "the role of such factors as baroque style, cultural upheaval, modern theories of art, technological advance, and other such matters that are the important concern of the critic, the art historian, the sociologist, and the philosopher of art and science will not generally be discussed here" (p. 3). In Winner's more recent *Invented worlds* (1982), the social dimension of the arts was also "omitted." This time, however, the reason was a bit different: "The influence of sociocultural factors on the role that artists carve for themselves, and on the ways in which art works are experienced is undeniable," Winner admitted. But "because there has been little empirical work on these issues" (p. 11), they could not yet be addressed honestly. Far from seeking to negate or deny the relevance of these factors, therefore, what Winner seems to have decided is that, in light of the state of extant research, their treatment would have to await the future, when more of the findings were in.

For both of these writers, the issue of context could essentially be ignored without incurring too much damage to the ideas being treated. Now, in certain circumstances, this point of view may be valid, particularly if the domain of creative activity in question is a relatively closed one, with its own fundamentally internal rules of operation. Social conditions, while surely not irrelevant to creativity in the domain of mathematics, for instance, are arguably less relevant than they are in the domain of the visual arts, which is more open and changeable. There is another way of thinking about this issue as well. To the degree that extant social conditions are so congruent with the process of creativity that they are hardly noticed, there may be little problem in assuming that they can be all but ignored; the creators in question would be blessedly free from obstructive noise, from constrictions on the purity of the process.

11

There does, however, remain a problem. The basic assumption of both Rothenberg and Winner (and many others, particularly those of a cognitivist bent) is that creativity can be seen as fundamentally *independent* of social conditions. Although it can certainly be *affected by* these conditions, as they acknowledge, the relationship at hand is understood in essentially causal terms; creativity, the dependent variable, is altered as a function of the various independent variables out there in the world. Amabile, in some of her earlier work at least, sums up this stance well: "Social factors," she writes, "can have a powerful impact on creativity" (1983, p. 3). If the root assumption we have been exploring is indeed a valid one, however, it is not quite right to say that creativity is *affected by* social conditions. Instead, it would seem more appropriate to say that creativity is *constituted through* these conditions, assuming its very shape in line with and as a function of both the specific nature of the *domain* in question as well as the specific nature of the *field* – that is, the structure of social organization through which those working in the domain carry out their activities (see especially Csikszentmihalyi & Robinson, 1986). If, therefore, we are interested in understanding creativity in the domain of art – not as it takes place in the laboratory but in the concrete experience of human beings living in the world, replete with its structures, norms, and demands – we must try to see what is happening both inside and outside the person of the artist: in the discourses and practices called "art" and in the institutions that serve to organize them for those producers and consumers involved. Inquiring into "extraindividual" factors in the study of creativity and its conditions, therefore, is not optional; if we are to resist reifying creativity into a trait, ability, or process that exists independently of these factors, it is imperative.

An important point follows. If creativity is most appropriately regarded to exist in the context of a system of influences, a given creative act can never be seen as taking place ex nihilo, out of nothing. It is true, I suppose, that someone who has gone mad with paintbrush in hand may, by contemporary standards, come up with a "work" that is deemed of value by others and can perhaps be labeled as "art." The same may be said

12

of children or animals; even though they may know next to nothing about what art is and even though there may be no discernible influences on their "work," it is possible that, through their own sovereign acts of imagination, they will "create" something others deem worthwhile. These kinds of anomalies aside, however, creativity must be seen as taking place in and being conditioned by some sociocultural context: a *tradition* of some sort, that serves to situate a given act in relation to what has already been done (see Gadamer, 1979; Hauser, 1979; MacIntyre, 1981).

In case we suppose that this root assumption is merely an academic one, it may be important to note that it is of much broader significance than initially appears. For if the tradition of a given domain is being called into question or in the midst of being destroyed or abandoned or recast, such that people are left fundamentally to their own individual devices, we may well find that the process of creativity is made much more difficult. If tradition is indeed the ground of creativity, those who aspire to create in the relative absence of tradition may experience their acts as being ground-less, both experientially (as in nausea, existentialist style) and morally (as in lacking any defensible rationale for being). Furthermore, those who aspire to create in this sort of context are also likely to find that it is much more difficult to determine what *is* creative: In the relative absence of consensually established standards, wrought out of a tradition, it may be difficult to figure out who and what are the "real thing." In short, if creativity involves the transformation of a given domain of expertise, and if that domain has become fragmented or incoherent, then it will be that much more difficult to know precisely what constitutes a meaningful contribution. As has already been suggested, these sorts of problems have been very much a part of the contemporary art scene. And what they show, generally, is that the ex nihilo version of creativity is deeply problematic for both theoretical and practical reasons.

Another way of framing the issue at hand is to say, quite simply, that creativity takes time. If inherent factors are insufficient to account for creativity, it follows that "raw talent" requires

13

time before it can be brought to maturity. Gruber (1986) has been adamant about this issue, especially as it bears upon the distinction between giftedness and creativity. Although it may be interesting to study giftedness in itself, by looking, for instance, at those children who demonstrate certain abilities that deviate significantly from the norm in a particular domain, it is only when we can account for the transformation of these gifts into creativity that the concept of giftedness is useful. A simple example should suffice to clarify this point. There are happy babies, well-coordinated babies, smart babies, and so on. Perhaps there are even a few "talented" babies, at least by babylike standards. To my knowledge, however, there have been no wonderful baby artists (or philosophers or mathematicians or chess players). In order to become one of these, it is necessary not only to develop physically, cognitively, and emotionally but also to have some working knowledge and command of the specific domain of expertise (art, philosophy, math, chess) to which one's (inchoate) talents may be put. "Even Mozart," Weisberg (1988) notes, "who began his musical studies around the age of four, did not . . . produce a masterwork until he had been working for 12 years," the implication being that "an evolution away from the prosaic seems to occur even in the work of the greats" (p. 170). Csikszentmihalyi and Robinson summarize the issue well: "Talent cannot be a stable trait," they write, "because individual capacity for action changes over the life-span, and cultural demands for performance change both over the life-span and over time within each domain of performance" (1986, p. 264).

What is implied is not only that creativity is most appropriately studied across the course of time, in the context of both developmental and sociocultural changes, but that it is most appropriately studied in the "natural habitats," so to speak, of creative individuals themselves. Because I do not wish to sound parochial about this matter, let me hasten to acknowledge that experimental work pertinent to creativity can, has been, and no doubt will continue to be done. Getzels and Csikszentmihalyi (1976), for instance, have done important experimental work bearing on real-life creativity, demonstrating that assessments of work made in the laboratory setting bear some relation to artistic success. Likewise, Amabile, in a number of experimental studies on the conditions of creativity (e.g. 1979, 1982, 1983), has acquired information that is unquestionably pertinent to what goes on outside of the laboratory. To be honest, I am not quite convinced that most studies of this sort are actually about creativity, pertinent though they may be, for as a general rule they involve so-called creative tasks rather than processes designed to yield works that will be entries in a real world domain and field. Pertinence, nonetheless, may be worthwhile in its own right. But if creativity is indeed socioculturally constituted, and if there is any interest in imagining how extant conditions of creativity may be changed for the better, then our attention must turn to the "unique creative person at work" (Gruber, 1989; see especially Wallace and Gruber's edited [1989] volume, *Creative people at work,* for a variety of perspectives on the same).

One qualification deserves to be mentioned in this context. According to Gruber and others, it is only logical that we pay special attention to the "very great." This way, we will know that we are inquiring into creativity and its conditions in the genuine item. There is another reason that has been advanced for studying the great as well. As Rosenberg and Fliegel have written in their (1965) portrait of *The vanguard artist,* for instance, "We had heard much about alienation and the artist and suspected that that dreary topic would certainly have a bearing on our study. If so, and no matter what alienation might mean," they continue, "we wanted to control for its presence among artists embittered by failure. If successful artists were embittered, their condition could not be a by-product of sour grapes" (p. 7). Along with Gruber, then, the idea was that it was better to turn to successes than failures.

My own perspective on this matter is different. To derive a comprehensive understanding of the conditions of artistic creativity, it is necessary, I believe, to examine not only the lives of successful artists (however this might be defined) but unsuccessful ones as well. By dealing only with problems encountered by those who have fared well, there cannot help but be the tendency to smooth out these problems or perhaps even erase them: The life of the creator, arduous though it might have been, culminates in the grandeur of success, of triumphing over adversity and meeting desired ends; history thus becomes another mythic tale of the hero. Furthermore, the idea may be perpetuated that this is how it *must* be, that there *is* no success except after those trials and tribulations that have become so much a part of the mythology of creative individuals, artists especially.

Simpson (1981), for instance, in his sociological study of the SoHo district of New York, suggests that financially unsuccessful artists are more likely to "parade their existential precariousness" than successful ones; it is in the face of their diminished self-image that there emerges the need to maintain what he calls their "symbolic marginality." The result, he argues, is that the artistic "mystique" is perpetuated more by them than those who have been successful; these latter individuals simply do not need the "mask" of alienation in order to continue thinking about themselves as creative. Even with successful artists, however, there are certain guises that seem to be adopted with some regularity. "Hostility toward the market and the dealer," for example, "reassures the successful artist that he has not compromised his aesthetic standards or 'sold out' to get where he is" (Simpson, 1981, p. 80). In a somewhat puzzling psychodynamic twist, particularly for a piece of work that aspires to be sociology, the alienation of both unsuccessful and successful issues is in large measure reduced to mere posturing; marginality is primarily symbolic and hostility primarily a defense against the recognition that one may have acquiesced to demands that in more innocent times could only have been construed as an anathema to the personhood of the artist.

I am not suggesting that the phenomena referred to in these studies are illusory. Some unsuccessful artists undoubtedly fall victim to both "sour grapes" lamentations as well as any one of a number of rationalizations and fantasy constructions that can serve to steady their precarious selves in the midst of their thwarted desires. Likewise, some successful artists, in virtue of

16

their shame and guilt over capitulating to some formerly loathed other – the market, the critic, and the bourgeoisie more generally – no doubt maintain a certain amount of hostility so as to ward off these painful feelings. But to reduce the problems implicated in these phenomena to the mere psychic ploys constructed by artists in order to hold onto their ostensibly withering identities as a general interpetive strategy is not only to psychologize what may be very real social conditions, it is also to *exonerate* these conditions by relegating them to the status of the imaginary.

The issue at hand is not merely a question of interpretive choice, which would imply that it is ultimately arbitrary whether an essentially psychological or an essentially sociological perspective is employed to explain these phenomena. It is a question instead of examining the data closely enough and contextually enough to be able to differentiate, with a reasonable degree of certainty, which phenomena derive predominantly from within (from intrapsychic ploys and the like) and which derive from the outside, from conditions that may be shown to have enough concreteness to warrant their being considered bona fide social facts.

Returning to the question of who is to be studied in learning about creativity and its conditions, my own conviction is that, whether the perspective employed is mainly psychological or mainly sociological, it is only by studying *both* the great and the not so great, the successful and the unsuccessful, that we can begin to outline the requisite conditions. With this in mind, the present study employs a prospective methodological approach, in which the individuals being studied have been selected on the basis of *beginnings* – their aspirations – rather than *endings*. The narratives we shall be exploring, therefore, comprise more than "comedies," stories of rescue and transcendence. They comprise an entire range of plots, including ironies and tragedies, stories of misfortune, decline, and loss. By studying those who wished to become successful artists rather than only those who did, we will therefore be able to secure not only the chartings of the stars, the cream of the artistic crop, but those people who have been destined to become more ordinary, from the hobbyist to those with no significant artistic accomplishments at all. Interestingly enough, it is the casualties that may prove to be more instructive about the conditions of creativity than the successes; and there is much more to what they have to say than bitter regrets and idealized sorrows.

There is one final reason why at least a portion of creativity studies ought to be carried out in reference to the actual lives of creative individuals. To the extent that our interest in exploring the conditions of creativity is not only *theoretical*, nor even only *practical*, but in fact *political*, such that it is infused by a hope that these conditions can be changed for the better, it is that much more important to look at creative people at work, in their real surround. For even though creativity may sometimes be facilitated by encouraging people simply "to change their minds" about their activities, it may be better facilitated by imagining how to change this real surround itself. Indeed, it is by working at the juncture of these two worlds, the inner and outer, as they are located in the place of the creative person at work, that we will seek to discern what *social* conditions yield the most optimal *psychological* conditions for creating works of art. If "individuals share too deeply in the life of society for it to be diseased without their suffering infection" (Durkheim, 1951, p. 213), they may become compatriots in health as well.

TOWARD IDENTIFYING THE CONDITIONS OF CREATIVITY

An important question follows from the issues just raised. If we consider creativity not as a sui generis, purely intraindividual phenomenon, but as a joint product of both intra- and extraindividual factors, on what basis are we to go about the task of articulating its conditions? If creativity was a discrete process or an inherent ability, affected this way or that by extant conditions, the task would be relatively easy conceptually: With this discrete process in mind, the task would simply be one of determining how to bring it about. If, on the other hand, the nature of creativity itself varies as a function of extant sociocultural conditions, doesn't this imply that we need to make certain value judgments – indeed, *moral* judgments – about both what optimal conditions of creativity are and what optimal forms of creativity itself are? In speaking of problems or pathologies of creativity, aren't we necessarily invoking some notion of what health, normality, or optimality might be?

There are at least two ways of dealing with this situation, both of which are employed in the present work. First, rather than adhering to some fixed conception of what *we*, psychological researchers and theorists, believe creativity to be, it may be useful to adhere to what the people being studied believe it to be, however variable. In this work, for instance, I am not especially interested in who is or is not creative, as judged by some external body; I am more interested in what might be called, for lack of a better way of putting it, "perceived" or "subjective" creativity. I do not mean to suggest that it is irrelevant to call upon the services of external bodies that might help to differentiate the more creative from the less creative; it is simply not the approach I employ. One basic way to address the issue of what the (optimal) conditions of creativity are, therefore, is to listen carefully to what people are saying about them, whether directly or, as in the present case, indirectly, through reconstruction.

The task at hand does not stop here, however. For aren't people likely to talk about entirely different, perhaps even incompatible, conditions and forms of creativity? If we remain *only* at the subjective level, in other words, we will probably have before us an interesting multiplicity of subjective accounts, none of which are to be privileged over any other. If we have any interest in saying something more objective and critical, therefore, it becomes necessary to commit ourselves, cautiously of course, to those values and virtues we are prepared to defend. If I did not care about artistic freedom, about unalienated rather than alienated experience, or about the desirability of artistic activities that are in the service of good rather than evil, survival rather than extinction, communication rather than silence, there would be few meaningful conclusions to be drawn.

19

The truth, however, is that there *are* meaningful conclusions to be drawn, and far from necessarily being a function of the personal tastes and predilections of those carrying out the research, these conclusions are better seen as entries into discourse and dialogue, subject to critical scrutiny on the part of those who wish to enter the fray. In seeking to identify the conditions of creativity, therefore, I avow the irrevocably evaluative and moral dimension of this project. To identify the conditions of creativity is of necessity to speak of the optimal, the ideal; it is to make a claim about what constitutes more and less worthwhile forms of creativity and how they might be brought about.

I focus especially on the material side of social reality, that is, on those dimensions of social reality aspiring artists must negotiate in order to be viable. Included are phenomena that are overly rooted in material life, such as the need to "hustle" one's way into legitimate locales for showing one's work, as well as phenomena that may be seen as covertly rooted in material life, such as the need to conform to specific artistic practices or to "package" one's work so as to make it consistently identifiable and differentiable from the work of others. Without considering the specifically aesthetic to be a mere outgrowth or epiphenomenon of material life, as some Marxists may be inclined to do, I shall nevertheless show how powerfully the material conditions in which these individuals have lived and worked have affected their personal and artistic worlds. Marx*ism* aside, then – this work is not, fundamentally, a class analysis – the shadow of Marx looms large in many of these pages.

As against authors such as Rosenberg and Fliegel, along with Simpson, who appeared reluctant to locate the roots of creative hardships in real social and material conditions, my claim is that these conditions are not only real but are at the very heart of the problems reported. Whether one is mainly secure or insecure, psychologically open or closed, there actually *is*, among other things, a powerful and often capricious art market, including dealers, who, armed with the knowledge of what moves and what does not, pressure "their" artists into quite specific modes of artistic creation. These negative conditions, far from remaining at a comfortable distance from one's artistic activities themselves, often seem to make their way right into these activities, determining what they can and cannot be. Referring once more to Rosenberg and Fliegel (1965), who suggested that what went on in the studio itself was something of an oasis from those sources of alienation that lurked outside it, the unfortunate truth is that for many of the people being studied here it simply was not so. The alienation of some contemporary artists frequently knows no boundaries; there is no safe haven for one's creativity to remain untouched, unsullied.

In advancing this line of argument, I emphasize that although they may be more pointed or pronounced than they have been at other times, many of the problems to be considered are continuous with those faced earlier in history. Cheatwood (1982), for instance, reminds us that the familiar notion of the artist as isolated from his or her social environment began during the early part of the Renaissance and emerged in full form during the Romantic era. Beardsley (1966) too maintains that the alienation of the artist from society is one of the earliest themes of Romantic thought. Bringing this idea a bit more up to date and attempting to offer an explanation for this phenomenon, Tax (1972) sees the primary source of artistic alienation in the emergence of the capitalist system. It is only since then that "the artist has been put in the position of producing for a *market*, for strangers far away, whose lifestyles and beliefs are completely unknown to him, and who will either buy his works or ignore them for reasons that are equally inscrutable and out of his control" (p. 22). In short, we ought not to think of the modern era as the point of origin for the schism between the artist and an inhospitable social world; alienation is nothing new.

It is nonetheless "impossible," Herbert Read (1969) has written, "to conceive of a society without art, or an art without social significance, until we come to the modern epoch" (p. 16); never before has there been such "aesthetic impotence." In a similar vein, Poggioli (1968) contends that "the modern artist works in chaos and shadow, and is overcome by a feeling that language and style are in continual apocalypse" (p. 127; see

21

also Berger, 1972; Butler, 1980; Cork, 1979; Fuller, 1980; Gablik, 1984). More darkly still, for some there is the tragic suspicion that art today may exist "not because society needs it or depends on it, but because by some freak of nature artists still exist" (Herman, 1978, p. 121). Before we issue the news of their extinction, however, there remain some things we might wish to think about.

In light of the ideas that have just been discussed, one final strand of my argument is this: More optimal conditions of artistic creativity cannot obtain to the degree that many desire unless the social and material bases of artistic activities are significantly transformed. Because the revolution of the proletariat is unlikely to come about, in the near future at any rate, I am not about to call for a violent overthrow of the present system; this is neither the time nor the place for manifestos. I am also not entirely comfortable claiming, however, that "deliberately and soberly changing one's mind about the nature of truth and reality, and about what is really important" (Gablik, 1984, p. 128) is the most suitable response to the problems at hand. Acts of will alone cannot always change what goes on in the world. In turning our attention to the social and material bases of artistic activity, on the other hand, we may have a better chance of imagining how some changes may be brought about.

THE PLAN OF THE BOOK

The problems of artistic creation to be addressed will be approached "concentrically"; that is, we will be moving gradually from those problems that are closest to the person of the artist to those that are farthest away, including especially the productive and organizational realities of the field of art and the aesthetic realities of the domain of art. Chapter 2 will inquire into the conditions of creativity as they pertain to the "persona" of the artist, specifically, to some of the widely circulated and widely held mythical images of artists (e.g., the artist as genius, as decadent, as God) and creative people more generally in contemporary American society. My aim is not merely to describe these images, however, interesting and revealing though they be; it is to show how they become operative, psychically, in determining the space of creativity. As we shall see, there were some artists for whom these images were advantageous; they gave these people some of the desired fabric for the construction of their identities as artists and allowed them to carry out their activities with a greater sense of mission than might otherwise have been possible. For many others, however, these images proved to be inhibitory or even destructive in relation to both their artistic activities and to their personal, familial, and social lives. The result for some was either a difficult and painful career or the abandonment of art altogether or, more positively, a process of realization: that they were carrying out their work or living their lives in ways that, in virtue of their unreality, were alienating them from their real concerns. Only when these mythical images could be identified as such, therefore, could they open up the space of creativity.

Chapter 3 will examine the interpersonal relationships these aspiring artists had during the time in question, including those with friends and lovers, family members, and especially their artistic peers. The interpersonal sphere seems not to have received much attention in the literature. Among other possible reasons, it could be that, because many of the relevant phenomena have been pursued elsewhere (e.g., in the sociology of work, family, and community life), researchers and theorists of creativity have turned instead to other things, more field- and domain-specific. It will become evident, however, particularly when we explore both conflicts of women artists and conflicts inherent in the art community, that a consideration of the interpersonal sphere is not to be omitted. This is because the pursuit of art, especially insofar as it is tied to the mythical images being considered, can often involve modes of living and working that render interpersonal relationships extremely problematic. Even though these modes of living and working may have begun in Bohemia, for many they surely did not end there.

Chapter 4 will inquire into what was earlier referred to as the "field" of artistic activity, that is, the social and organizational dimensions of the domain of art itself. To a certain degree, references to the field will have been made already; there is no understanding either the mythic role of the artist or the dynamics of the art community outside of the field of artistic activity itself. Nevertheless, in this fourth chapter I focus my attention more pointedly on both the various demands made by these artists' respective art worlds themselves as well as on a number of other worlds – those of art education, commercial art, and "craft," among others – these individuals have inhabited. The main set of issues to be dealt with has to do with the motivation to create and how it may be affected by the productive and consumptive apparatus of art. Because it is not a particularly new idea that "intrinsic motivation" is generally preferable over "extrinsic motivation" when it comes to creativity, I do not spend too much time on this aspect of the issue. Of greater theoretical interest is the familiar, but not well understood, notion of alienation, which in the present context refers not only to the constriction of the space of creativity but to its corruption and deformation: In becoming complicitous in the inner workings of the hand that feeds them, artists and their activities can become prey to a kind of self-betrayal, which in many instances reduces these activities to ploys or machinations, designed fundamentally to yield commodities.

In large measure, there is no escaping the commodification of both art and artist, particularly for those who seek to enter the field in some significant way. Contra the myth of "discovery," it is rare for artists to be found by interested parties. Moreover, even if one is found, it will be only a matter of time before one becomes a part of the productive and consumptive apparatus of art. As for the select few who might be lucky enough to gain a measure of fame and fortune in their endeavors – which might lead some to suppose that they can now be "free" to create what they wish, to call their own artistic shots – this too is rare; when one fares well vis-à-vis the art world, there will more than likely be an increased demand for more of the same. It is nevertheless the case that there have been devised ways of dealing with this situation so that alienation, if not entirely eliminated, can at least be reduced. I shall therefore be working in this chapter toward identifying negative conditions of the field and showing how they might be rectified.

Chapter 5, which moves more fully into the domain of art, is in an important sense an extension of the fourth chapter. This is because in recent years, there seems to have been a profound conflation of the field of artistic activity and the domain of art itself. Again, I have no illusions about the fact that the same may be said of times past; what art is and what creativity is will always be tied, to a greater or lesser extent, to goings-on in the field. As suggested earlier, however, there is good reason to believe that this has happened to an unusual, and unusually problematic, extent during the course of the past few decades.

One of the primary reasons is the much-fabled "freedom" that accrued to artists during this time. Two interrelated issues deserve mention here. The first, which presumes that this freedom was real, is that in virtue of there existing a pluralistic art world – or at least a more pluralistic art world than had existed in times past (with pluralism referring broadly to the attempt to cast into question any and all modes of artistic activity that aspire to the status of transcendent primacy or absolute superiority and to affirm, in turn, the irreducible multiplicity of these modes) – there also existed both the need to devise one's own unique strategies of artistic creation and the need to become "different" enough from others that one's work had a chance of being noticed, and sold. The result, for a number of artists, was twofold: In addition to the sense of artistic groundlessness discussed earlier, what also happened in some cases was that artists had to devise a signature or "brand image," a "logo," that would serve to identify their work as *theirs* alone. Framed another way, in the relative absence of a cohesive artistic tradition *outside* themselves, they effectively had to create one *inside* – a "self-tradition," we might say, that would allow them to demonstrate that rather than just ambling along in this direction or that, they were indeed heading somewhere, playing out an important and innovative artistic project. For some, this project was quite real. For others, however, it was more like a mock project, leading to mock creativity and mock development. So much for freedom.

25

The second issue, which puts a different spin on these problems, has to do with the fact that despite the art world becoming more pluralistic than it had been earlier, it was nowhere near as pluralistic as some had assumed. Indeed, as many of the artists considered here were to learn – women artists especially – the domain of art actively excluded certain distinct modes of artistic activity from its purview. In short, despite proclamations of pluralism, not just *anything* could be deemed art, but highly specific things, especially those forms of art that sought to question and critique the domain itself. As for those forms that were less self-critical (such as the "old" representational kinds of work, for instance), they seemed to acquire the status of a taboo; they were deemed retrogressive and out-of-date. Some artists were therefore doubly unfree. For alongside their being coerced into the production of variations on set artistic themes, the very style and content of their work could fall victim to coercion as well. As for the result, it was only when they learned how to *resist* this coercion that they could expand the space of their own creativity.

Also to be explored in Chapter 5 is the alienation of artists from the viewing public. In line with the various modes of artistic activity many had come to adopt over the course of their careers, especially those who aspired to partake of the climate of artistic pluralism by devising their own arcane strategies of creation, they sometimes found that their initial motivations to create had become buried or lost: Whereas they had hoped at one time to communicate meaningfully with others, the very arcaneness of their work seemed to prevent them from doing so, the result being that their own "audience" was limited to the few fellow members of the club – which, of course, were most often the "elite," the denizens of "high culture."

Without deciding that the art they created had to be for *everybody* – it was clear enough that one could not please everybody and that there were some defensible reasons for resisting the "kitsch-y" demands of popular culture – some of these artists realized that art designed for the private delectation of a select few compromised their innermost aims. An interesting thing sometimes happened as a result of this sort of realization:

The desire to expand the space of communication served to expand the space of creativity itself. It wasn't so much that these artists were creating *for* a wider public, which would have led to a kind of means–end, rationalized mode of artistic activity (as in "Let's make it simple"). Rather, they had begun creating more with others in mind, we might say, than they had earlier. It could be argued that this was merely a matter of assuaging their guilt, that they felt badly about casting aside the "little people" and that their own predominantly middle-class values led them to become more inclusive with their work. This is probably a valid argument for some cases. My own inclination is to say, however, that what surfaced for most of the people who sought to expand the space of communication was their own sense of human expressiveness, relatedness, and responsibility, along with their own desire for community: their interest, in short, in practicing fidelity to the others in their midst. It was only in becoming less self-involved and self-enclosed in their artistic activities that they moved forward, creatively and communicatively, in their work.

The sixth and final chapter of the book has two distinct aims. The first is reconstructive: On the basis of the pathologies of artistic creativity identified in the preceding chapters, I shall articulate more optimal conditions within which artistic activities might occur. Some of the cues for this reconstruction have been taken from the artists themselves, especially those who have been able either to withstand these pathologies or to transcend them. As I indicated earlier, then, one of the ways in which I try to articulate what may be considered optimal is to follow the directives of the individuals this work is about, to see what they believe needs to be done to expand the space of creativity. As I have also suggested, however, a further way is to "read" the inverse of the pathologies that have been identified and, with these readings in mind, to formulate theoretically – and with certain avowed moral commitments in hand – what these remaining conditions might be.

The second aim of the final chapter is to imagine ways in which the transition from theory to practice might be made. I shall not resort to utopianism here: "If only this; if only that."

27

Nor, again, will the end result be a manifesto uttering the death knell to the bourgeoisie. Instead, by considering some plausible ways in which we might see the social and psychological conditions of creativity change for the better, I hope to say something of value both about art and creativity and, perhaps more important, to those who aspire to create art. Although facile solutions to the problems at hand are out of the question, there is reason to believe that the future is open to change.

ON INTERPRETATION

In order to describe the nature of the research project that was undertaken and to outline some of the demographic characteristics of the group being studied, I have provided an appendix. This appendix is the only portion of the work dealing with numbers. Without going into detail about why this so, suffice it to say that a quantitative approach is not my chosen mode of dealing with the available information. If my foremost aim were to offer robust generalizations applying to the entire population of aspiring artists, perhaps a more quantitative approach would be called for. Likewise, if my primary interest were to predict – for instance, those factors that lead to success or failure – this too would call for a more quantitative approach. Because I am interested in neither of these, however, my treatment will be qualitative and interpretive. Let me therefore bring this introductory chapter to a close by offering a few words on the problem of interpretive inquiry in the social sciences.

Although I hope and trust that the presentation of the materials to follow will be both "methodical" and believable, I have not employed a discrete method – in the sense that much of contemporary social science uses the term. Earlier on, when the research project began, I did flirt with the notion of doing a "content analysis" of some sort, mainly to comply with my elders, who were much more given to quantification. I even developed a comprehensive qualitative coding scheme, designed to be a kind of compromise between a content analysis, which would have relied essentially on the frequency of statements pertinent to a given topic, and a full-blown interpretive study. In the end, however, I elected to do the latter, mainly because I became convinced that an interpretive or hermeneutic perspective on the information at hand would indeed provide not only a more interesting and compelling read, but a more valid piece of work than would otherwise be attainable (see, e.g., Gadamer, 1979; Habermas, 1983; Ricoeur, 1981; also the volumes edited by Messer, Sass, & Woolfolk, 1988; Packer & Addison, 1989; Rabinow & Sullivan, 1979).

Despite the fact that this work is mainly about the social conditions of artistic creativity, with particular attention being paid to those conditions that exist outside the person of the artist, it is important to note that most of the information at hand is derived from these persons themselves, from the stories they tell about their lives. Strictly speaking, therefore, I will be dealing neither with social reality in itself (as an organizational sociologist might do) nor with experience in itself (as a phenomenological psychologist might do) but instead with *recollections* of experience, as disclosed in language. This indeed is why a hermeneutic approach is called for: The data take the form of *narrative texts* to be read and interpreted (see Franklin, 1989; Freeman, 1993b). These texts, insofar as they document psychological reality – the world of one's desires and frustrations, one's hopes and regrets, one's victories and defeats – will therefore be the vehicle for pointing us in the direction of social reality.

Now, it must be recognized that in dealing with narratives of this sort we are faced with a unique historiographical situation: The data themselves are *already* interpreted by those individuals whose narratives they are. On some level, of course, this situation is part and parcel of most forms of historical inquiry. If the object of the inquiry is human action or language, then there is some sense in which meaning precedes the arrival of the interpreter; it is the actor's or speaker's own before it is anyone else's. But in the case of narratives issuing from the interview setting, there is the additional problem of both the interpreter and the informant being removed from the experiences discussed. Again, life-historical narratives consist neither of experiences themselves, which are long gone, nor of material documents or artifacts, able to point to the past. They consist instead of recollections: selective and imaginative renditions of the present meaning(s) of past experience (see especially Freeman, 1993b).

What researchers interested in this sort of information must interpret, therefore, are the informants' own interpretations. They are thus *doubly* removed from the things they may be most interested in, namely the realities not just of the perceived past but of the past (or, more appropriately, the "past present") itself, however problematic this idea may be. I am interested in artists' recollections of their experiences in the art world, for example, to learn not only about their perceptions, their own subjective realities – though these are often important and revealing – but also about the art world. My aim is to move, therefore, from the level of individual (recollections of) experience to the broader social level signified and expressed therein. In short, I am proposing that this information can indeed tell us something about the worlds in which these individuals lived and worked and later described to us, the researchers.

For some, this proposal might be considered untenable. First off, it might be argued, it is difficult enough to rely on interview data that are *not* recollective. Because these data consist only of words, as opposed to observable actions for instance, they may be as much about language as about the world to which language refers. They may also be as much about what the informant thinks the interviewer wants to hear as about what he or she truly thinks, feels, and believes. With recollective data, this argument might continue, the difficulties are even more pronounced. And this is because recollection, as I have already stated, is selective and imaginative: Far from re-presenting the past "as it was," recollection may more suitably be seen for some as a kind of creative fictionalizing, as much a *con*struction as a *re*construction.

"We do not *live* stories," Hayden White (1978) has written, "even if we give our lives meaning by retrospectively casting them in the form of stories" (p. 90). Our lives, from this perspective, are really only what we experience from minute to minute, day to day, and year to year; meaning is imposed on the contingencies and the chaos of life from without, as it were, when we take the time to narrate, to render a story out of the discrete episodes of the past. This theme has become a familiar one, both within historiography as well as the study of life history. Again, life-historical narratives, woven through the imaginative process of recollection, are seen by many to be either fictive "impositions" upon the (real) data of the past or just plain fictions, these ostensibly real data being constructed as well. Because these narratives cannot pretend to resurrect the experiences of the past in their original, pristine form, then it must be the case that the facts are being "tailored," as White puts it, to fit: If they are going to be part of some cohesive narrative, then they are going to need to enter in smoothly, to be recast in such a way as to become an integral part of the story being told. To make matters more problematic still, there is in addition the distinct possibility that the stories people tell of themselves will be essentially false, mythicizations, perhaps, of what they had been or become. Interested in maintaining not just a consistent past but a worthwhile one, people may variously become larger – or, depending on one's need for self-punishment and the like, smaller – than life itself. As Vaillant (1977, p. 197) has flatly put the matter, at some point or other during the course of our lives, "maturation makes liars of us all."

With these two basic sources of "distortion" in mind, it comes as no surprise that there may be disjunctions between the data of immediate experience and those of recollection: To be alive to the historical significance of events as they happen, one must know to which later events these will be related; and these are descriptions that actors themselves cannot give at the time of experience. This is why we can say that a certain experience or stage of life was significant even though it was not experienced as such at the time, or why what we thought was a clear understanding of a situation was ultimately not so clear at all, but rather confused, naïve, or illusory. This is also why it is no contradiction for us to say that while these events themselves may be dead and gone after the moment of their passing, their *meanings* can remain very much alive, especially as new experiences come along and retroactively transfigure them by supplying a new context for interpretation.

But given that life-historical narratives cannot pretend to represent the past; and given that the narrator is inevitably involved in shaping the information at hand; and given as well that the specific manner in which this is done is a function of culture-specific plots, changing psychological needs, desires, and so on, what exactly *can* they tell us about? If it is not the actuality of the past that is being depicted, then what is? Finally, how can we begin to speak about the "objectivity" of the information in question?

In the process of recollection, as it is frequently embodied in life-historical narratives, what we often see is an interpretive movement wherein meanings are at once lifted out of the past and created anew; neither strictly "found" nor strictly "made," they often carry with them the conviction that they have somehow existed previously but never in as fully realized a form as they are now. Stated another way, the process of recollection is often one of *finding new meanings,* new patterns and metaphors for articulating the shape of one's life (Lakoff & Johnson, 1980; Olney, 1972; Ricoeur, 1983). And what this implies is that disjunctions between the data of immediate experience and those of recollection, though they certainly *may* reflect fictionalization or even outright distortion, do not necessarily do so. In addition, they may testify to the development of insight and understanding into issues that may have earlier been clouded by confusion or mystification or self-deception.

In response to the first of the aforementioned questions, then, what life-historical narratives can tell us about are the ways in which old meanings have been replaced and superseded by new, and hopefully "better," more comprehensive ones. Many people in the present study, for instance, spoke about what they had come to realize were their illusions and delusions about themselves and their possible place in the world of art, how these may have been corrected by the demands of the market, and how they may have had to rebuild a more adequate series of anticipations, expectations, and plans of action. Others realized that being an artist, or being a specific kind of artist, was not really what they wanted at all, that they had been directing their lives more in terms of an image – the life of the artist – than a reality, the practice of art. We shall hear from them shortly.

It should be evident from what has just been said, moreover, that what life-historical narratives can tell us about frequently extends well beyond the psychological plane: Illusions and delusions about one's place in the world of art may have been realized as a function of its cold realities. Similarly, in living one's life largely through an image instead of reality, there is an immediate reference made to the possible currency this image may have for society and to the type of society that perpetuates it. The realization of one's self-deception sometimes became concomitant, therefore, with the further realization that one had become ruled by external forces, manifested in the form of pseudo-desires. In any event, for the time being I want to reiterate that life-historical narratives, in addition to being a primary vehicle for understanding the trajectories of individuals' lives, may also be seen as one of the primary means of access to social reality, their very biographies serving to signify and express the worlds through which they have moved.

In response to the second question, in fact, which was concerned with what it is that narratives depict or refer to, it may be that narratives of the sort being considered here are better vehicles of representation at the sociological level of analysis than the psychological (see especially Bertaux's 1981 edited volume *Biography and society*): While the hard and fast facts of career transition and the feelings accompanying them, for instance, may be relatively uninforming from a strictly psychological point of view, representing but the faintest outlines of what some individual is "really about," they may well portray certain social realities in full relief. Furthermore, we, as researchers, may have easier access to these realities, for they are ones that we participate in as well.

Finally, in terms of the question of objectivity, especially as considered in relation to the aforementioned "distance" of recollective data from the experiences they seek to be about, my own conviction is that more often than not this distance is a productive one. In line with what has been said about the possible development of understanding through recollection along with the ways in which the meanings of former experiences may progressively be articulated and corrected throughout the course of one's life, the central idea here is that this distance may actually be the requisite condition for attaining a degree of objectivity vis-à-vis one's life that was unattainable in the flux of immediate experience. Ongoing interviews or observations can surely provide useful information at times; there is no denying it. But they are in no way necessarily "truer to life" than the kinds of reflections to be dealt with here. As many of the individuals with whom we have spoken readily attest, the truth often takes a great deal of time to mature.

One last point may be worth mentioning before moving ahead. Interpretive social science, to the extent that it aspires to yield theoretical knowledge, frequently moves from subjective to objective contexts of meaning (see, e.g., Berger & Luckmann, 1967; Geertz, 1973; Schutz, 1967). Thus, the focus on subjectivity, psychic reality, whatever we wish to call it, though often crucial for this approach, is by no means the whole of it. Indeed, as with any text, the interest is not only in what the *author* himself or herself may have meant by a particular utterance but what the *text* itself means: We want to understand what is being said and what this something may be about. This greatly expands the interpretive field. For in moving beyond subjective meanings, localized in the person of the author, we immediately have before us a much larger range of possible interpretations, emerging in line with the essential openness of discourse itself.

As concerns the present work, therefore, we will not rest with subjective meanings alone. Perceptions of experience, as

34

recollected by the individuals being studied here, will remain front and center; they are the "results," if you will, and their description must come before anything else. From there, the task will be to extend their reach, through interpretation, to the social realities constitutive of them. Let us now begin to explore what these individuals have had to say about their lives and their work in and out of the world of art.

Chapter 2

To be an artist

THE (AL)LURE OF THE IMAGE

"THE WORLD OF ART," says a flyer for the magazine *ARTnews*, "has never been more fascinating, more rewarding, more fun." What should we call this new fascination? "A cultural renaissance? The latest showbiz extravaganza? A sign of the times? Whatever you call it, something new and important is happening in America today." The evidence is as straightforward as can be: "Go to any major art opening these days, and you're likely to rub shoulders with more celebrities than at most Broadway or Hollywood premieres!" Or, if you wish, "Join the auction sale of a new Jasper Johns painting, or a De Kooning, and watch the bidding go up, up and up – past the million dollar mark!" Or, a bit more subtly, "simply follow the Saturday crowds to a popular art gallery and feel the electric excitement that fills the air!" Okay, I'll subscribe! "Yes," the flyer continues, "it's true. The art world, once the special preserve of a fortunate few, has now exploded into the mainstream of American life. It's a cover story for *Time* or *Newsweek*. A hot topic for the TV talk shows. A new leisure time activity for millions of Americans." It is, in short, "One of the most extraordinary cultural phenomena of our times." It is indeed.

The mystique of the artist, frequently manifested in the form of either grandeur or alienation, has had currency for many years. In part, Marx and Engels (1981) have suggested, this may be a function of the channeling of creativity into individual persons: "The exclusive concentration of artistic talent in particular individuals and its suppression in the broad masses which is bound up with this is a consequence of the division of labor" (p. 109). Rather than there simply existing those who paint or sculpt or what have you, alongside the other productive activities with which human beings might become engaged, there arose "painters" and "sculptors," who came to define their very existence through these identities, such that they would be singled out for their uniqueness. With the advent of communism, of course, this would all change: Creative activities would be woven into the fabric of life itself, and not only for "particular individuals," but for those "broad masses" in whom these activities are ordinarily suppressed.

As we know, it hasn't quite turned out this way. Rather, the artist has become a locus for both creative activities themselves and, more importantly for present purposes, images of what it might mean to live a life inspired by the need to create. As noted earlier, one of the primary images associated with the person of the artist was that of the alienated recluse, working away in terrible yet beautiful obscurity, a man (most often) possessed, who refused to capitulate to the coarse demands of bourgeois life. It may be worth nothing that this "refusal" was in large measure ordained by these demands themselves; those who were not particularly productive laborers, as judged by the standards of commodity exchange, would more than likely be relegated to the margins. The image, in this respect, may have served as a compensation of sorts for the loss of capital; at least artists could know they were being true to themselves.

More recently, in any case, the stock of culturally based images seems to have shifted somewhat. To some degree, the myth of marginality has remained alive and well (as has, for many, the reality of marginality); a number of the artists considered here, for instance, will tell us about just how operative these myths were, particularly early on in their careers, when they were expected to be on the margins. But what has also happened, beginning, by most accounts, in the late 1950s or so, is that the myth of marginality has taken something of a back seat to other, more "positive" images of what it is to be an artist.

Money was surely bound up with this shift. There was a

painting of Franz Kline's that had sold for $1,200 in 1957, for instance, that brought $25,000 some three years later. One day in 1959, Willem De Kooning apparently sold all his paintings and suddenly found himself $150,000 richer. Meanwhile, Adolph Gottlieb, among others, who had also begun to reap the benefits of the sudden infusion of capital, began throwing parties in the Hamptons, Gatsby-style, filled with artists, buyers, and gallery owners, not to mention bartenders and maids. The suddenness of this shift is what deserves emphasis here: "Poor Jackson (Pollock) started it all," De Kooning has been quoted as saying (cited, along with the above, in Elkoff, 1970), "and he died before the money came." Indeed, had Pollock been able to hold out just a few more years and witness this strange transformation, perhaps the end result – his violent and untimely death – would have been different. It is difficult to say; as it turned out, many of his fellow Abstract Expressionists, who had at one time coexisted peacefully, had apparently become more hostile to one another as some of their careers took off. Some of the earlier innocence was gone.

The idea of innocence lost notwithstanding – innocence wasn't worth much anyway – alongside the myth of marginality, there also emerged those sorts of myths associated with a kind of decadent grandeur, those that would attract the attention of the paparazzi, who would eventually turn their cameras the artist's way: "The American artist," Myron and Sundell wrote in 1971, "became the hero of the sophisticated sixties, rivalling movie stars, politicians, ballplayers, and astronauts for public attention" (p. 192). Recall the National Endowment for the Arts figures cited earlier, describing the remarkable increase in the population of active painters and sculptors in the decade following. It would of course be facile and unfair to posit that this surge was tied in some concrete way to the emergence of the artist-hero; there were lots of other reasons to become an artist too, not the least of which included those bound up with the communitarian ethos that had been spawned by events ranging from the antiwar movement to Woodstock. All the same, there is little doubt that many wanted a piece of this new action.

By the mid-1960s, writes Lucy Lippard (1984, p. 162), "the small number of highly visible artists who made it offered a false image to all of those art students rushing to New York to make their own marks, and to have nervous breakdowns if they didn't get a one-man show within the year." The dream of artistic success, as difficult as it might be to realize, had apparently become a part of at least some artists' desires. Even if the work came first, it was no longer sufficient to simply carry out one's activities patiently and let the chips fall where they may; one had to pursue actively success and notoriety, as early as possible: The sooner one was on the map of the art world, the better.

More problematically still, however, what seems to have happened in the intervening years is that, for some, artistic desires have become virtually inseparable from these other concerns. "Look at the hordes of young people who come out of art school seeking glamor of recognition as artists," the art critic Carter Ratcliff (1988, p. 145) has written. "How can we understand them – or our interest in art, for that matter – unless we acknowledge that aesthetic aspirations cannot be formulated in our culture without formulating, in the same instance and with the same art, a desire for market success across the board, from the review columns to the collectors' living rooms?"

As Ratcliff suggests, the desire to create art is frequently indissociable from the desire to be an artist, of the kind that we hear and read about. This ought not to be construed exclusively in terms of a crude desire for money either. In addition, there has emerged the desire to be a particular kind of person, leading a particular kind of life. With the "glamor of recognition," perhaps a new identity will be born, one that will be vastly more interesting than the one possessed before. Whether the myth in question is one of marginality or glamor, therefore, it is clear that the images to which it refers have come to be a profound source of allure for many. The fact of its allure, however, is not all that we need to learn about. We also need to see how this allure has become operative, for better and for worse, in the lives and work of aspiring artists.

THE CONSTRUCTION OF ARTISTIC
IDENTITY

It must be emphasized first that there were some people among the group we studied who were largely untouched by the myths and images being discussed. Whether detached enough to ignore them or insightful enough to transcend them, these people were able to carry out their work in such a way that extant images were beside the point. For many others, however, the clutches of these myths – again, for better and for worse – proved difficult to escape. Let us begin by exploring briefly those for whom these myths and images provided a formative influence on the construction of artistic identity.

By bolstering their own sense of themselves, as people and as artists, the myths and images at hand convinced some that they were indeed extraordinary, doing something exceptionally meaningful and important, and that it was their responsibility to share their "gifts" with others. One man described himself as an "eternal child," who was "constantly learning and looking at new horizons with that wide-eyed amazement at things." Here is the myth of the artist as primitive, blessedly free of those civilized, adult fetters that serve to bury the primordial power of the visual world. Others noted that artists are generally "heightened beings," who "feel things stronger" and "tend to observe more than other people." This didn't necessarily make things any easier, personally or artistically. But it could provide a measure of consolation when things got rough: One always had one's identity.

Consider the following story, of a woman – we will call her Gloria Adams (the names to follow will be fictional as well) – who has been working at her art consistently since attending school. There had been problems, she said, from the very start. School itself had been difficult because it was unclear what her teachers wanted. "The Abstract Expressionists, they were all in vogue, and then you would get a C because you did something realistic. And then, you would go to Naturalism, and you would get a C because it was abstract." There were too many mixed messages back then; "it didn't make any sense at all." So finally, she had said, " 'The hell with it.' " She never wanted a part of this faddishness anyway. There was also the problem of getting into galleries, which was nothing short of "impossible." What's more, "People don't know what we're going through," especially in terms of "the desperation of not selling work." Galleries wanted money for themselves, not artists, and the result was that it was a sad situation for people to face.

It was particularly so for women, Gloria felt, because they were all but banished from reviews and the like. In her own case, for instance, it was mainly other women and "sensitive people" who liked her work: "You really have to be sophisticated enough or sensitive enough to see the things that I see in something," and the fact was, "there are very few people around like that." Nevertheless, she went on to say, "You can't think about anyone else" when you're creating your art; "either they like it or they don't." Her response in this context, she believed, was the only appropriate one: "I don't give a damn," she said.

What she did give a damn about, however, was the oppression that issued from her own family, especially her husband. They had made a deal, apparently. He was supposed to become a doctor and leave her enough time to do her own work. But when it came time for him to own up to his part of the deal, he would have no part in helping her along. Not only had he refused to give her the money needed for her to buy materials, which was "heartbreaking" enough, but he had even gone so far as to say, " 'I'm going to make you fail.' " He never really cared about her work at all, she felt, until she got good at what she was doing. Not that his lack of support stopped her, she was quick to add, but she greatly resented his attitude toward the entire enterprise. "How dare you do this to me," she had said to herself. Her children had also been a source of trouble. For in addition to demanding a great deal of time and attention, particularly when they were small, they too seemed a bit suspicious about her activities. " 'When are you going to sell something, Mother?' " they would ask. And, " 'Must we have all this

41

crap here?'" Why did she need all of these materials? Why was she trying to do all this work anyway? Why couldn't she be like all the other mothers?

The only consolation was that she was an artist; she was lucky enough to be "born with it." Artists "are always watching people in motion. They watch nature. They watch trees. They look at everything much more than everybody else does" and "tend to observe more than other people." As for the process of making art itself, she added, "When an artist creates, it's like being God," even if only "in a very small way." In spite of all the hassles she had faced, they were ultimately of little consequence, for she was fulfilling an obligation, a calling. "A lot of artists feel that way," she noted. The shame of the situation was that others, even significant others, didn't quite see it this way. In their own estimation, her calling was something entirely different, and judging by what she said, they did everything in their power to let her know. In this case, therefore, the mythic dimension of the artistic identity served to relegate some significant conflicts to a lesser status than they might otherwise have attained; there was always a measure of umbrage to be taken under the shadow of the muse.

"We must imitate God," another woman said. She was unsure "if anybody personally, in the genes, was an artist," so it was difficult to know where exactly her own seemingly extraordinary abilities came from. One thing she did know, however, was that she was tremendously fortunate to have them. "It's such a joy" to be an artist. "And get paid for it? What greater heaven could there be?" Here, the myth of the sacred being, with a direct line to God above, finds its instantiation, the picture being one of abundant pleasure and fulfillment. This is not to say that being an artist was completely devoid of pain, she went on to qualify; there were also the inevitable bouts of depression that artists faced due to their greater intimacy with the ups and downs of emotional life. But this was hardly cause for lament: "I know this is part of the price of being an artist."

In another particularly notable instance of this myth, a woman remembered how she responded when she learned that her mother was dying of leukemia. "I kind of enjoyed it," she admitted, somewhat tongue-in-cheek. "It was like I could say things about death." When she was younger, death had seemed to be an intrinsic part of the territory of the artist, and it behooved her to assimilate it into her artistic activities as best she could; she would dare to enter those existential arenas where those less sensitive and bold refused to go. So it was that a sadistic pleasure in watching a loved one suffer brought with it the magic of masochism, in the form of a self-inflicted pain only special people were allowed to feel. Subjectively at least, this woman's own mythical image of the artist seemed to play a formative role. Whether it helped her art is another question altogether. It should be noted that she wound up rejecting this mythology later on in her career. When asked about what she had been doing over the years, her answer was straightforward. "It's real simple," she said: "art and teaching." She was pleased about this too. Although her hope had been that teaching would be more of a "backup" than a full-time (pre)occupation, she had never really seen herself as one of those who would gather fame and fortune. Dying mothers aside, art, as it turned out, was simply something she liked to do.

Another mythical theme she was interested in casting into question had to do with the notion of originality. It was true enough: "You're always wanting to be original." But, she said, you never really are. Even one of her boldest and most innovative ideas, which was to try to cross the decoratively tacky with the sublimely elegant, owed its rationale to all of the endless squabbles "everybody's so worried about" that went on in the art world: concerning what was fake and what was real, what was craft and what was fine art, and so on. There really was no deciding these sorts of issues, she felt. Instead, she would be "dualistic," drawing on both the sacred and the profane, bringing them into dialogue in whatever ways seemed appropriate. Hers was "the art of bringing things together in new situations," which is what most artists wound up doing anyway. The main thing differentiating her from other artists was her attitude. She was a populist, who would go to junk shops with her friends, who preferred the "unsophisticated" aspects of art, and who bristled at the adoration sometimes lavished upon her by those who saw artists as deities. Sure, she reiterated, "I want to break rules." In large measure, this was how being an artist was defined in this day and age. "But I don't know if I ever do."

Far from experiencing this state of affairs as confining, however, all this meant was that there was little reason to suffer under the stifling pressure of the desire to be one-of-a-kind, to be Unique, an Originator, breaking all the rules in order to reach some (allegedly) higher purpose. The fact of the matter was, art had no purpose. This is what made it so exciting: In the absence of any overarching purpose or end, the artist was face-to-face with freedom itself. It is with these sentiments in mind that we can begin to understand why this woman tended to "hide" from exhibiting her work in the standard way. She simply was not a stern enough "disciplinarian" when it came to her art, she explained. People were always asking her why she didn't try to sell her work, why she wasn't more successful, and so on. There were the usual fears, but beyond these, she didn't really know why, other than that she found the whole scene rather boring. What she also suggested, though, was that showing and selling more than she did presently would probably compromise her freedom. She was plenty "dutiful" when it came to teaching because there were responsibilities involved and she got paid for it. But "I'm not always that dutiful about art." It would no doubt remain this way too; she had come a long way from her earlier days of beautiful suffering and pain.

Further myths were operative as well. As one man avowed, "We walk that line between sanity and insanity every day." This is the myth of the artist-madman, always on the edge, and while it is widely known by both artists and nonartists alike, its hold may be no less strong. Walking this fine line was not all that being an artist meant for him either. In addition, there was something downright extraterrestrial about it: "We have the ability to fantasize," he said, "to the point where we have out-of-mind, out-of-body experiences." Even if it is a bit unclear what exactly "out-of-mind" experiences are, we can safely assume that only extraordinary people have them. This man may be extreme in his beliefs. At the very least, though, being an artist, said another person, "puts you in a little bit less of an ordinary situation." This is why "it's sort of an ego trip in a way," why "there's a certain magic in being an artist."

Those who have been shut out of this magic may even seek to cultivate it, as if it were an acquired skill. "I wanted to be an artist," Lynn Winters recalled; "it's just that I didn't really know how." Things had been very difficult early on in Lynn's career. At first, she didn't have a studio and was therefore forced to do her work in the kitchen and dining room. There had also been several moves, due mainly to job opportunities for her husband, which slowed down her progress as well. And then there was the decision to have a family, which had brought her art to an abrupt halt for some two years. Finally, though, after several years of sporadic work, there was a breakthrough. It was time, she had learned, "to be more modern." Copying nature had proved to be a dead end, she explained; if she was going to be a full-fledged artist, she would have to find a more up-to-date approach. This is exactly what happened: "I was getting to the point where I was becoming more contemporary."

Lynn had been determined to hold onto her art no matter what the cost. This was especially difficult in her family, she went on to note; there was sometimes the feeling that she was more committed to her art than to them. But this is how it would have to be. The only problem, still lingering after all these years, was that although she always knew she wanted to be an artist, she was "always trying to find out how." Perhaps certain things had to be given up, she came to feel, particularly since she was still so far behind those artists whose work and whose life she sought to emulate. Sports would have to be given up, and sewing. And her husband.

Despite the fact that Lynn had gradually come to like her own work and felt good about what kind of work it was, there was the sense that much of what she was striving for was over her head; as contemporary as her work was becoming, at least in appearance, she still did not really understand its rationale. It just wasn't personal, she said, and as a result she came to feel "mixed up," occasionally even reverting to more representational art, however retrogressive she felt it to be, for the sake of doing something that felt like her own. Even though she began to "think more like an artist," there still remained something troubling about where she seemed to be headed. She'd "better do something naturalistic" once in a while, Lynn had said to herself. In fact, perhaps the most appropriate thing she could do was maintain two styles: "I'd have an experimental style and I'd have a more naturalistic one." She liked things that moved, she had realized, things that were alive, but for a time they didn't seem appropriate to include in her paintings. Learning to work flat, she explained, had been like a "scientific discovery," and she followed it through as far as she could. But the resultant works were apparently too dead for her liking. She would therefore insert images of birds in them sometimes, to bring them alive.

What also helped in Lynn's process of becoming an artist was a book she had read on "what an artist's life was like." Despite all her contemporary gestures, she felt that she was still feeling her way along, like an "amateur." She began to rely on art magazines as well, hoping that she too would eventually be able to achieve – not to mention understand – what all of these modern artists were talking about. At least one thing was becoming clear, in any case, and that was that before she could go out and show her work, she would have to get her own personal style together more than it was. "I really feel that you have to have a cohesive body of work that's interrelated," she said. The problem, however, was that she simply wasn't ready for this yet. Indeed, once she tried to "put a label" on her work, it "stops the meaning right there." She would therefore have to endure the heterogeneity of her work for the time being, her goal being to achieve a measure of stylistic unity and coherence organically rather than artificially. "When I first started out," Lynn added, "I was too anxious to have a meaning in my work," and what resulted was a "superficial meaning." Maybe she had to learn to see meanings "in between" the works, then; maybe that would help things along. She didn't really know.

What she did know, again, was that in order to acquire the sense of artisthood she so desired, she had to break away from the "traditional middle-class environment" in which she had lived. Her husband and her children not only wanted her to be a traditional woman, connected to her allotted roles as wife and mother but, interestingly enough, a traditional artist as well. If she was going to insist on being an artist, then the least she could do was accessible, realistic work. They also felt that she should earn something from it, which would make her appear more professional in their eyes. But no; it was impossible to acquiesce. She had "taken too much art history" to go this route, and it was too late for her to do the kind of work that would please them. She wanted to grow too fast, Lynn admitted, and the direction in which she was heading made her husband in particular extremely uneasy. "Everything was all right," she claimed, "until I decided I wanted to become more contemporary and abstract." This was *his* problem, though: "You have to be yourself," she insisted; "you can't be someone else."

There are many different ways to interpret the information this woman has provided. On a cursory level, it may have been that the art she grew to embrace was indeed the source of many of the problems she and her family encountered. There was the sense, perhaps, that she had gotten a bit too wild and unruly, too isolated from the real world: Here they were, a nice middle-class family, and mom's going off the deep end with her art history–fed abstract painting that hardly anyone can understand, including, perhaps, her. They had tried to possess her and she had struggled to break free.

Relatedly, perhaps there was the feeling that she was above the rest of her family, that she was better than they and wanted more out of life than an average existence would permit. She must have been unhappy caring for all of us, they might have said, to go to such great lengths to cast their entire way of life into question. It wasn't good enough to raise a family and do some art when time permitted; she had to do the real thing, which meant that they would be cut off from some of the comforts to which those in more normal situations had access. For the most part, her children were around "regular" people, which, she implied, she was not. It was no wonder, then, that there would arise some friction over her chosen pursuits. All told, it could be that her family begrudged this woman her autonomy: You have to be yourself, she had said, even if this means sacrificing some of the needs and desires of others.

At the same time, it may also have been the case that despite her protestations about the need to be herself, something else altogether was going on. Perhaps her family had to listen ceaselessly to her fantasies of penetrating to the very heart of artistic modernity. Perhaps they saw her reading those books and magazines as if they were instruction manuals, telling her how she might become the artist of her dreams. Perhaps they saw how mystified she would sometimes get at her very own creations, and felt that the pride she had experienced upon becoming "contemporary" was somehow hollow. With this hypothetical scenario in mind, it could also be that just as Lynn had grown into this idea of being herself, in others' eyes she had become someone else entirely, someone chasing a fantasy, an elusive image, of just that sort of self-fulfillment that would lift her out of the doldrums of an all too average life.

All was not lost, however. The fact was, she had rushed into her marriage, just as she had rushed into art school; again, she had felt that she was behind everyone else and had done whatever she could to try to catch up. She was always on the fringe of things, Lynn said at one point, one of those people who always seemed to "miss out" on what was happening. This had been painful and perplexing, and it was important, she said, to try not to put so much pressure on herself. But the project of becoming an artist was nevertheless one in which missing out was unthinkable. Whatever it would take to catch up with those who had fled ahead, both personally and artistically, was what had to be done. Yet it was unclear whether things would work out as she hoped. The divorce had been traumatic and had left her anxious and depressed. It was tough enough to stay whole psychologically, let alone worry about her still-dispersed artistic self.

Although the images this woman sought to realize may well have worked for her on some level, if only as a vehicle for giving her a dimension of self-worth in relation to her art that she was apparently unable to acquire elsewhere, it is unclear whether we are to regard them as truly formative. If in fact she goes on to do more and better art, then perhaps these images will have been of service. If the end result is a broken family and little else, the story would be quite different; time will tell. What we see in this case above all, in any event, is precisely the double-edged dimension of these mythical images. While on the one hand they could often serve a positive function, particularly for those whose artistic identities were either fragile or insufficiently developed, they could also yield some serious and often harmful unintended consequences.

It could of course be argued that there is nothing mythical at all in what these artists have said; perhaps they are just extraordinary people telling it like it is. For some, this may be so. But the very fact that a number of these artists were ultimately able to identify these myths for themselves and to see how they had infiltrated their lives and work – unbeknownst to them – should suffice to show that for some their presence was quite real. By and large, those for whom these myths functioned positively never had this sort of awakening; there is rarely the need to be awakened from a dream that is going well. Those for whom they were decidedly less positive, however, often met these myths face-to-face.

HAVING WHAT IT TAKES

For some in the group, the decision to leave art early on may itself have been tied to the mythical images they held. Despite their initial desires and despite the fact that they might have thought, at one point, that they had the requisite talent – "golden hands," as one man put it – they came to feel that something was missing. This man just didn't have a "super talent" like some of the others, so he knew it would be an uphill battle the entire way. Another person, who felt that she only had "medium talent," said that although she might have been able to compensate for her deficits with her great drive, she still knew that there was just so far she would be able to go. For another, the sad intimation that she was "never going to be doing great art" was enough to stop her virtually dead in her tracks; if there existed a ceiling to her creative process, a limit beyond which she would not – indeed could not – go, then there was little reason to keep on.

Notice what is being said here in relation to the idea of artistic development: To the extent that one believes development to be finite, owing to one's seemingly limited capacities, the process itself becomes foreshortened; since forging ahead will, to a greater or lesser extent, inevitably be an exercise in futility, it may be preferable to step aside and make room for others. Some of these people, of course, might have been perfectly justified in doing exactly this; perhaps they simply didn't "have it." But it is also important to recognize that these intimations of the alleged finiteness of their artistic development were often tied as much to internal realities, such as nagging fears and doubts about who and what they were and might become, as facts. In other words, the assumption that their work would never measure up to that of others, far from necessarily being rooted in a veridical appraisal of their talent, may have been rooted instead in both an illusory image of what both they themselves and these others could do.

Perhaps the most prominent of these internal realities was a thoroughgoing lack of confidence in themselves and their work. Several people said that they were never satisfied with the work they were doing; it was always somehow subpar. They were thus unable, from the very start, to gather the kind of conviction and faith requisite for continuing surely and hopefully. For some, this lack of confidence was very much with them still; they found themselves "inhibited" and found the attempt to share their work with others "embarrassing." One woman, for instance, noted that in addition to the problem of the sacrifices that would have to be made if she were to become a genuine artist, she was never really happy with what she had done. If she was going to go through the arduous struggle she had envisioned, then she would have to be significantly better than "okay." And given that there was no assurance that she ever *would* be better than okay, it seemed wise to move on. Another woman described herself as having been "chicken" in the earlier years, which greatly slowed her progress. She had thought back then that this was temporary, that she would eventually get back to her art with vigor and confidence. After all, she went on to recollect, the potential appeared to be there: "We were all going to be great . . . we were going to be famous." It was a good group of people too; they all had "the right kind of spirit" and were "dead serious" about their art. But it was precisely this spirit, she implied, and the fears and insecurities it brought in tow, that had made setting out so painful and difficult: "The idea of failing was horrible."

There could also be the feeling of being in limbo or "treading water," waiting for something, anything, to happen – "those painful years . . . when you're first out of school, when nobody could give a shit about what you're doing except your two or three friends." It is during this time, this woman said, that one can only go on "steam and hope and dreams and honesty about the fact that the work is not really ready for exposure." Again, the issue here has to do in part with where one stands – or where one *imagines* oneself to stand – in relation to others. With everyone appearing so sure of where they were headed, added one man, it was difficult to maintain the conviction that his own art was valid; in the absence of affirmative responses to what he was doing, others' confidence could not help but diminish his own. For him, as for a number of others, it had been unclear whether the work would *ever* be ready for exposure. Some began to pull back, to withdraw; it made for less disappointment and regret.

Interestingly enough, a woman who turned out to be among the best-known artists in the entire group noted that she had not really been interested in becoming established during those early years; she knew that it was premature. The desire to become an established artist – which, she insisted, is not to be equated with a blind search for glory – comes not so much from others and their responses, important though they may be, but from "a belief in your own work." This, of course, takes a great deal of time. But it was imperative to remain patient, this woman emphasized; she herself had been fortunate enough to see the need to ride her artistic immaturity through rather than parade it ostentatiously, as certain others had, with an ill-conceived exposure of both her work and herself.

Some never got this far. They were "never aggressive enough," admits one woman, "never had enough self-confidence" to wait things out. She was just too shy, she "didn't have the guts for it," and, rather than operating on the assumption that her situation might change, by the age of 21 she knew she would have to make a living some other way. The truth is, she really had little idea of what it meant to do art back then. Her own perceived artistic immaturity was not the only factor responsible for her having become disenchanted years ago. She had also come to believe that the art world was a "racket," a political struggle in which you inevitably had to "sell yourself." And she had been entirely unprepared to do this sort of thing. Indeed, she still felt that "it's perfectly idiotic for a young kid, so little of themselves that they know, to put themselves into that kind of situation," as if "they're going to live and die on the art work they produce." For all intents and purposes, this woman left art before really even giving it a chance; it was just too much to ask of someone as naïve as she had been. The desire to be an artist still remained, she noted. Her fantasy was that when she turned 50 or so, she would move to a small town and live out her dreams. Until that time, however, she would have to sit tight and have faith enough to believe that they would someday come true: "I'm still hoping, I'm still hoping."

As the statements we have been considering attest, one of the most salient problems people faced after art school was a lack of confidence in their own work. This meant different things for different people. Some simply didn't believe that they had what it would take to become an artist; adopting essentially nativistic theories about their own capacities, or lack thereof, they felt that, were they to go on, they would be plagued by the fact that their work was forever destined to be inferior. They could therefore either leave art completely, as some did, or go on, knowing – or at least believing – that no matter what they did, they would never be the artists they wished to be.

Others were more temporary in their convictions. They realized that they were immature as artists and that it would take some time before their work was good enough to believe in. If those in the first group were the "nevers," the ones of whom we are speaking now were the "not yets"; their lack of confidence, however well founded it may have been, was a passing phase, a developmental given that had to be accepted and endured. These people, in short, had enough developmental humility, we might say, to acknowledge their own weaknesses without losing sight of the future. Because they knew there were no short cuts to greatness, they would have to learn to withstand their own assaults. There were others still whose lack of confidence apparently had less to do with their work itself than with themselves, as people. In some cases, in fact, even if it was patently clear that they were doing good work, they might still have felt left behind somehow; they could never quite measure up to the unreachable standards they had in their minds. Premature casualties and the like aside, many in the present group did indeed believe they had what it takes to become an artist and set out right away to become one. Let us now turn to some of them, beginning first with those who sought to realize the marginal existence they had heard so much about.

THE TERRIBLE BEAUTY OF PURE MARGINALITY

One man admitted that he got into art because of the "the legacy of the bohemian artist and what that means to society." He thought that he would be "starving and fighting hard, doing all sorts of great work that no one was aware of." The myth, therefore, was one in which he would be working against all odds, free, but hungry and alone: the reclusive genius, painting away in the darkness of obscurity, until the day the world would finally get to see what had been going on. Perhaps it was this myth that led to his early departure from art after a stint in London, where he had been "kicked out" for having no money, and then the Bay area in California, where he had essentially become a full-time artist-dissident, living hand to mouth. He finally got tired of everything and decided to stop being an artist, for a while at any rate.

"I thought that I would just love to be an artist somewhere in a garret," a woman recalled, painting ceaselessly, alone and unnoticed. Unfortunately, she said, "it didn't work out like that": She had to settle for living comfortably. As another woman said explicitly about poverty and how it is frequently viewed by artists, "There is a whole mythology involved with it and it's really destructive." She too had once been "attracted by the bohemian life-style," especially the alleged openness of artists, their freedom from the countless constraints those less fortunate had to withstand. What she found, however, was that while some artists may well face fewer of these constraints, the ones they manage to escape are for the most part insignificant. We shall be hearing more from this woman in the next chapter, when we inquire into the art community. For now, suffice it to say that she had expected things to be vastly different than they in fact were.

Being a painter, said one man, was indeed bound up with "the hero thing"; it meant existing in a "continuous state of the martyr." He was someone who would endure on behalf of those who could not. "People never understand how you could sit there, like you're in a pilot's chair, and just stare at a color for a while." It would be a strange and sacrificial existence, he had thought, filled with emptiness and desolation, but, ultimately, he had asked, " 'What could be purer than being an artist?' " We shall be hearing from him later as well, particularly the tales about his family going on welfare and his suicide attempt, not to mention his seemingly earnest desire to put the people from the New York art world on an island and blow it to smithereens.

Earlier in his life, another man, Jack Murillo, had wanted to be someone like Van Gogh, "on some taut emotional string," always close to the breaking point. When there were art openings, he would be so excited he'd be "panting at the mouth waiting for the door to open"; he couldn't wait to see the latest thing. Sometimes, in fact, he would get so excited in the name of art that he would get into fights. He even had the distinction of having slugged Chicago's leading Abstract Expressionist. Art was all he used to think about. It was enough to destroy his first marriage and, for all he knew, the second one, too. He had been too involved, too serious, and, on account of this, had treated his first wife badly, selfishly, and uncaringly; however innocent she might have been, her very presence thwarted his desires. Quite a few other men in the group, and several women as well – though decidedly fewer – related similar scenarios: There simply wasn't enough emotional room for a commitment both to art and to another person; one of them had to give.

As for his art, Jack had done quite well for a while. He was on the "inside," with a good gallery connection; he had exhibited at the Art Institute and a variety of other well-known museums, and his paintings had found their way into some important collections. There was even a piece in the permanent collection of the Metropolitan Museum of Art in New York. Furthermore, although he continues to question the idea of whether originality is really possible – you usually wind up doing something, he believes, that is tied in one way or another to other artists; you "mix" something in that's your own – he was still convinced that, on some level, some of the things he had done not too long after school were indeed "firsts." One time, for instance, he "had an idea about reality, or something to do with reality, if you read all those awful books," and it became manifested in the form of exhibiting an entire city block. There were all kinds of press releases, posters, and so forth. He had apparently "conned a whole lot of other artists to give [him] money just so they would see their names on the posters." This too was exciting but not altogether successful. Rich people, whose names he had gotten from mailing lists, had come to witness the event, as had school kids with clipboards, anxious to see what all the fuss was about. Some of them wound up getting angry, though, and returned to their fancy cars; as far as they could tell, there was nothing there. He thought it had been a "stroke of genius," and perhaps it had, but all that was over now.

Even though he had once been a part of it, Jack had grown disenchanted with the whole scene: "the self-promotion, sales, gallery trip openings, shaking hands, backslapping, politick-ing your way into a slot so you can live from it." He just wasn't good at doing all these things, he said; he had tried it, because it seemed to be a part of the territory, but always withdrew and played it safe: He couldn't bring himself to be a "suck-up." What he came to feel was that getting ahead in art had less to do with talent than with skills at financial manipulation, skills he neither possessed nor wanted to possess.

There were other problems as well. After a horrible job as a commercial artist, he, like many others, decided that teaching might be preferable; at least then he would maintain some con-tact with art. Upon finding himself in the mountains of Ken-tucky where his first teaching job had brought him, however, he felt that he was losing exactly that contact with art he had hoped to maintain. He therefore moved back to the Midwest, where he was more comfortable, and even became "teacher of the year." But when he shot his mouth off one time too often, as he was prone to do, he was sent packing. Back to Chicago it was, for another teaching stint and a resumed involvement with commercial art.

Jack knew what the dream was: "'All right, I don't care what happens; I'm going to be a fuckin' artist. I'll get on a Greyhound, I'll go to New York, I got ten bucks in my pocket . . . somehow I'll be able to get into what I want, hit it.'" Well, he said, "I never did that." There were some regrets, he admit-ted; after all, that dream had once been his. But they were fewer than they were 10 years ago: "Like dreams about ex-wives, they slow down." All these changes he was describing seemed minor, he went on to say, not very dramatic, not worth talking about. If you're looking for myths, he implied, you'd be better off looking elsewhere; there was nothing exceptional about the story he had to tell.

In fact, if there was anything mythical at all about his life story, he went on to suggest, it was that he had done certain things entirely backward. James Rosenquist, for example, had begun as a billboard artist, only to make the transition to fine art later on in his life; he had moved forward and upward. But

Jack, who had recently become a billboard artist himself, was doing just the opposite. He could live with this, he said; echoes of that former excitement were still there: "When those painters blow that thing up forty feet long, they're making that painting for *me*." But there was something about the position in which he had found himself that left him feeling very uncomfortable as well. "If you do commercial art," he said, in most people's eyes "you're just an asshole who advertises a product – crass, banal"; you're another cog in the wheel of corporate America, hawking your wares. "Fine artists," on the other hand, "throw paint around, do whatever they want, live on some kind of pedestal, and what they produce is crap and doesn't mean anything." So it was that he found himself, some 20 years down the road from when he first began, engaged in a perpetual and painful battle, between what he had come to be – an accomplice in the decidedly impure, capital-driven world of the marketplace – and what he had aspired to be, however meaningless he tells himself it is.

One of the foremost challenges Jack faced was living with the reality of "hopping over the fence between commercial and fine art . . . and regulating [his] life and thoughts to be harmonious." It hasn't been easy. His decision, in fact, was to abandon painting altogether for the time being. He couldn't look at it or touch it, for all of his ambivalence, his regrets, and perhaps his shame immediately stared him in the face: to think that a man who had once been capable of genius, or at least something like it, should have been forced into this awkward position. My sense in speaking to him was that he actually quite liked designing billboards; that wasn't the main problem. The problem instead was in the fact of his aborted project to become a fine artist and, more painfully still, in the image – conferred not only by others, but by himself – of a man who ostensibly had capitulated to "going commercial." Note the irony of this situation: Despite having become disenchanted with the commercialization of fine art, and despite feeling still that there was something just plain absurd about commerical artists being considered "assholes" and fine artists being put on a pedestal –

57

the dividing line between what they each did wasn't nearly so firm as some might believe – he could not quite shake the profound allure of being an artist. Hence his fear to look and touch.

Regrets aside, when asked how pleased he was with his present situation, he was quick to answer: "happy as a fuckin' clam"; he didn't know "how any man could be more fortunate." Would he ever paint again? Yes, he'd certainly like to, in fact he "can't wait" to, but it would undoubtedly be some time before he was ready. Would he have done anything differently if he had known the outcome? Probably not. The truth is, "I think we behave like robots; I don't think there's much choice involved." Sure, he said, "I can look back and read all kinds of lists of mistakes I made, but I think given the conditions at the time, I'd do the same things again."

In some respects, Jack's attitude might be considered a healthy one. There was little use in creating odes to what might have been – had he been wiser, stronger, more confident, or what have you; he did what had to be done. At the same time, however, it could be that his own thesis of inevitability and fatalism, his own conviction that things could only have been as they were, is a kind of rationalization, a defensive justification for the way his life turned out. The primary reasons why he left art, he said, were practical ones; he had to make a living, support a family, and so forth. But these concerns, he admitted, also gave him something of an out, a "back door." And not only had he slipped out this back door, but the new door he had entered represented the very antithesis of what being an artist was at least *supposed* to be about – namely, damning precisely those tawdry visions of bourgeois existence strewn across billboards and the like throughout the land. He had all but become an accomplice to the crime.

He felt like an entirely different person lately. There was a painting still in his apartment somewhere that he had hoped to finish, but he had no idea what to do about the "damn thing"; it just sat there, untouched. Strangely enough, the processes responsible for creating fine art and the processes responsible for designing billboards were not all that different. "I wouldn't call it an opposition of styles," he said; "it's an opposition of two

58

kinds of philosophies." What Jack suggests, in other words, is that it was the *meaning* of the two processes that were problematic for him, the aura that surrounded them: Whereas the first would lead to contemplation, the second would lead to consumption. And once you dive headlong into the production of commercialized objects, whose very existence is designed to serve some other's ends, it is no easy task to return to creation for creation's sake. Again, practically speaking, there may not be all that much difference in this context either; fine art often serves some other's ends too and it may be no less rooted in the world of marketing than the things being advertised on billboards. But the awareness of this fact was of little emotional consequence: No matter how happy and fortunate he told himself he was, he couldn't wait to sit before that unfinished painting and know what to do.

It can plausibly be argued, I think, that the man we have been discussing has engaged in a kind of "reaction–formation" defensive maneuver. He had been passionate about creating art and especially about being an artist, wound up doing something philosophically opposed to his previous values and ideals, and subsequently came to be alienated from the very objects he had once loved. Perhaps in due time he will succeed in "working through" his defenses, as psychoanalysts sometimes say, and be able to face those objects once again. There may be a cost to this. For he may find that there is little choice but to split himself in two: a billboard artist by day, a fine artist by night; two distinct selves, a producer and a creator. Until that time, in any case, he will have to continue hopping the fence between these two worlds and hope that he remains agile enough to make it work.

To claim that this man sought marginality probably isn't quite right. Even though he had once sought to emulate Van Gogh, his dreams weren't really of dilapidated garrets per se; they were instead dreams of purity, of a mode of existence unsullied by the dirt, the crude commerciality, of American life. This purity of which he spoke was itself a myth; and this myth, juxtaposed against the tawdry realities of billboard life, made him feel, deeply, that he had done himself wrong. In this case, therefore, the myth at hand not only affected adversely his own artistic activities – which, again, he was still interested in pursuing at some point – but stopped them completely: Going back to what Marx and Engels said earlier regarding the concentration of talent in particular individuals, one can say he *was* no longer an artist. Thus the space of his own creativity, despite his desire to keep it open, had closed, and would no doubt remain so until he found it within himself to demythicize what being an artist was all about.

Another man, Gary Keane, related a similar scenario. Most people had the same idea – "The Plan," as he put it: He would get a good teaching job and would have time enough left over to dedicate himself to his primary goal, which was to be a fine artist. Unfortunately, he said, "it doesn't work." For one, despite the fact that he had thought teaching would be wonderful, it turned out that he couldn't stand it; the time demands were greater than he had assumed and, more important, he found that he just wasn't that interested in it. "What I really like to do," he learned, "is make stuff," and "if I can't be making something I'm not really happy." He therefore decided that he would go into advertising, which, though it was a significant step removed from his initial desires, would at least allow him to do more hands-on sorts of things.

Gary had no idea at all that he would wind up where he did; the idea of going into advertising had never even entered the picture. But upon recalling some design work he had done for a photographer while still in school, which had actually been quite satisfying, he came to feel that he would place himself in a better situation than the one he had been in as a teacher. "It's a happy medium," he said. "You're not a total fine artist, but you can keep doing things that are similar and you can use a lot of artistic judgment."

The only problem was his lingering desire to be a fine artist. For when he was working on his art, he would torment himself for having capitulated to doing commercial work; he would experience tremendous guilt over what he had done, and for about 10 years he would go back and forth between the two endeavors, trying to justify in his own mind their respective rationales. But he was never really able, he said, to keep them in balance. "I just didn't have enough time to devote to it . . . didn't have the right priorities." He therefore elected to give up fine art completely; the guilt had proved to be too much to bear. Things became much easier afterward. He had finally calmed down and learned to live with his choices, the result being that, "Everything seems more justified now than it did before."

What also happened, however, was that upon being able, finally, to put things in perspective, he found himself thinking about art more than ever; he felt that he really could do both again and have it be all right. He was still able to see what the "real values" were in life, and art certainly represented one of them: "If you're going to be make any contribution to life or whatever, art is really it." He knew he would have to include it in his life in some fashion; there was simply no way he could give it up forever.

One of the problems he had experienced during those 10 years was that he had been a "total perfectionist." Back then, he had believed, it was either all or nothing; it was unthinkable that he could have anything less than a complete and total commitment. But he had "gotten away from that perfectionism: 'I have to have the right studio, the right tools, the right mood.' That's all past now." He would no longer wait for "the right time," as he put it, because he finally realized that "there *is* no right time." It wasn't necessary to conform to the idea and ideal of the single-minded artist, the purist, committed to art alone; that was just a romantic image he would have to set aside if he ever was to do anything. He had to go ahead and do it, without thinking about it or talking about it, without ruminating obsessively about whether his chosen path was or was not justified. "Now," he said, "I feel like whatever you want to do is possible." Maybe he would sculpt again after all.

There was no great urgency, however. There was a sense, in fact, in which advertising was liberating, even more liberating, perhaps, than fine art. "I used to think about the art work as fishing: You do the art work, put it out there, wait for a nibble." Now, despite being part of "cold-hearted industry," he could avoid these sorts of situations. Furthermore, there were so many artists, he said, who were so "cloistered," who always seemed to get "hung up on one idea." As an advertising artist, though, he might work with 20 ideas in a single month, and sell 20 different products. It was true, of course, that the work he was doing didn't represent any "great, meaningful statements on life," but when he thought about all the different things people did to make a living, he couldn't help but feel that what he was doing was "pretty terrific." And again, the fact of the matter was, as far as the actual process of making things went, it really wasn't all that different from what he had done as a fine artist. When he went to a big art exhibit a while back and saw how similar some of the works were to pieces he had done in conjunction with advertising, in fact, he started to feel that there was something markedly artificial about the hard and fast line of demarcation that had been erected between fine art and commercial art, and about the "supposed superiority" of the former over the latter. Why should he feel so guilty about what he did anyway?

There were some differences, of course, since he was mainly responsible for the execution of ideas rather their conception, and he also was aware that there wasn't as much freedom in commercial art as there was in fine art; the bottom line was, the products had to sell. Upon showing us a great big styrofoam pumpkin he had recently done, and then a wooden turkey, he admitted that there was no way he would have even thought about doing such things when he was in art school; they would have been deemed too banal and tacky to deserve any consideration. But things had changed. You've got to be someone who lives, Gary had realized, not just talk, like a lot of artists did. He would have lunch with local cops; he had come to have a new reverence for the commoner. What it came down to, he suggested, was that he really didn't need the whole art scene anyway. It was tremendously important to be an artist – that much he had already avowed – but it was too far removed from life itself, what with all its incessant discussion of ideas, its deliberateness, and its complicity in elitism.

An additional reason for Gary's falling away from art had to do with his background. "I was a middle-class kid," he explained. "My parents didn't have any money." He had never begrudged them this, he said, and he had never gotten upset about it either. But he had been left with a heavy load: "You start out, got a goddam paper route, got a job in a drug store, job on the beach . . . you're always thinking about making money." He was still able to feel that this ethic was valid, "but God, the price you pay toward your artwork is horrendous." He could never quite reconcile the idea of being engaged in a pursuit that was so much the antithesis of what he had learned was "real" work. The fact that his wife had been employed full-time when he was still doing free-lance art didn't help much either. Here he was, the supposed breadwinner, the Man of the Family, indulging himself in this personal odyssey while his wife was providing for the family. This couldn't help but affect his ability to do his art and feel justified about it. And while the guilt virtually vanished when he went full-time himself, so too did his art. It had been a no-win situation.

There was no denying it: "When I went to the Art Institute, I thought I'd died and gone to heaven." But he was nevertheless ill-prepared to step into the role of the artist. He had never understood "that there were definitely two parts" and "that there was nothing wrong with wanting to be either one or keeping them in some kind of balance." Only now, some two decades later, was he able to see how thoroughly he had internalized these cultural contradictions, and only now could he imagine being able to strike the desired balance. He didn't have to become an Artist in order to do art; that was someone else's requirement, issuing from one of those purist myths he had heard so much about. The only real requirement was that he do what he felt was right.

This man had been caught between two opposed ideologies. On the one hand, there was the ideology of the totally committed fine artist, who would settle for nothing less than constant immersion in his or her work. Also a part of this ideology was the notion that fine art should have nothing at all to do with crass commercial considerations and the like; the artist was precisely that sort of being who knew that there were more important things to life and who would work fiercely and independently to make sure these things achieved primacy over all the rest. Given this man's failure ever to become this being, he had been left feeling tormented, even ashamed.

On the other hand, there was a kind of Protestant work ethic in the picture as well, that had been wrought by both his humble upbringing and, later on, by the culturally based expectation that the man of the family should be doing something more productive with his time than fulfilling his own romance-laden dreams of becoming an artist. What he most seemed to want, therefore, was that which he knew he could never justifiably have. Not only was being an artist too self-indulgent, but it ran against the grain of that sort of homespun populism that was closer to his roots. Fundamentally, he felt he was more like the local cops with whom he had lunch than the fine artists he had once emulated.

The only way Gary would be able to sculpt again was if he defused these two sets of ideas. First and foremost, he would have to stop being such a purist and perfectionist, always waiting until everything was just right, and would have to convince himself that creating art did not necessarily require all of the accessory images he had earlier adopted. If the desire arose, then he might as well just go with it, guilt-free, and do what he could. Second, he would have to convince himself that it was perfectly justifiable to engage in activities every now and then that didn't have quite so much utilitarian value as activities were supposed to have; it was okay, he would have to learn, to balance the instrumental with the expressive, even if it meant having to account for himself to his friends, who were undoubtedly demanding something else. He knew full well, he said, that most artists were frowned upon, like they were "some kind of nitwits," because they weren't "trying to make a billion dollars"; he knew that "the business of America is business." But he also knew that he "could be the richest man in the grave too." Somehow, therefore, he would have to find a place for those passions that had once moved him so. Judging by his own words, Gary was on the way to doing just this; he had begun to gain a hint of what the necessary balance might look like. But it was also clear that, given the ideological structures within which he had become entangled, it would take no small amount of psychical effort for this man to be able to sculpt again.

BEING AND DOING

In at least one case, of a rather different kind, we are able to see how images of purity and marginality can become fused with visions of grandeur. We have seen hints of this fusion already; artistic purity, manifested in the form of the untainted fine artist who serves as the antidote to the poisons of bourgeois life, can have as its correlate the fetishization of the superior being – a kind of Messiah complex, as one man put it. In the case to follow, this dynamic is more pointed still. Indeed, what it serves to demonstrate, among other things, is that myths of marginality and myths of grandeur are intimately connected with one another: The garret is replaced by the pedestal.

Samuel Palesky provided a virtual catalog of reasons for why he was unable to paint as he would have wished. Prior to attending art school in the early 1960s, he had worked full-time as an editor for a publishing company in Chicago. While in art school, he moved to part-time, and upon graduating, resumed full-time responsibilities for several years. Graduating from art school in 1964, at the age of 45, he was among the oldest students there. He was also late to marry due mainly to what he described as an elusive search for perfection, for the one and only woman who would match the intensity of his fantasies. Although it is difficult to say whether he found her, he did get married in 1967 and moved with his wife to the small town she was from. It was a great place to settle, to raise a family perhaps, and to do some serious painting. He felt that he had succumbed to "wandering in the wilderness" artistically due to the change of venue, but his new wife and, eventually, his new son helped to make the transition less painful.

Despite the fact that their new home was about three hours from Chicago, Samuel chose not to give up his editorial job; the long commute and the hassle involved in staying in the city for several days did not suffice to incite him to leave. The job, he said, remained important, both financially and emotionally; it was the one thing where he was truly needed. Furthermore, there was also a certain amount of creativity involved in what he did. It wasn't the sort of thing he would want on his tombstone, he explained, but as jobs went, this one wasn't bad. Not surprisingly, however, he grew more and more to feel that his life was being split into two distinct arenas: work and art. Although he continued to maintain a studio in Chicago, he felt that he was unable to be creative while he was there; it was too unsettled, too temporary. After a day's work, it was also difficult, particularly because he was getting on in years, to commence doing his art; he was tired and preferred to rest. "When I leave here," therefore, he said, referring to his home in the country, "I'm artistically dead." He did a sketch once in a while on the road, but that was all. As a general rule, half of every week was "lost."

When he had lived in Chicago, he had a number of paintings in shows, a solid gallery connection, and had even won a prize for his work. With his move, however, he was just too far away to remain involved with the Chicago art scene. As for his artistic involvement out in the country, he had been fortunate to be able to establish another gallery connection not too long after his arrival; it had lasted 6 or 7 years and had generally worked out well. But after this, the gallery had been forced to go out of business, leaving him high and dry.

From that point on, he said, he felt that he couldn't really sell much more than watercolors – "little representational things" that might find their way into people's homes. The locals' artistic appreciation was "nil," and the visitors who would occasionally come through town on their country outings were not about to shell out too much money for an unknown quantity like himself. As he reflected further on this situation, the picture darkened even more. The story really wasn't all that different when he had the gallery connection. He recounted one opening, for instance, when the rain was coming down so hard that only four or five people showed up; the countless unopened bottles of champagne served as sore reminders of what his artistic life really was. In fact, when it came right down to it, he went on to say, this opening wasn't much different from those that went on when the weather was just fine, and in bigger places than this one. There had been another opening many years back, for instance, at a well-known art center in Chicago, where everybody, himself included, felt that they were important, that they were on the cutting edge of American art. But this was simply an "illusion"; it was no more important than the scene out in the country. "What difference does it make? You have a good time, and if nobody came, then so what?" You go back to your editorial job the next day anyway.

Samuel was unable to see his former excitement as genuine. Because he knew that these openings, despite the incredible sense of possibility they presented, could lead to nothing, his past appeared foolish to him, inflated with the grandiosity of youth: to think that he had assumed he was part of something big, something promising. The reality, he suggested, was that he and his fellow artists had gotten caught up in the mythical wonder of the moment, and no matter how much joy and exuberance there had been, it had all become bathed in the bleakness of the situation in which he ultimately found himself.

Like so many others, his plans had been "to do a lot of painting, attract a gallery, and be some kind of success." But apparently, it was not meant to be. Commenting on those people in his home town who do the "pretty little watercolors," he said, "more power to them. If this is what truly makes them happy, I envy them, I truly envy them." It wasn't for him. He also envied the person who could "produce a body of important work and not have any encouragement, do this on his own and plug away." He wasn't talking about rewards but a climate, an artistic environment that would allow him to feel that he was part of something beyond his singular self. It was difficult to feel this out there in the woods. The people he envied most, however, were artists like Picasso, Braque, and Chagall, "who, aside from the commercial success they all achieved . . . were able to do what they really wanted to do superbly, to find themselves." Of these artists, he said, "Hell, they touched brush to canvas and they knew basically where they were going; they already

67

had a road map in their mind and it was just a matter of kind of working out the details, moving a certain amount of furniture around, so to speak." It didn't matter when you found it, he continued, "whether you're a Giorgione who dies of the plague at thirty-one or thirty-three, who finds it early and dies early, or whether you find it when you're sixty, or whether you're somewhere in the middle and lose it. But you've had it; you've been there." The problem, he went on to say, was that "it wasn't that simple for the modern artist." Indeed, "After Picasso, what is there left to do? In other words, it's all been done." He therefore found himself "distracted" when he faced the canvas; his fear was that he was "never going to find it."

Samuel's search for himself and his art had become fraught with anguish. He described himself as looking frantically for that elusive formula which would allow him to gather both the creativity and the recognition that might have accrued to him at some other time or place. He was always "trying to find some new way," he said, but like so many of his artistic forays to date, it seemed that they each turned out to be "less an avenue than a blind alley." So much of what he had done was "untrue," he felt. He had wanted at one point, for instance, to be "literary" in his art, clever and enigmatic. But he could never make it work, neither for others nor for himself. So, "why try to do clever things that are trying to catch the public eye that won't catch the public eye anyway? Why not do things that are truer to what painting is all about?" He had always faced this sort of problem, he recollected, even in the case of the painting for which he had won that prize, back in the 1960s. "At that time," he said, "I had no qualms about that: If it helps, it helps." But it was too late, and too unjustifiable, to do "clever things" now.

These memories brought up a further problem that he had to contend with. The ideal condition for creativity, he said, was "where art isn't beholden to any commercial considerations, where you don't have to make a living at it, where you don't have to please a customer, where you don't have to please a dictator." If it wasn't for the lingering gaze of the public eye, in other words, the situation would be vastly improved. There would be no rules, no dictates; artists would able to remain true to their own hearts. Yet there would still remain problems. For without the public eye, "you're on your own." The dilemma, therefore, was that if artists painted expressly for others, as he had sometimes done, the creative process would be deformed. But if artists created strictly for themselves, they would be left in a kind of vacuum, devoid of support and encouragement, which became problematic in its own right. The issue, again, was not to be reduced to the mere absence of rewards. The issue had to do with tradition, which, he believed, "we don't have now." In short, Samuel felt that he was forced to suffer some of the plight of modernity itself: "The contemporary artist," he asked, "what does he have?" The answer was, "He doesn't have anything really; he has to find his own way." The result of this situation was that "the luck of the draw" led to recognition; you "have to be in the right place at the right time." In the absence of meaningful standards of value, this was all one could hope for.

Samuel realized how easy it was "to take a cop-out and say the world treats me poorly" and that "I have every right to cry in my beer." He had heard himself whining, it seemed, and he had no desire to project his countless problems onto the world alone: "A person is partly responsible for his own plight." Furthermore, given that "the muse of art is a stern mistress," who "demands devotees who burn with a pure flame in her service," it may be that he simply hadn't been motivated enough to achieve what he wanted. Sure, he said, he could blame his tendency toward distraction on his family, as he sometimes did, but he also admitted that even if he didn't have a family he would have found some other distraction. "Maybe," he even said, "it's that I've always felt that I don't have that much to offer, that I allow myself to be distracted." Maybe he was "trying to avoid getting down to basics, wrestling with the unknown." Maybe he wanted to be spared the "inevitable," which had to do with his failure at successfully "fighting paint and fighting an idea, trying to make it work." Or maybe, as Fernand Leger once stated, "You can either have a great life or a great painting, but not both."

This might be true for some artists, but the notion rang somewhat hollow for him. The fact was, he just didn't respect himself. Whether it was trimming the Christmas tree or going out shopping with his family or going to visit people, he would always say, "'Well, that sounds pretty good.' So I'll put down the brush, put down the pencil: 'Yeah, great, let's go. I'll get back to it again. I'll get back to it. I'll live long enough to get back to it later on.'" Look, he said, "What I have to express I can express in the time I have"; it would be utter delusion to contend otherwise. He was insightful enough to acknowledge that he himself had played a significant part in his failure. But there was no denying that "the world is a cold, cruel place." Hadn't he on some level been forced to become this distractible? Weren't these tendencies themselves signs of the times? "I'd like to do more work," he said, but since "there's nobody waiting in the wings to get it," there was little reason to try.

He didn't feel that his goals were that grand; all he wanted was "to make a little ripple in the art world," to have a gallery connection again, sell an occasional painting, get an occasional review. Of course none of this would be success in the "real" art world, he noted, but from where he stood, "two inches high," that was all that he could hope for. But it wasn't realistic to expect this; he was too far away from meeting this goal, and time was starting to run out. The tragedy was that in some ways Samuel's entire life had become a distraction. He was no longer able to do anything without feeling that he was merely defending against the knowledge of what he ought to be doing: trying to create the art he could not create. Even if there were no distractions at all, he reiterated, and even if there were people waiting in the wings, he would still suffer the plight of the modern artist, "adrift amongst the shifting sands." It was a terribly awkward situation. Like so many others, he said, "I don't know what the real me is." And the truth was, "I don't know if I will ever know."

The main problem, he concluded, was that the climate within which artists were to create just wasn't conducive to it. "This isn't the era of the artist," as he put it. "This is the era of the engineer, the technician." Maybe someone who was "extremely gifted" or a "wealthy dilettante" could pursue a life-

70

time career in fine art; he knew that there were people who had been able to make a go of it. "Art," however, "can be a real burden to those of us who have not supreme ability or supreme pushiness or supreme good luck or a combination to excel in 'real' terms." They were forced to "move ahead without very much outside help, direction, or interest." Although he was ob-viously a "failure," he wasn't about to complain too much. Af-ter all, he could have been dead. "I see all these brilliant achievers who cork off at sixty or fifty-five or even earlier," he said, and they paid the price for their achievements. "I look at myself as a failure," he said again, "but I'm a *live* failure." This too rang hollow. For being an artist, he said, is ultimately "what it's all about. It's the culmination of mankind; it's the flame." The artist was "godlike," he said, "the Prometheus, pulling down the fire," and he just hadn't risen to the occasion. He had hoped to be a God, but instead became a man, and by his own lights, not a very successful one at that.

It may be that this man was such a perfectionist and had such an inflated image of what being an artist meant that he had no choice but to fail. To this extent, he might have been a victim of his own fantasy, peopled as it was with romantic heroes from days of old. It might also be that the quality of his art itself was such that, no matter what the conditions, he might have stopped short of his goals. He himself said as much when he admitted that he did not have the "supreme talent" that some others have. In the case of both of these interpretations, the pri-mary locus of responsibility for his own failure would devolve upon Samuel himself, the external factors he adduced being little more than projections, designed to assuage the terrible re-alization that he had indeed been the architect of his own destiny. Along these lines, a "better" man or woman, less gran-diose perhaps or less willing to reify artistic talent into a gift from God, might have faced the same conditions and fared sig-nificantly better than this man did; he or she would have tran-scended these conditions rather than buckling beneath them. Given his own refusal to completely disavow his own part in what had and had not happened, he himself might have agreed; he knew that the world he was indicting derived, at least in part, from his own constructions, his own discolored interpretations.

But what led this man to construct the world as he did? Acknowledging that intrapsychic factors played some role, I am still prepared to say that the most fundamental dilemma of which this man spoke – which had to do with either bowing to the demands of the public, which would compromise the integrity of his own inner voice, or listening to this voice, which was so dim as to be barely be audible – was quite real. As regards the first horn of this dilemma, he felt alienated by what seemed to be demanded of artists in this day and age. In the relative absence of a shared set of artistic values and ideals – a "tradition," as he put it – he felt that artists were often forced to devise gimmicky schemes to catch the public eye. As others told us as well, there was the need to stand apart from other artists rather than with them because what was required, most of all, was a significant enough difference in one's work as to make it marketable. He may, of course, have been indulging himself in a kind of nostalgia in supposing that in times past things were different, but he was convinced nonetheless that much of what passed as artistic creation fell short of what "true art" was all about. If left to their own devices, he suggested, artists might indeed ascend to the heights of the gods; they might be able to tap into that realm of existence which lay beyond the petty concerns of the earthly world. There were few, however, who had the psychic resources to do this.

As regards the second horn of the dilemma, Samuel also felt that being left to one's own devices was no less problematic than painting on demand. For what artists faced was the burden of fashioning their *own* traditions, of creating their own singular universes of language and meaning. On some level, again, this situation is no different from what it has always been: "The artist," he said at one point, "can create something out of basically nothing." How, then, are we to understand his complaints in this context? If the true artist could create something out of nothing, why was the situation he described any more precarious than it had ever been?

The answer is a straightforward one. In the past, Samuel suggested, enough had existed in the tradition to allow artists to forge ahead with a sense of directedness and conviction. They didn't really create out of nothing but out of something; firmly rooted in the ground of their lives, they had a sufficient degree of faith to allow them to become like the gods they emulated. For modern artists, however, creating something of nothing meant just that: Devoid of an existential foundation and devoid of those gods who might allow one to feel that artistic creation still partook of the divine, they had been forced to face a kind of ontological vertigo, rife with uncertainty about whether the project of finding one's true self, as both artist and as individual, was a valid one. So it is that when he looked to the God within, all he saw were blind alleys and dead ends. However deluded he might have been about the origins of his problems, therefore, it may be that he was being ruthlessly honest in proclaiming that he simply did not know if there was anything really there for him to express. Romantic images aside, to create out of nothing was all but impossible; it was tantamount to an act of magic, like a beautiful white dove appearing out of nowhere.

Even with these interpretations, however, my inclination is to say that this man's artistic activities were curtailed primarily by his mythicized expectations of what a true artist was and did. *Being* an artist, he said, was tantamount to being a God, and *creating* art nothing less than the godly act of giving life. Whatever truth he may have expressed about the ugliness of the field, the absence of a discernible artistic tradition, and so forth, it was largely his own inflated images of the artist that led to his demise.

Psychodynamic interpretations may be appropriate here as well. It could, for instance, be argued that it was his own intrapsychic "issues" – his perfectionism, grandiosity, and so forth – that were really (which is not to say exclusively) responsible for how things turned out. Because this case is particularly extreme, there is some reason to entertain this idea. But it can still be said, without contradiction, that the images in question were a primary means by which the space of his own creativity was constricted. In addition to the division of labor, the emergence of the Romantic era, and so on, these myths may in fact have gained some of their currency because they mesh so well with intrapsychic needs and desires, at least as they have become constituted in the Western world, with its profound emphasis on the individuated subject, able to make her or especially *his* mark: The project of individuation, of finding oneself, coupled with the project of attaining the heights of artistic godliness, would seem to make for a particularly explosive – and destructive – situation for those falling short of it. We need not be reductive, therefore, in calling attention to this mythical dimension with which we have been concerned; "overdetermination," as Freud called it, is the rule. Indeed, the case we have just discussed should serve as an apt reminder both of how labyrinthine the nexus of contributory factors can be and of how thoroughly enmeshed with one another they are.

THE ROAD TO GLORY

Other artists had a much more enlarged view of their own artistic abilities and their own prospects for success than Samuel had. Early in their careers, many of them believed that they were either fully formed artists already or that they soon would be. Their futures appeared to be theirs for the asking and development a mere matter of potentiating what they perceived to be their own extraordinary abilities. In recollecting his anticipated future, one man glibly stated, "I would have been the next Messiah, what else?" After the ritual trek to Europe, where he would become steeped in Culture, he would return with even more ammunition with which to blow away his fellow countrymen, with their sorrily American values and ideals. "I thought I'd come back from Europe and make a name for myself," he admitted. Unfortunately, though, "it's been difficult to even get to first base." Now that she had settled into a solid teaching job, which had proved to be compatible with her art, one woman had time to think about being an artist more humbly than she had earlier. She used to think she was

74

more "special" than other people. "We all want to be whis-
pered to by some unnamed muse," she said. And then there
was her "captivation with living the part": She too had seen
herself as a kind of Messiah. But times had changed. Art, she
came to believe, rather than being some divine gift from above,
was instead a learnable skill, having to do with "our basic drive
to find patterns and likenesses around us." She also came to
believe that it was important for people, her students especially, to see art in these terms. But if they were anything like she
herself had been, there would have to be a good deal of
demythologizing for this to be possible.

"I felt I had this gift to give to the world," added another
woman. Thankfully, she said, her teachers at the Art Institute
thought otherwise: "'Your gift ain't there yet,'" they told her.
"Until you go someplace like the Art Institute," said yet another, it's easy to "have an illusion that you're the greatest artist
that ever hit the world, and that you don't really want to
change anything you already do because you might louse up
your inherent genius." If you are lucky, as she was, "it sinks
into your stupid head that all you're doing is standing in your
own way." Notice that those artists who saw their futures as
bleak, owing to the perceived ordinariness of their artistic abilities, and those who saw their futures as bright, owing to their
"inherent genius," faced a similar problem: The process of their
own development was brought to a standstill. If you've already
got it, they seemed to say, then there is nothing more to be done.

Let us move toward concluding this chapter by exploring
two final cases, both of which show, in quite different ways,
how one's creativity and development may be restarted. Seven
or eight years before Tom Davison was interviewed, he had
apparently undergone a total reevaluation of his artistic aims.
He had painted earlier, he said, but not seriously; he came to
feel, in fact, that he had done his work more out of habit than
anything else. For reasons that were unknown to him at the
time, he kept getting lost during the process of painting; he felt
he had no sense of self whatsoever. What he decided to do,
therefore, was adopt a regimen of painting self-portraits, of
which he did some 30 or 40; perhaps if he was able to behold

himself face-to-face, he would gradually learn just who and what he was. This went on for approximately 5 years, and the paintings had no destiny other than to serve as possible vehicles for his own self-reflection. He didn't try to exhibit them or sell them; he just looked at them, with the hope that he might come to terms with his alienation.

What he needed to determine, most of all, was whether painting was for him or whether instead it was for "some romantically linked view of the artist as being special to a community." Becoming an artist, he suggested, had some obvious allures, particularly during the time in question. The artist, it had seemed, was someone who was able to partake of the sacred in an all too secular world, someone who was indeed "special," extraordinary, who possessed just that sort of identity worth having. This is what he himself had desired. Moreover, he had greatly desired acceptance, applause, write-ups in the papers, and, of course, sales. He had therefore set out to do exactly that sort of work which might bring these desirable things about.

But he wasn't aware of these issues back then; for all he knew, he wanted to create. After completing the aforementioned series of self-portraits, he realized that, yes, he had been operating "out of some rather masklike values: The kinds of things I had done," he said, "were not based on my inner need or even personal goals so much as what I thought others wanted to see or what others thought was good, valuable." He had even stopped doing art at one point for 2 years; he was so worn out from trying to paint authentically, whatever that might mean, that he "couldn't touch it."

Tom went on to enumerate some of the problems he had come to identify. For one, however alienated he had been from his own artistic processes, it used to be the only thing he felt he had in life; like a number of others with whom we spoke, he had been "crazy, off the edge." Fortunately, he said, "my view of what I do now is far less important than what I saw before." Another source of problems lay in the contradictions between what the School of the Art Institute had emphasized, particularly in regard to the value of nonobjective art, and what the little community college where he taught had emphasized, which was decidedly less radical. He became more and more confused over these contradictions, he said; the styles with which he had been working did not feel natural, they were never really cohesive and integrated, and they couldn't be understood by him, let alone by others. The way he described this situation was that he had learned to maintain a social self, but it was excessive; there was nothing that felt rightfully his. He had been insecure, he admitted, and had apparently done what would be deemed acceptable. This too has come to pass: "My concern for what will be acceptable . . . is no longer even a question." This is not to say that he does not want his work to be acceptable, for he surely does; but if the issue of acceptability was foremost in his mind from the outset of the creative process, it could not help but dilute its integrity and authenticity.

After his 2-year hiatus, Tom's aim was to bring the two strands he referred to, the nonobjective and the objective, together. He would create forms, but of an unidentifiable nature, and thus try to articulate the interplay between what is and isn't real. Later, however, he came to feel that these issues did not really matter anyway. "Painting is fiction," he said; "it hasn't got anything to do with truth. It's honest, but it's not reality except as an object." He realized that this may sound somewhat "glib," but he felt that these realizations had proved healthy for him, leading to a much more realistic view of art, both personally and socially: Art should be a creative outlet, a vehicle for discovery and play, a means to escape social and cultural confinements. And the way he had treated it earlier, he suggested, was precisely *as* one of these confinements; again, it had been seen as the epitome of human endeavors, the greatest thing one could possibly do, the result being that the "Hollywood-type romanticized images" with which he had been invaded had prevented the possibility of his doing anything meaningful.

"Painting," he realized, "doesn't have to be fixed according to the rules of the world, the universe, the laws." It used to be, for instance, that "imitating something seemed taboo," particularly when he was in art school; it was deemed archaic and unmodern. One had to do what one was told; only then would it be possible to become a bona fide artist, a member in good standing of the much touted Art World. His own self-deception, he implied, was not strictly his own fault; indeed, it was almost as if this was required on some level: In order to succeed, he was apparently told, he couldn't remain who he was; "the style was more important than the reason for doing it." What young artist had enough sense of himself or herself as to be able to withstand these directives? He had been the dutiful student, eager to find the key to the future, like many of his friends. But the result, ironically, was that he had wound up moving farther and farther away from whatever creative impulses he might have had to begin with.

It was only when Tom was able to identify the strictures and prohibitions that had been operative in those earlier years that he was able to create. With the maturation of his own conviction in his work and his self, which led to a diminished concern for what was acceptable and stylish, he felt that he was finally able to free up some of his creative energies. The illusion he had lived was not complete; he really did want to create. But it took no small amount of time before he could fully believe this. What was important, he said, was to remain in touch with what he thought was right and, more specifically, to abide by the internal workings of his paintings and his own true desires rather than by external values.

What had happened, in fact, was that his paintings had come to be about exactly the sorts of issues with which he had been dealing, even if unwittingly, for all of those confused years. He became "curious about perceptions, habits, conventions, how we learn to see the world the way we do, the things we're taught when we're very young, the things we learn through mimicry." And what it all came down to, he concluded, is a view "that the kind of reality we have is one that we make – which puts *us* in charge." Nobody would determine for him any longer what is real and true and valuable and what is not; the task of the painter is to determine this for him- or herself.

None of what he has told us should be taken to imply that rewards are irrelevant or that he did not desire them; he still had "plans" for making a living from his art someday. But these rewards were at last in their proper place. The goal now was subjective rather than objective success, his foremost desire being to do some good paintings. Indeed, if he could adhere to this goal, he suggested, objective success would be that much more likely to follow. He still had a way to go before he would be able to live off his art. Teaching tended to interfere, as did his children, despite their being virtual "models" of spontaneity and creative expression. Perhaps if his wife got another job, he would be able to quit his own and paint full-time. All he could do for the time being, however, was wait, consoled by the fact that, after all those years of false starts and mock creativity, he was ready to go out on his own and do some honest painting.

Tom's story, like several of the others that have been discussed, is as much about the artistic field and domain as it is about Hollywood-type images; integral to playing the part, he indicated, was the desire to become well connected in the art world as well as the desire to do the kind of art that would further this end. Once again, therefore, there is little need to point to the mythical images that had become operative in this man's life and work as being *the* source of his own artistic stasis. It is nonetheless clear that it was only when he worked through the existence of these images, as they had become signified in the faces that gazed back at him in the portraits he had painted, that he could move on to be someone and do something real.

Paul Monte's story is a bit severer. "I had a game plan," he recalled: "I was supposed to have had my first one-man show in New York by the time I was thirty." He was exactly the sort of figure that Lippard had spoken of; seeing all the commotion being made over those who had managed to make it, he was determined to follow in their tracks and climb to the very peaks of success. Unfortunately, it didn't work out that way. Quite the opposite, in fact: "I started at the top and worked my way down." What led to his downfall after such a promising start?

Things had gone extremely well for Paul during school and shortly thereafter. Indeed, he had become convinced early on that greatness was a whole lot easier to attain than he had supposed. "I had always heard that artists were supposed to strug-gle," he said. "Well, at twenty-one I had my first one-man show," and by 1965, at age 24, he had found himself "sitting on a stage with Robert Rauschenberg and [Richard] Pousette-Dart receiving an award at a black-tie opening in Washington, DC." He had also received loads of commissions, his paintings had found their way into the distant halls of foreign embassies, and private collectors were eagerly buying up his work. As for his life in New York, where he had naturally come to settle, it was wonderful; he would go on all-out binges in his work, filled with emotional catharses, the wildly abandoned artist, able, apparently, to have it all.

In the first case study of this man, Getzels and Csikszentmihalyi (1976) referred to him as "the artist of the hour" in virtue of his unique ability to arrive at a suitable mid-dle ground between both professional and lay audiences as well as between his personal life and the vagaries of the art world. So much for all the horror stories that are the lore of the modern artist: If you are confident in what you do and do it, it appeared, all will work out in the end.

But as he was able to see some 20 years later, there had been a lot of "front" as well; he had tried too hard to impress people back then. There was always the sense, he said, that he was in the middle of doing something big, filled with romance and excitement. But it was just this, he believed, that led to his des-cent. His early success proved to be crippling and inhibiting, he felt, rather than liberating: "I couldn't match it," he said, "I couldn't maintain that." Thus, any success he managed to gath-er subsequently was always "diminished" somehow; it was anticlimactic and disappointing. Perhaps, he suggested, this was why his life became filled with alcohol and drugs; why his marriage failed miserably; why he looked toward new rela-tionships to "save" him from his fall. "I was the director," he said, "and I hired actors and actresses to fill parts . . . I used people and I manipulated them."

Meanwhile, he had become something of a Constructivist in his art, his paintings becoming progressively more hard-edged, geometric, and fastidious. With these paintings, he said, he offered proof to the world that he was all right, that he was still able to keep everything in order. But what it really showed, he came to feel, was that he was slowly but surely going out of control, the paintings serving as a kind of inverted reflection of the "flimsy structure" he was trying to build in his life. The fact is, "I talked a good game," but in his own eyes, "I didn't do anything." The main problem, he went on to explain, lay in the clash between the persona he had adopted as an up-and-comer and his inner realization that much of this was fortuitous and false, a bastardization of what it meant to be an artist. The result was that he eventually went through a lengthy period of mourning, over the future that had been lost on account of his having tried to seize it prematurely; he became obsessed with what might have been; he couldn't quite believe that he had frittered everything away. A good portion of these years, he said, was a complete blur, utterly self-destructive; it was a vicious cycle of blame, self-pity, rescue, failure, excuses, and lies. And very little had gotten done: "I knew that I couldn't do anything and didn't want to make a fool out of myself by try-ing." He stopped showing his work for some 10 years.

It was only after a period of rehabilitation that Paul was able to drag himself out of this terrible morass. Ultimately, he said, he went back to square one, to much the same point at which he had begun, back in 1966. There was no longer the burden of trying to attain an impossible goal, only daily involvement and hope; there was no longer a desire to impress others, only to express himself. At its best, he said, "the art form takes for granted that . . . people are going to see it"; so there was no need to "hit them over the head" or "logo-ize" his work, as he had done earlier, so that they knew it was valid and that it was his alone. The goal was instead to do good work, nothing more. This required discipline and diligence, he realized, not wild abandon; he would no longer wait for the muse, as he used to, or wait for everything to be just right, for it had become pain-fully clear through his ordeal that significantly more than divine inspiration was needed if he was to succeed in more authentic fashion than he had. Most important, he would try to paint, as best he could, without having it become confused with fame and fortune. There was still the need to maintain a certain level of egocentricity, he clarified. You've still got to be able to say, "'You're goddam right I'm better than anybody else'"; without this, it would be impossible to get anywhere at all. But it was no less necessary to refuse to let that egocentricity lapse into grandiosity: The art world was entirely too unforgiving.

It may be that Paul was still deluded when we last spoke with him. As implied earlier, he was convinced that if one was forthright and sincere, success would follow. And some success did in fact seem to be returning: He had established a gallery connection, he was gaining something of a reputation, and he was once again getting some commissions, just as he had earlier. There was less invested in the fine art side this time around – he had taken to doing some commercial work in addition, perhaps as a way of removing some of the financial and emotional strain of devoting himself exclusively to what was arguably a higher calling – but it was clear that it was still his foremost concern. He even spoke of the idea of immortality in this context, the sense of being "special" that being an artist brought with it, and the sense of playing an integral role in the creation of enduring cultural values; none of this was to be denied. But it had to be put in its proper perspective.

Would it be possible? Would he be able to prevent himself from slipping into grandiosity? Would he be able to prevent his own creative process from being confused with fame and fortune? I have no doubt that all of these things are possible; there were plenty of other artists in the group at hand who were forthright and sincere and who were indeed able to minimize, if not completely avoid, many of the traps into which this man had fallen. But we ought not to be too harsh in our condemnation of those who succumbed to these traps, for the most salient of them may come to possess people in the form of dreams and fantasies, which, upon being actualized, all but acquire a life of their own.

MYTH AND CREATIVITY

To the best of their ability, aspiring artists must keep a vigilance over their desires; they must remain aware of what their motives truly are. This in itself may be seen as an important condition of creativity. Clearly, it is no easy task to accomplish. Unless it is, however, artists may find themselves being punished for their duplicity and find themselves inhabiting a world that is opposed to their innermost aims.

As the best-known artist of the group insisted, many artists who had managed to make it had little romantic attachment to either the process of creating art or the idea of being an artist. When I interviewed this man and asked him to describe some of the dynamics of his latest work, he immediately told me that some of the questions with which I was armed were off, that they presumed too much about how meaningful things were. It's not like "lost weekend with the brush," he said. It wasn't that art was intrinsically meaningless, he qualified; there were times throughout the course of history when the mystique that surrounded both the creative process and artists themselves may have been justified. But to retain these notions now, he implied, would be utter delusion. If you are aware of who you are and what you are doing and you understand where we are as a society, he said, "you can live with yourself." But it should be evident by now that it was extremely difficult, for many, to achieve this kind of awareness.

I close by outlining two further conditions for artistic creativity and, by extension, artistic development. The first is simply that the artist must believe that development itself – taken here in the broadest sense of progressive change or transformation – is in fact possible. To the extent that one believes development to be fundamentally *im*possible, or, more likely, to be finite, to have a definite ceiling as a function of one's limited abilities, the process itself becomes foreshortened: As noted earlier, it may be difficult to keep on, knowing that the "end," so to speak, may be near. Likewise, to the extent that one believes development to be fundamentally *unnecessary* or inevitable, owing to the (ostensible) fact that it is only a matter of time before one's extraordinary abilities will rise to the surface, the process becomes foreshortened again: There is little reason to work diligently to forge the future if there is not much more to be gained than variations on what nature has already provided. A corollary here is that aspiring artists – like the researchers and theorists who study them – must avoid conceiving of the development of extraordinary artistic abilities in naturalistic terms, that is, bestowed upon certain people by God or by genes. The very assumption that one either *has* these abilities or *does not* have them may itself preclude the possibility of development.

The second condition for artistic development, very much related to the first, is that artists must be aware of and indeed have the power to *defy* those myths that are most operative in their lives and work. For some of the artists we studied, the ability to identify and to defy these myths meant the end of being an artist. Having realized perhaps that their desires were more closely connected to the image of being an artist than to the reality of creating art, they may have decided that other pursuits were preferable. But most others gathered what they could of their remaining artistic selves and, ultimately, seemed to have their creative energies liberated. Again, it was mainly in retrospect that this last group of artists could identify these myths; it was largely through their own praxis, their own real activities as people and as artists, that they were able to form a new consciousness of who and what they had been. We might call this process one of *desocialization*, for at the same time that the social determination of their ideas and practices became exposed as such, their coercive power often diminished, the socialization process effectively coming undone. Only when artists succeed in differentiating the mythical images that surround them from the process of artistic creation itself, therefore, are more optimal forms of creativity attainable.

"I don't think it is as sacred, or should be as sacred, as people make it out to be," one woman said of art; there is work involved. "I'm a small businessman," another artist said. "I have suppliers I have to deal with for new materials and new equipment, and insurance problems, labor problems, transportation problems. It's a business," he emphasized again, "not a flake-out." There were some who apparently were not aware of this aspect of being an artist. "People think artists are either independently wealthy or they get their materials out of garbage cans or nothing costs any money." Furthermore, there were also some, particularly young artists, who assumed that he was always having wild orgies up in his loft, as artists were wont to do, and they would feel bitter that they didn't have what he had. What they didn't realize, he said, was that there was a history behind his work, and that it was one of labor, not glamor.

"Art gets elevated to a position it doesn't belong," said one woman; "it's put on such a pedestal." And the result was that people like herself, who were uncertain whether they wanted to ascend to such heights – and whether they could – were left feeling that if they couldn't have it all it would be better just to forget about it. Had this mythology not permeated, indeed constituted, the very frustrations and fears and anxieties she had experienced early on, when she first caught a glimpse of those single-minded heroes she knew she would never be, maybe she would be doing a bit more now. But because it had seemed that there was little possibility of her ever doing anything else but fall short of the expansive goals she had in mind, there was no other way. The situation of the artist was strange and contradictory: "Sometimes," she said, "the artist isn't given his due. Sometimes the artist is made some sort of hero. Neither seems very real . . . or right."

Chapter 3

In the company of others

TO BE AN ARTIST, WITH AND AMONG OTHERS

This chapter will explore two different, though not unrelated, dimensions of the conditions of creativity, that of interpersonal relationships and that of the art community. As noted in Chapter 1, there has not been much attention devoted to these sorts of issues in the literature, at least not in the psychology of art and creativity. Despite an increasing recognition of the importance of both field-related and domain-related factors in the constitution of creativity, the more "informal" sphere of interpersonal relations has gone relatively uncharted. There are some obvious reasons for this. The sorts of issues we shall consider in relation to family, for instance, such as the difficulties of balancing the demands of work and home, are no doubt familiar to many already. Likewise, in regard to the issue of community, particularly as taken up by the likes of Bellah and company (1985), it has become clear enough that our own society has suffered as of late; it has become no easy task to forge ties that truly bind. My goals in the present chapter are therefore relatively modest ones. In trying to show how these issues have become operative in the lives and work of aspiring artists, I will try to add to the extant picture and thereby develop further our understanding of some of the central problems besetting both artists in particular and the modern self, living in the company of others, more generally.

To take but one example, it should be noted that many of the more sordid tales tied to the mythologization of art and artist were told by *men*. Far from implying that the ideas of which they spoke were entirely alien to women, it appeared that men were more inclined to pursue "the hero thing," as one man put it: Most of their models were men, and many of these models had sought to make their own highly individuated marks on the world, no matter what it took. As for the men in the present group, some of whom we heard from in the previous chapter, we have already learned how their own dogged pursuits could lead to their forsaking the relationships in which they had become involved. For some, it was all or nothing; anything that got in the way had to be shoved aside. There was also, you may recall, one instance of a woman doing much the same thing; if she was going to be an artist – a true artist – certain aspects of her family life, including her husband, would have to be abandoned. Perhaps the book on artists' lives she had read had told her as much.

I do not mean to take this approach too far. These sorts of perspectives have a tendency to reify both femaleness and maleness. Moreover, there are too many exceptions; generalities can be all too facile. Qualifications aside, it will become evident in the pages to come that the mythologization of which we have spoken can be plausibly tied to the dynamics of both interpersonal relations and the art community. The reason is simple: There is no separating out one's designs and desires as an aspiring artist from the actual activities in which one is engaged; and these activities both affect and are affected by the company of others.

For contemporary aspiring artists these relations can be particularly difficult and troubling. For many, the practice of creating art, particularly in the early years, could be terrifically important, so much so that virtually all other pursuits were relegated to a secondary status. "You lived for art, morning, noon, and night," one man said; it was extremely intense. We might also recall the man who found himself "panting at the mouth" when the latest exhibit opened, or the man who was "crazy" and "off the edge," so deeply was he committed to an all-out, no-holds-barred personal and artistic project. One woman said that if she had found herself early on in her career unable to do art, she would obviously have to kill herself. Fortunately, she no longer believed this; art could be important without it being a life-or-death situation. Even if she was a prisoner in Siberia, another woman added, there was no question but that she could continue to do art. "It's so tied up with the identity, my own identity, that I would not know who I was if I was not able to do something creative." It's "like breathing," she said.

The commitment to art therefore demanded unswerving attention for many of these people, a kind of tunnel vision that for some absolutely forbade any and all distractions from entering into their midst. As we have also seen, there were some who tended to flee from this straight and narrow path – from the "stern mistress," as one man put it, who demanded "devotees who burn with a pure flame in her service" – and threw obstacles in their own way in order to prevent themselves from meeting the muse head on. Others realized that they were simply unwilling to sacrifice the comfortable, family-oriented lives they had always envisioned in the name of art. There wasn't enough time to devote to it, one man had said. Another had his own studio after leaving school, but "never really seemed to accomplish anything there"; it was "always too far to get out of the easy chair and go to it." In addition, "working all day . . . transforms your outlook on life, your starry-eyed ambitions." As an auto mechanic, this man's own eyes were too tired after a day's work, and he didn't have much energy; there was no way he could begin "pounding on a hunk of rock" as he had earlier. Even more to the point, though, "What it amounts to," he added, was that "I like to eat." This was the main reason why he never became "a full-time starving artist."

There was also a woman who recounted how "dreary" it had been during the Depression and who insisted there was no way she could ever bring herself to lead such a tenuous, fragile existence as that of the artist. She had seen too many people whose "eyes were lost," and she didn't want to end up a "little old lady in sneakers." Her experience of the Depression, she said, had made her unwilling to forget the possibility of growing old without grace. Art remained important for many of these people and there were frequently some regrets for having abandoned it, along with guilt for having capitulated to the niceties of middle-class life. But they could live with this: If the decision ultimately came down to choosing between art and life, as it did for a number of people, there really was no contest.

For those who chose to remain in art in some fashion, however, the contest was often an ongoing one, a perpetual series of threats and assaults, adjustments and compromises that despite being largely expected – most were warned about these sorts of things ahead of time – were no less difficult to endure and work through. Intimate interpersonal relationships and family life proved to be problematic, at some point or other, for almost everyone involved: The diffusion of their energy and commitment could not help but constrict the space of their own creativity. Those who elected to abandon these relationships, meanwhile, often had their own share of problems, not the least of which included guilt – particularly in the case of men, who were generally more likely to move in this direction – over leaving others behind.

Problems tied to community are not so obvious and expectable as those to which I have just referred. This is mainly because the art community – should we choose to call it that – seems to have its own unique characteristics and dilemmas. There were many, for instance, who believed that becoming a member of this community would either be a venture into Bohemia, a free and easy counterculture serving as an oasis from the banality of ordinary life, or into a variant of Hollywood, a circus of the stars. By all indications, it was neither of these things. Before we go on to see what it was, let us explore in greater detail some of the dynamics of these individuals' lives with and among others.

BLIND AMBITION, AND ITS ECHOES

A number of people in the present group did indeed opt against committing themselves to enduring intimate relationships, including marriage. In one somewhat extreme case, a woman gathered the conviction that she seemed "to have a deficiency" in regard to these relationships. It wasn't that she was completely uninterested in being with someone, but that she was unable. After years of painful questioning, denial, and self-accusation, she had finally grown more comfortable with her solitary status: "I've finally quit hassling myself with trying to make myself more like other people and just figure, 'Well, I'm one of those eccentric loner types.'" She "would not have been a good wife" and "would not have been a good mother" anyway, for she "would have always felt this commitment pulling against it." There was only one choice, therefore: "Fuck it," she said. "Art's more important."

For most others who had remained single, however (there were a total of 8 out of 54), their decision was wrought not so much out of their alleged inability to have relationships; they simply believed that art and intimacy didn't quite mix. Basically, they felt that there was enough to worry about without a spouse to care for and kids running around. Marriage, said one man, would have been boring, and though he regretted not having children, they were not worth all the dismal routines they and their mother would bring along with them. If he had gotten married, he wouldn't have remained an artist; he would have been a teacher rather than "free-marketing." In some fields, like politics, he said, you need a wife. But not in this one. Marriage "imposes too many restrictions," another man agreed, though he also acknowledged that this belief may only be a "defense mechanism." In either case, being an artist, he said, had made him critical and judgmental of people; it's "part of the training of the artist." Although he certainly tried to "temper that with a little humanity every now and then," he too got bored easily. He had "no problems with females who are in the arts themselves, or who require the same kind of privacy" as he did, but they were apparently not that easy to come by.

Another man had finally found himself in a serious relationship now that he had left art. It was much easier, he felt, "without that involvement with yourself," without that "self-absorption" and "self-indulgence." It was too important when

90

he was younger to do the work and pour his entire being into it: "The art focus made me less capable of having more complete relationships." His movement away from art had therefore allowed for the possibility of his entering more connectedly into the world of others. Likewise, said yet another man, who believed he was going to be "one of America's great painters," things had been very different years ago. "In school and when you first get out of school, you want all the recognition you can get: You're painting for a definite audience, you want recognition, you want to hang in a gallery, you want to make money so you can buy more materials and keep painting and make a statement. . . . Then all of a sudden you get married and have kids: There's all the recognition you need in your life. Now you're established. Now you can have fun with your paintings." Two issues deserve to be emphasized here. First, he had become less driven in recent years and, on some level, less egocentric. Family life, he said, "lets you forget about yourself and be more concerned with other people." Second, despite the fact that painting had become but a "little meadow" he could visit, he could at least do some frolicking while he was there. Whether his art improved – that is, whether he had become "objectively" more creative – I cannot say. But he was enjoying art more.

According to one of the women who chose to forgo intimate relationships, marriage just wouldn't work, because if she continued to do art it would only be "salt on the wound." She told a story of a friend, who, upon hearing her husband's car coming up the driveway, would immediately dash to the nearest chair to hide her work. Like the woman whose husband had been fiercely determined to make her fail as an artist, the fact of her being an artist was apparently construed as such a radical endeavor, such a threat to the man's values, that there was no choice but to banish – visually at least – her art from her life. There was little reason to follow in this woman's footsteps.

For a select few, it should be noted, artistic activities seemed enhanced by relationships. Even when he "wasn't fit to live with," one man's wife was always there, supportive and accommodating. Another man said his wife definitely helped him with his art in that she was a "stabilizing force." She would get upset at him once in a while, to be sure ("you can become very selfish as an artist," he admitted), but she served as a kind of mortar for both his life and his art; she kept him together. Another man's friends told him that if it wasn't for his wife, he would probably be dead. Still another man's girlfriend tried to keep him "from going crazy." Like the other men's wives, she seemed to serve in an almost nurselike role, soothing and comforting her nervous and crazed creator-man.

For women the situation was generally different. One woman, whose husband was also an artist, said that although they had run into some serious difficulties together (they did, after all, get divorced), her husband had for a long while been a remarkable source of both encouragement and discipline; he had "poked and prodded" her to make sure that she would live up to what she was capable of and really get somewhere. Sadly enough, it was this support that may have led in part to the demise of their marriage, for once she got on track he seemed to become less a husband than "this fellow engaged in the same thing you are." It was an unintended but perhaps inevitable consequence of her progressive actualization as an artist. Another woman was also glad to have married an artist. "I think it would be hard for a woman to be married to a nonartist and to continue to make art; you would have to be a very strong person," she said. Judging by what women in this situation had to say, she seems quite right about this. She could never have gotten married to anyone who wasn't in a "creative field," another agreed; it would just be too difficult for most men to accept and, consequently, too difficult for her to thrive.

These relatively fortunate few aside, art and close interpersonal relations have not mixed smoothly; well over half of the people in this group cited what they considered to be some serious difficulties. Subjectively, it was the artists themselves who were often at fault. Most centrally, and in line with the aforementioned selfishness and single-mindedness, many people – again, particularly men – realized that they had treated their mates poorly: "badly" and "uncaringly," as one man from whom we have heard put it. There was also the "director," who had "hired actors and actresses" to perform on his own personal stage. "I couldn't have existed for another person," another man said. He had been quite successful, owning a condominium, a studio, and a beach house; he had all the fixings, in other words, of a provider. His wife got the short end, however; little did he realize that his entire mode of life was "driving her crazy." In addition to trying to "force" her to do things for herself, perhaps to remove some of the burdens of his own preoccupations, the fact was that she was afraid of him, of his art, of the wildness that surrounded it. He was now alone, his marriage having reached a sudden – at least to him – breaking point, and he was extremely humble about it. He was thankful to be able to feel "the real pain of going through the divorce and not having it frosted over with liquor and numbness." His ex-wife seemed to jar him awake.

Even if one was aware of the damage being incurred, certain problems could still remain, such as "stopping everything for an exhibition and the other person not understanding it." The "price of success" for this man consisted of the time, the frenzy, and the refusal to be distracted that were part of being an artist, at least for those who were serious. As for his own marriage, which also ended in divorce, he could only say: "In retrospect, it was an act of masochism." Another man noted that his (first) wife just didn't like having to deal with his art all the time, while still another referred to his wife, during the time he was busy with shows especially, as a "canvas widow." He joked about this, but it was also clear that his guilt was real.

For some other men, there was the more general problem of practicality. Their wives might have initially supported their being artists, but they had also assumed that these idealistic young men would eventually settle down and start making some contributions to something other than their own careers. This situation finally came to a head for one of these disgruntled wives. She had been "on [his] ass" to make it, one man said of his wife, but it wouldn't happen. Needless to say, there was considerable pressure to create works of art that would facilitate attending to practicalities and appease those who wanted more. The irony was that this sort of pressure rarely seemed to culminate in anything but repetition, in an ever-renewed inability to do what needed to be done. Whether the problem revolved around selfishness, drivenness, or the failure to attend to practical affairs, the result was frequently guilt and regret. Now that things had settled down and they had grown up, these people gathered the ability to reflect on their former cycles of self-indulgence, the pain it could inflict on others, and the further pain that gradually but inexorably came back upon themselves, ugly reminders of their sins and shortcomings. For many of them, it was not easy to confront their art day after day with vigor and conviction: Others were losing out.

WOMEN ARTISTS AND THEIR ODDS

Art "didn't really become a career," one woman said, because she refused to let it. She always felt she would "have to sacrifice more than [she] could sacrifice for art." She was a woman, she said, which meant that she was "raised to think we should be concerned and interested in other people." It also meant that she would never be able to "close the door," as it seemed the true artist had to do. The whole thing was too "intense" and "draining" for her, given all the other things she wanted to do, like raise a family; and because she refused to go about the business of being an artist "half-assed" – she didn't want to "sort of do it" or just be an "okay" artist – she was better off leaving it behind altogether. She had become a therapist instead; and while it was nowhere near as "all-consuming" as being an artist had been, at least she wasn't "up in the air" anymore, struggling to keep in balance all of the different facets of her life that had clamored for attention. This woman wasn't sure if it was even possible "to combine anything with being an artist," certainly not a "truly sharing, invested marriage." This was why, she said, the best artists were the most single-minded. It was also why they sometimes were not the best people: Their "disconnection from everything else" led to a "narcissistic" outlook and a world that was "very narrow and small." Ultimately, she implied, art school and a career in art were for men. Women may still be going to art school, she realized, but many seemed to be "passing through," getting just that dose of narcissistic self-fulfillment that would no doubt be unavailable later on.

Although this dose may have been better than nothing, it wound up exacting a serious cost for a number of women artists. This cost was different than the one that men often incurred. Rather than selfishness, these women often came to feel that they had been too self*less*, too caught up in everyone's needs and desires but their own. Not unlike what Carol Gilligan (1982) has discussed in her work on women's development, they had been unable to see that they too needed time and attention, that they were as deserving of care as others were. This in itself was troubling for many of them, for rather than going ahead full steam and forging the life they had planned, there was often capitulation, and then regret. If many of the men suffered guilt, over what they had done and who they had hurt on account of it, for women there was often remorse and, sometimes, shame. Too many sacrifices had been made; they had been too weak; they had left themselves out of the picture.

Once again, it may be instructive to note an exception to the rule. According to Marsha Riddell, "there's a definite advantage to being a woman if you are an artist." What she wanted all along, she admitted, was a successful man: "I always dated successful men, always looked for them." Very seldom did she date artists. The reason for this was that she knew they would never be able to support her; and "it would be a terrible situation to be married to an artist who needed all the things" she did. They "would just be disruptive to each other." Another trait she looked for in a man was the kind of aggressiveness and drive that led to concrete results. Because she had found herself to be "poor" at coping with the outside world, particularly the world of art, she was attracted to just the opposite, those who could deal with the challenges the world presented. She was "wonderful at raising babies and making sculptures and making a house – all the very female things – but going out into the world and selling yourself and being businesswoman" she was "terrible at." This was why she "always looked for a mate who had that quality." She was pleased that her (second) husband was so good at "pushing" her, encouraging her "to be more aggressive," at "shoving" her out into the world. She was also pleased that in addition to being pushed and shoved, she had acquired that degree of financial security which allowed her to pursue her work essentially free from the problem of livelihood: The kind of man who could teach her the skills of hustling and coping with the outside world had learned these skills himself. As it turned out, this woman was one of the most successful artists in the entire group, able to create her art relatively unhindered by many of the concerns other women had.

A number of these other women indicated that they were not nearly so willing to be pushed and shoved by their husbands. Rachel Colworth, for instance, felt that her husband didn't understand her need for privacy and her desire to keep her art to herself. Getting married and having children changed her life more than she had expected. Back around the time of art school, she said, "I saw myself at some future time in an enormous studio, working, lots of mess, small children on the floor, completely occupied with painting." But it didn't turn out this way. Her husband was a gifted musician, who had begun his career sometime near the age of 12. Consequently, there was little question about whose career would get priority: "Everything has been done to facilitate that career." This made sense on some level, she admitted; after all, he was the one who was bringing home the paycheck, which was no doubt more sizable than hers would ever be. But the situation was a difficult one. What also made things difficult was that one of her children was born neurologically impaired, which meant that extra time and energy would have to be directed toward her care. Activities with this little girl were "the center of our life," and the result was that for many years there was no possibility at all of creating any art. Not surprisingly, "I felt badly because I wasn't doing what I had set out to do." There was always a sense of "personal guilt" over her own self-betrayal, and this despite the fact that she had little alternative.

Psychologically, Rachel's art was still very much with her. She couldn't do it as often as she would have liked, but when she did, it was "intensely personal." She wanted her work to be "beautiful and precious," her primary aim being to "make things that I liked, that made me happy, that I would enjoy. . . . I know," she said, "that I'm conveying something that is very dear to me and very deep within me." She looked forward to the day when she would be able to do more than was presently possible. A studio of her own would certainly be helpful, she noted; it would "separate the two parts of my life that need to be separated." But it was not clear when this would happen.

Aside from lack of time, there still remained a problem with her husband, who was continuing to pressure her to be more professional about her art. " 'Have a show, sell them,' " he had said; "and immediately there were some hooks on those things already." She herself was "not really of a mind to put together a show and try to sell it," she explained; "I don't see it as really being important outside of myself." She was not against making money, she clarified. She had done a children's book, some magazine illustration, and so on that she was more than willing to be paid for. These activities were approached "with a different attitude"; they served a specific function and deserved compensation. With her own personal art, however, there were "no strings attached," which is how she wanted it. "I think in a very, very real sense I'm a closet artist," she said; there just wasn't that desire to show and to please others. Whether this was out of insecurity or of her misgivings with the commercial aspect of this process, she could not say.

The most troubling aspect of this problem was that Rachel felt that the only way she could ever truly justify her artistic activities in her husband's eyes was to make money; only then, she suggested, would he take her seriously. Again, he never really understood her need for privacy and self-expression; he wanted to see her "do something that [would] have some kind of financial success attached to it." But this was exactly what tarnished the process of creation itself, what turned it, for her, into a mere means to an end. Perhaps she shouldn't have given up the teaching job she had had earlier, she mused; at the very least, it might have conferred on her the financial independence and sense of significance her husband seemed to want her to have. The result, in any case, was that Rachel had been forced to cut short her own development as an artist. Hers was an "old-fashioned household," she said, and she had proceeded as she had because it was obviously the most appropriate and practical contribution she could make. That this wasn't quite good enough for her was a problem in its own right; there continued to be a sense of shame over her own martyrdom, over her own sense of missed opportunities. That this wasn't quite good enough for her husband either, however, made things infinitely worse. The one dimension of this woman's selfhood that gave her the satisfaction and integrity that she desired was apparently insufficient and illegitimate. There was no room in this life for simple pleasures.

Several other women told stories of sacrifice. Chris McKay, whose husband had been an up-and-coming young artist himself, indicated that there had been an element of sacrifice from the very beginning of her and her husband's careers. Because he had been off and running, and the two of the them had been broke, the decision was that he would get to be an artist first. He would have the first 10 years, they had agreed, she the second. But what happened, apparently, was that "after ten years, we forgot about that." She was not particularly bitter about this, she emphasized; she could have resumed her art, but never did. There had indeed been some accusations back then that she had been "dominated" by him by being made to play second fiddle, but she herself never really felt this way. "Everybody else feels a lot more strongly about my stopping than I do," she said. For the most part, she just wasn't that interested in it anymore. We will hear more about why this was so later on in this chapter, when we consider the issue of community.

Things may have been different if she had thought more of herself. Art was the very "nucleus" of their relationship, Chris said, and the fact was, "He was better than I was. I knew that. What I didn't know was that I was better than everybody else anyway, which I know now, in retrospect." At the time, however, "it just seemed convenient and realistic to stop for a while and pick it up later." Some bitterness eventually crept through her words: "He expected me to wash dishes and clean the house and do laundry, and I asked him, then, would he build me stretchers. And he said, 'If you want to be an artist, build your own stretchers.' And I thought, 'Oh, God, he doesn't want me to be an artist.'" At this point she had asked herself, "'Well, am I going to live with this contention and jealousy or just give it up for a while?' So I just gave it up." Perhaps this was wrong, she said, but again, she really didn't have many regrets. The only source of dissatisfaction in relation to her abandoning art were the comments of her friends. "It was very frowned upon to have children," she said. "That was the period when people weren't supposed to have children." As a result, "I met with a lot of negativity in my community and among my friends," all of whom seemed to think that she had betrayed herself. But this was their problem, not hers; many of these people have trouble thinking about anyone or anything but themselves and their careers. Now that Chris had taken to working with computers, she had become convinced that she was better off than she would ever have been as an artist, not only financially but emotionally. Her husband's talent, his lack of encouragement, and his double standards may ultimately have led her to a better way.

Her life was nevertheless in "absolute flux." All of a sudden, she said, she had realized that she hadn't been very happy, and it was time to start dealing with that. Partly, this realization was a function of her new occupation as a computer programmer; after all these years, she said, she discovered what she had been missing. As opposed to most artists, she explained, her fellow programmers were "real bright and have a lot of breadth of knowledge and a lot of interests," all of which provided some welcome relief from her previous life. Although her activities were a bit more regimented now than they had been and she was still "kind of a drone" at her new job, things were generally looking up. She really felt that she had been asleep over the course of these years and that, all of a sudden, she "just woke up." It was an extraordinary time for this kind of interview, she noted. If we had tried to speak with her in the not too distant past, she undoubtedly would have had very different things to say. "But now that I'm awake," she said, "I feel I really have to make an effort to try to find a way to do something about my own life." It had to do with being independent, she went on to explain: "I've been a devoted wife and mother for many years and now I think it's time for me."

Another woman also decided to "submerge" herself for a while because her husband was apparently a better artist than she was. This was probably why she too "gradually tapered off and stopped"; once you're down, she implied, it's tough to get back up. The problem came down to this, explained one woman: "Men have wives who usually take care of them, more or less." Women, on the other hand, "don't have wives." Her feeling was that "men don't understand what you're saying and they don't realize what you do to make them comfortable and what you give up so they can have a peaceful house when they come home." She had to do things for herself, she realized, but she felt badly if she didn't do all the things that were expected of her. Sometimes she thought it was a mistake to get married and be an artist.

To make matters worse, her husband, like a number of others we have heard about, was annoyed at her being an artist. When she had a show a while back, "he didn't even go down to look at [her work] hanging up." This hurt her tremendously. She believed that he felt threatened and envious because he assumed she had so much more freedom than he had. But she really didn't: He himself saw to it. All too often, she would just get "a funny feeling from him," a feeling of hostility and condescension, fused together. "Some men are really threatened by creative women and they tend to belittle what you do, not in a real apparent manner, but in certain things they do or don't do." She "took it" for some time, but decided that it wasn't right for her to do this; at the same time that she was feeding his insecurity and playing the role of accomplice to his play of power, her own shame mounted. If she was going to be able to do her art freely and comfortably, then something was going to have to be done.

Similarly, there was a woman who believed that her husband

was consciously happy that she was an artist, but unconsciously resentful that she wasn't "darning socks." When another woman began to date after her husband passed away, her
artistic activities always seemed to interfere in some way. She
told her suitors that she would probably be painting if they
came over to visit, but they never thought she meant it; they
assumed everything would be put aside for them. Another
woman's husband never shared in chores, which she "could
understand," but to top it off, he resented her art as well. When
she would become inaccessible and moody, yet another added,
her husband felt resentful. There could be no "truly sharing,
invested marriage," she believed, if one of the partners was an
artist. The last important painting Claire Harris did was in
Chicago, not too long after she left the Art Institute. Either she
"was going to stop then" or she "was going to move on." The
painting was "like the end statement of everything I worked
on," she recounted, and there haven't been any statements
since then, only "exercises." Deciding on a "definite conclusion," she gave the painting to her husband-to-be, as if it was a
ritual offering, signifying the death of her artisthood and the
birth of her new life. Maybe she didn't have a clear enough idea
about herself since that fateful time to make another statement
like that one, she said.

The situation was more difficult in the case of Donna Streeter,
who was married to another artist. She was not going to get
married, she noted; her career had always come first. Everything was fine for a while. But when her husband stopped
working several years ago and started complaining about how
much time she was spending doing her art – and this despite
the fact that he had been warned from the start that it would be
this way – things took a turn for the worse. There were constant
arguments over who got priority, over how much money got
allotted to each of them, even over the choice of which kind of
davenport to buy. "It's like my whole reason for marriage is just
going down the tubes," she said. He had never really been convinced of her seriousness and commitment until recently, she
went on to say, when she finally sold a piece of work for a respectable sum. Prior to this, it had apparently seemed as

though she was dabbling, that she was bluffing her way through the process of becoming an artist. The result was that she spent a lot of time "biting the bullet." When the sale came along, therefore, she was greatly relieved. In some ways, it was "the best thing" that could have happened for the relationship: "He knows now I'm in it." What he also knew, and apparently didn't like, was that she would become that much more involved with her art. Indeed, now that she was finally coming into her own, the marriage was in jeopardy. Sadly enough, it seemed as if the only way to massage her husband's wounded ego was to curtail her own success. But there was no way she would do this. Not only had success been too long in coming for her to cast it aside in order to keep the peace; it was too late for self-denial, and time instead to accord herself the dignity she deserved. Donna proved to be fortunate in this respect: At least her present crisis, painful though it was, had emerged as a function of what she had done in the world.

CONFLICT AND COMPROMISE IN FAMILY LIFE

Approximately three-quarters of the individuals in the present group who had families reported problems affecting their ability to do their art. These problems often revolved around the responsibilities that having a family entailed. Of particular concern was the time taken away from art because of all the other things that had to be done, particularly when their children were young. This is not to say that they regretted having families – very few did – only that conflicts had arisen, conflicts that often called for a measure of compromise in their own artistic endeavors.

We begin once more with the men. Between working a full day, which many of them did, and trying to spend time with their families besides, their art often suffered. "There was no time," said one man. "It made me stop," said another. In the midst of trying to put together a new house in a new city, working 12 to 14 hours a day, added one man, he had hardly any time or energy left for his art. Another artist used to go on 24-hour painting binges, getting so involved in his work that he would keep on going until he couldn't any longer. Once he had children, this proved to be impossible. Yet another man did binges of a sort even still, but they were a combination of both painting and work. As a single parent, who was trying to paint as well as work full-time, it wasn't easy to get everything done. To add insult to injury, he felt guilty too. Going days without sleep tended to sap one's energy, and the result was that he and his art were getting shortchanged.

His family served as "influential preventatives," said one man. There was also a man who used to get terribly angry if he had to pick up his kids at school. The flip side of this, again, could be guilt: over being free-lance while one's wife had a nine-to-five job; over going down to the basement to work after dinner, when everyone else was upstairs, together; or, more seriously, over preventing a life from even coming into being. This man was on the way to the abortion clinic with his wife, when all of a sudden he was overcome with anguish over what they were about to do. "There was an instant," he said, "when I realized that the life I wanted over the next few years didn't include this life that was coming into being and that I was going to trade the idea of what I wanted over the next few years for this life." They turned around and went home. Later on, with his daughter on welfare, a different kind of guilt surfaced: "'You can't take that kid's dreams away,'" his wife told him. "You ask yourself: 'What kind of great artist are you if you let your child be on welfare?'"

For others, family life may not have presented many problems at all. They "sometimes wish we were a regular American family," one man said of his children, but beyond this, all was basically well. Having a family had no big effect on another man because he was a "fairly selfish person," who tended not to care what they thought anyway; if other people wanted to suffer, that was their problem. Finally, though, there were some whose family always took precedence over their art, and their involvement in art wasn't so great that they had to face the kinds of conflicts and compromises that others did. "I would be completely satisfied with my life," one of these men said, "if they put on my tombstone that I was a good father and husband. That's all."

For men, therefore, it generally seemed that the degree to which family life invaded the space of their own creativity was a function of the degree of commitment they had to their art, to their family, and to reconciling the two. Again, finances entered in; having to earn a living was a distant cause of many of the problems we have been considering. In any case, it seems as though one of the most basic tasks for men who wished to continue doing their art alongside their families was to remain committed to the former without forsaking the latter. If this was not done, it could often come back to haunt them, perhaps invading the space of creativity in an even more injurious manner than their most dreaded compromises.

For women, again, the story seems to be different. Their lives often changed tremendously upon having a family. Along with many of the men we have encountered, women occasionally had a measure of guilt tied up with the feeling that they weren't pulling their weight or that more had to be done for their families than they were doing. Conversely, one woman was home for a year attending to her family, but found that she "could not justify it." Being a mother could apparently be experienced as an indulgence too; she felt that she should be contributing to the household in a more substantial and concrete way than she was by going out and earning a living. But most problems for women had to do with what they had forsaken as aspiring artists by choosing to have families.

Many of them were simply weary. Without her family, one woman said, perhaps she could have made it as a bona fide artist: "Conceivably I might have become a more major type of artist rather than [one who does] the kind of small, somewhat decorative things I'm doing." But even this kept her busy, she was quick to insist. "I really am not keeping a nice, lovely home for my family," she said. She had thought it would be easier. Another woman had heard from so many of her friends "that once they had a family they just gave up because they figured, 'How on earth can you combine everything and still try to do something?' " She was determined not to let that happen; she would continue at all costs, as in fact she has. But having a family still slowed down her artistic activities greatly. There were all those years of "playing nursemaid" to everyone, when she "had to pay attention to everyone else's needs." When her husband had problems, she found that she was unable to do her own work; the expectation was that she would be there for him. But she finally "got sick and tired of being the one everybody depended on to take care of them." There were too many sacrifices, she said, and though many of them had passed in recent years, she didn't feel good about what had happened. Another spoke of her artistic activities being brought "almost to a standstill" when she had a family. Hers was a particularly difficult situation. On top of the fact that her husband had been largely unsupportive of her work and that she had given birth to a special-needs child, she felt that she hadn't really wanted a family in the first place. Her "dreams," she said, "were not to be a mother." Despite her recent divorce, which, while perhaps alleviating some aspects of her burdens, surely exacerbated others, she still felt that she was letting herself go personally. She was "kind of like in a dither," said Chris McKay, the woman who had recently become a computer programmer. "I haven't been on my own for so long I don't even know how to be anymore," she said. What's more, she felt guilty about the changes she had made, particularly her separation from her husband: "Any time anyone else has ever done it I thought it was terrible." It would no doubt be a while before she would get herself on track.

Although it was difficult trying to raise a family and create art, there was one woman who believed that it may just be a "romantic fallacy" to assume that combining them can't work. Artists who didn't have families might be spending their time in bars, she said. Not that it had been easy for her; far from it. "I came from a large family of girls," she explained, and "you put aside what you wanted to meet other people's needs." The task, therefore, was to try to create other values, values that were tied to the respectful recognition of everyone's needs and desires, including her own. "All I had to do was learn to say no," she said, which was a big enough challenge in its own right: "I am forty-one years old and still learning to do it." Marsha Riddell, who had earlier expressed the belief that there was a definite advantage to being a woman artist, told a similar story. She hadn't exhibited her work when her children were young, yet she had kept on working as much as she could. As for when her children grew older, the biggest problems apparently had to with their nagging questions, such as "'Why do you waste your time with this art work?'" We might also recall the woman whose children had wanted her to remove all her "crap." Even if the notion that art and family life could never be combined was a romantic fallacy, they too needed to create new values.

It was easy to be "torn in several directions," added another woman. Her children had also been bothered by her art, especially when she had to work extra hours putting together an exhibit. Nothing could have stopped her, she said, but there were often the "worst guilt feelings" when she put herself first. She remembered leaving the house when the children were sick, overridden with these feelings, but she had refused to stay put. It was "all work," she said. Her strategy is reminiscent of those strategies adopted by many of the men in the group: She would try to proceed with her own life and endure the side effects as best she could. It was preferable to feel guilt over acts of commission than shame over acts of omission; it was a different kind of emotion altogether, less bound up with one's being than one's circumstances. This preference notwithstanding, there came a point in her life – she too was the mother of a special-needs child – when there was simply no way to resolve the conflicting demands she faced. There had to be a compromise at that point, she realized; something had to be given up. Not surprisingly, it was the art that "gave."

Consider the following scenario in this context as well. Alongside an early divorce, scarce teaching jobs, and eventually a move down south where her new husband's work had brought him, Meg Carlstrom's painting had "gone down the tubes entirely." She had therefore decided to work in a paint store, where she could at least bring in some money. Of her earlier work, which was primarily in the Abstract Expressionist mode, she came to feel that it "just wasn't enough," that it was "a little too simple" and "too cheap." They were paintings, she said, "that could go in anyone's living room and that whole business," and she swore that she would "never do that again." It was good while it lasted, she noted. "I know it's not 'in' anymore, but it was then, and it was easy to have a good time with it." But what she learned was that, if she were to continue developing as a painter and do things that were closer to her heart, she would have to turn to some form of figuration. The problem, however, was that it was "a little late in the game to try to put all that together."

In addition to the problems mentioned already, there had also been a "problem baby," which had slowed her down a great deal. In fact, there was a period when she was raising her children that the few paintings she did primarily depicted the "experiences of weariness" that had come to characterize her life. She never knew, she said, just how much energy it would take to be a mother. Also relevant, however, was that she had a tendency to make the art "too important" and "precious." Rather than a "living kind of active thing" that could be incorporated into her life, children and all, she had somehow gotten it into her head that it was either all or nothing; there was simply no room for doing it when the opportunity presented itself. "I should have my stuff set up and when I have time I should do it," she admitted. There shouldn't be so much "hemming and hawing." The fact was, art was still like a "religion" for her, just as it had been when she was in art school. And one didn't dabble with the sacred.

Meg didn't feel that she had given up completely, however. In fact, now that her children were becoming more independent, she felt "closer and closer" to giving it another try. It was ultimately just a matter of commitment, she said. Even now, she could paint if she really wanted to; there was just so far she could go in blaming the circumstances. But apparently, she wasn't quite ready to do what needed to be done. She went on to reflect a bit about her own background, about why she might have been so reluctant to make the necessary commitment to her art. She thought about Chicago: the city, the gangs, the buses. She had traded her club jacket, she said, for a paintbrush, and everybody approved; she was going to do something with her life. But she wished that her family especially hadn't been so approving, that they would have pushed her a bit more toward recognizing the need for acquiring other skills, like "learning how to type or something." The problem, she said, was that all this approval made her feel "a little too special." And here she was, working in a paint store, in a job that meant nothing. If only she was back in Chicago where things were happening. She felt that she needed "a community of people talking the same language" to really get going. Instead, she was "stuck" in a place that was thoroughly alien to her desires and needs, still raising her children, and still preventing herself from doing what she did best.

She remained forward-looking. Giving herself up to her children was a "bitch," but it made her a lot larger; you don't grow up, she said, until you give up. And someday, hopefully soon, she would take the wealth of experiences she had accumulated through the years back to her art, which would no doubt be that much better for it. "I don't want to sound arrogant," she said at one point, "but I'm an artist: I know how to draw; I studied it. I know how to put things down. I know how to make things look the way they're supposed to. And so, when I walk around and look at things, I never – through all of this – quit looking . . . that has always remained. And thank goodness. Because if that were gone, then I'd have no right to be talking about any of this."

Meg's attitude seemed to work well for her. Even though she was not doing any art, she was able to comfort herself with the idea that she was still an artist; circumstances had simply been such that she had been prevented from doing as much as she would have liked. There was therefore little reason to be ashamed, resentful, or bitter; when the time was right, she would continue. It would all wind up being little more than a not too pleasant memory.

For many of the other women from whom we have heard, this sort of psychic maneuvering was less forthcoming. The reason for this, it seems, is that their circumstances were such that it would have been unrealistic and illusory to do so. Perhaps they would be able to do their art again on a regular basis at some point in the future, but they could not expect to become as involved as they had been earlier. Even if their children were growing up and circumstances were becoming more conducive to the process of artistic creation, there would still be a serious emotional toll to be outlived: years of sacrifice, whether readily accepted or not, couldn't help but be incorporated into one's beliefs, values, and prospects for the future.

Nothing that has been said here should occlude the fact that many of the women with whom we spoke were content with how their lives had turned out. It is nevertheless clear that others had become embittered over having had to relinquish their own artistic commitments and goals. While for some this presented only minimal difficulties, for others the toll was great. As was the case for men, the issue was one of balance. This balance, however, was on the whole tipped differently than it was for men, being more in the direction of sacrifice of self than of others. There was therefore a different array of emotions coming back to haunt them. It seemed as if these emotions were often more difficult to withstand as well, by virtue of what their sacrifices were: they had sometimes been forced to give up their very selves, or at least that particular sense of their selves that they at one time had found most central and worthwhile. Whatever they chose to do, in fact, only rarely could the space of creativity remain unconstricted. In the context of both intimate relations and family life, the odds women faced were indeed considerable.

It is difficult to identify in any precise way the origins of this situation. The division of labor, particularly as manifested in gender-related differences, is surely relevant here; despite the emergence of the feminist movement during this span of time, gender roles remained fairly set, as they are to a large degree still. To the extent that this aspect of the division of labor continues to be rethought and reworked, perhaps things will improve for aspiring women artists in the future; perhaps they will be better able to move ahead and actualize some of their own talents and desires. The mythical images that we considered in Chapter 2 are relevant here as well. If women believed that the pursuit of their art was an all-or-nothing affair, they might have had to opt for nothing; to do their art "half-assed," as one woman had put it, would only serve to confirm others' beliefs that they weren't serious anyway, that they were dabblers, seeking a little self-expression. Perhaps if art had been something other than an all-or-nothing affair, therefore, they might have been better able to integrate it into the fabric of their lives, as one part among others.

PLACE AND COMMUNITY

In addressing the more general issue of the art community, I begin by dealing briefly with the specific locales in which these aspiring artists have lived and worked. Some of the problems encountered in this context were obvious enough. There was, for instance, the problem of isolation. Depending on where their jobs or families brought them, they might have lost contact with art or felt displaced. One woman, for instance, felt that she was "out in the boonies somewhere, without anything." Things had gotten better recently since she had found a local gallery to show her work, but it was "still like being in the desert as far as art goes." People were "still so far behind in so many areas and so afraid of change and so afraid of things that are different," she said, "you begin to feel like maybe you're in the wrong place."

Like a number of other artists, this woman was a stranger in a strange land; she was a city sophisticate out in the "boonies," where naïveté, ignorance, and fear tended to run deep. This could work to their advantage in some ways. There really was no art community where one man lived, and the people, he said, were "vegetables"; they seemed backward and dumb. Admittedly, though – and it is unclear whether he realized the implications of what he was saying – he stayed there because he was able to have an effect. He didn't want to lose the little bit of notoriety he had been able to acquire, even if it was from "vegetables." At least 10 people in the bar where the interview took place knew about his work, he boasted; it reached them, which was rewarding in its own right. "You're here," another man said of the place where he had settled. "You may as well do your part in improving the climate in some way."

Upon moving away from the mainstream of art, it may also have been difficult to know whether one was doing valid work; there may have been different, perhaps less sophisticated, criteria for evaluation. At the School of the Art Institute, many people were doing abstract work, with Abstract Expressionism in particular being the reigning approach. But out in New Mexico, said one man, it would have been "impertinent" to do this sort of work; it belonged to the city, not the country. Another artist, who had been drawn to hard-edged, minimalist work also found this less "relevant" in Georgia, where he had lived for a spell; now that he lived in the rural Southwest, it had become less relevant still. The people out there – along, at this point, with himself – are "out of contact with the latest thing." From "sensory bombardment" for a trendy urban audience, therefore, he has moved toward "invited contemplation."

As we can see through these few statements concerning place, in order to avoid doing one's art in a complete vacuum, the ideas and aesthetic preferences of the "locals" had to be taken into account. Otherwise, one might have felt like an alien or intruder. In short, then, saving one's own artistic integrity in the face of the need to accommodate could be a difficult task to accomplish. With this in mind, it would seem that being in a hub of artistic activity, New York for instance, would be preferable. In many ways, there *are* no intruders in New York, and there is little risk of the same kind of aloneness that people feel elsewhere. Being in New York and places like it, however, brought its own share of risks and dilemmas, and these were often considerably more treacherous than the ones just described.

From the very beginning of their careers, a number of people in the group had in mind to make their way to New York: "You realize that New York is a place that simply cannot be avoided as a force, a place to go." Despite the fact that this man had a

111

good teaching job in the Midwest, it was just "too nice" there; it was "a place you could too easily put your roots down and stay forever." Once the opportunity presented itself, therefore, he knew that he would leave; it was "inevitable." He himself had no small part in this: "I brought people in during the two years I taught there, people from New York, as visiting artists. The handwriting was on the wall," he said. Others who were in Chicago around this time also felt New York calling. Chicago may have begun "closing in" on them, as one woman put it, or they may have realized that what it had to offer would never be enough.

New York proved to be as exciting for some of these people as they had hoped; it was, and is, the center of the art world. But it was also a difficult place to build a life, particularly if there was family involved. One man moved there with his wife and daughter and it was overwhelming; after a year of struggling, and of doing virtually no art at all, they turned around and went back to Chicago, where things were easier, less frenzied. The catch, however, was that it was too late for Chicago by this time; he was unable to stay there with conviction and a clear conscience; he felt that he was fleeing. After a short time there, then, he and his family made the journey east once again, only to face many of the same trials and tribulations they had initially. They still lived in New York at the time we spoke, and they generally seemed comfortable. But it had been many years since this man did any serious painting.

It's a nice place to visit, said another man, but there is no way he would live in New York; it's a "conceptual town," as he put it, and he found living conceptually to be difficult. People could become "very involved in the world of issues" living in New York, added one woman. It was also a place where it seemed as if everything, even the simplest errands, took an inordinate amount of time. "This is a city," she said, "where those errands can cost you a day." She has never quite understood why "there's a thousand times more hours anywhere else." As another man put it, "you never have time to do it all" anyway, but "New York is particularly that way." Along with this frenetic pace, there was the feeling for some that life got a bit too "func-

112

tional," too designed for maximum yield. Too many of his friends were like "business associates," one man said, and although this was useful in terms of making good connections, it could be sad too: "It always has the edge of doing it for a reason somehow, rather than just being a gesture, a warm human gesture or something." It was like, " 'Let's invite the Snits over for dinner tonight so we can get the contract signed' or something." School days were much more "authentic," he felt. "New York is a very isolated kind of world."

In terms of the art community itself, particularly SoHo, he continued, it had become a "real-estate speculator's world," where as living became more expensive the art world became more silly and superficial. "We come to New York," another man said, and "work our asses off to fix up a decent size space for a studio, a home, raise a family; and when it looks right, the landlord won't sell it to you." Just as you are settling in, after years of trying to make it your own, the landlord "raises the rent out of sight, forces you to leave so he can let a doctor or lawyer do their bourgeois, masturbatory, swinging SoHo pad." Some artists were able to remain there, mainly those who had been wise enough to buy early. But many had apparently been chased out by people with more money, especially those who wanted to delude themselves into thinking that their place of residence entitled them to avant-garde status.

A further, more fundamental problem many faced was that of coexisting with their fellow artists. One man, for instance, said that he just didn't like artists; they were too egocentric for him. The art community was filled with "glory seekers," he said. He himself was proud that he didn't look or act like an artist. He wasn't emaciated like some of them were; he was more like a workman, thick and strong. Another man, recalling his days at school, said that there were a lot of people "who were very free with their social attitudes in just about every respect" and were "really pretty degrading to themselves and to the people they were with." School itself had been a little too free for this man. Artists need discipline, he felt, maybe even more than people in corporations do. "People want in some cases to be alone so they can manipulate themselves any way

113

they want, very selfish people. A lot of artists are like that," he believed; "maybe they can get their creativity out better that way." But this, he felt, "isn't a good attitude toward society." These two men rejected the egocentrism and selfishness that they believed pervaded the art community. In certain ways, in fact, their own identities were forged in opposition to these traits. "There are just very few artists I would consider being interested in being friends with," added one woman.

The art community was too much for some of these people. As one man who lived in the Chicago art community admitted, art was the primary focus, all day, every day. "The whole dialogue around here is art. All the people are artists. It's all art, all about making art." It was a "real inbred group here," said another man of the SoHo community; all people talked about was their art careers, what they were doing, and what it was doing for them. But the problem had to do with significantly more than egocentricity, selfishness, and exclusivity of focus; it had to do in addition with what kinds of characters these art worlds had forced them to be. One of the men from whom we just heard enjoyed being part of his community and was thriving in it. He also knew, however, that "It's a small, petty world," filled with people "coming around with their broken wings, close to having a breakdown, shaky." These were often the people who eventually realized that they had made art too important and that other things in their lives had been forsaken along the way. It was an insecure world, said another man, "peopled by people who have actually built up these mechanisms to defend themselves and their friends, the people around them." He could no longer bring himself to respect these people or to care for them; they were often too pitiful and needy.

Chris McKay had much to say about this issue. Indeed, she seemed to be extraordinarily bitter about her misfortunes in regard to the art world and the art community. As we learned earlier, she had separated from another artist, she had dissociated herself completely from everything related to art, and had gone into computers, which, ironically enough, she found to be an infinitely more humane occupation than being an artist. It might have been difficult for most people to believe, but in all honesty, she said, she was downright happy to leave the art world. "Have you ever lived in a ghetto," she asked, "where everybody is exactly the same, more or less? This is my step out of the ghetto. I live in a community [SoHo] of thousands of artists," and for the most part, "I find it incredibly boring." Artists just "aren't that interesting," she added. In fact, many of them were "dumb"; they had a "weak grasp of what's going on in the world. They're so narcissistic they don't care anyway, and all they talk about is art and themselves." There was "a lack of intellectual thrust" to their entire existence and, again ironically, "a lack of humanistic ideas and concerns." Even in the heyday of humanistic idealism, in the sixties, the primary concern for many of them was "to promote their careers." And she had grown tired of the whole situation. It was "so nice," she said, "to have this opportunity to say 'artists are boring.'" She had been thinking it for a very long time. Admittedly, she herself had once been attracted by the alleged bohemian life-style of artists; it had been part of the draw of her becoming an artist herself. But artists, she came to believe, were "as rigid and narrow-minded as everybody else."

In Chris's own inner circle, one had to be career-oriented to survive; there was no other way. "Usually," she said, "you can judge somebody's career orientation and ability in building a career by how good their career is. It has nothing to do with their art," and "it has everything to do with how they can build a career and who they know." Once in a while, she qualified, "somebody who knows the right people is a good artist." But most of it was "crap," and she had "no idea why people weren't embarrassed about doing it." Even while there were obviously good artists and bad ones, by her own account there was hardly anyone who had risen to success who had not tried hard to do exactly that. No one simply fell into it or was discovered; they had to work at it, strenuously and probably to the exclusion of lots of other activities and concerns. Success, therefore, in her own eyes at any rate, was little more than a sign that there had existed a career builder, hell-bent on success; it couldn't possibly come about any other way.

Most social relations in the art community, Chris continued, were "indirectly centered on moving forward an inch," the result being that "artists have to spend a lot of time hanging out with everybody else, hoping that somebody will tell them about a job, tell them about a dealer, reassure them that their work is good. . . . So it's real insecure." It was this insecure situation, more than anything, that had provoked her to leave art, free of regret. It was "such a meaningless business" that there was no reason for regret; it was "decadent and corrupt, boring and disappointing." Everyone believed that they could make money and become famous and, as a result, "everyone has to find out who's top dog and kowtow to that person in the hope that they'll do something for him." As for the art world itself, it's "a simple, primitive structure." Artists who worked for "big people" were called "midgets," which more or less said it all. Again: "Who you know and how well you present yourself are far more important than originality, talent, and quality of work, at least as far as success goes. Art dealers create and perpetuate the market and control the professional journals and museums." Ultimately, Chris believed, "Nobody really cares. It's just to play the game" and "it has nothing to do with anything else." It was another hierarchically based power structure, filled with those who dominated and those who submitted. In this respect, she said, "Maybe it's just real life and that's how it is." She thought it would be different.

Another reason why Chris was devoid of regret was that she had no idea what she could possibly create at this point in time. "I can't even imagine what I would do if I wanted to make art," she said. She was such a romantic that she would "probably paint skies or something. . . . I'm not even fitted for this period of art." All told, neither the art itself that presently had currency in the art world nor the ugly, self-serving tactics that were required to gain success would be missed. Her situation was interesting, Chris went on to suggest. Now that she had moved away from the world of art and was concentrating more on her own needs, and now that she was creating a new vocational identity as a computer programmer, she finally was feeling bohemian. For being bohemian was ultimately about freedom, about emancipating oneself from oppression and subjugation, which is precisely what she was now doing.

In bringing Chris's story to a close, it should be reiterated that the recent and rather monumental events of her life surely colored her perspective on the past. There was even one point during the interview when she paused for a moment and admitted that some of what she had related was "probably more rationalization than real." Perhaps she needed to paint the darkest picture possible of the art community: If she were going to leave, there would have to be some pretty good reasons for doing so. But we ought not to discount her story. For what she has told us, above all else, is that the art world was nowhere near as sacred as she had thought it would be. Indeed, it was actually more profane – more self-serving, more uncultured, more insecure – than many other walks of life that were customarily regarded as inferior. The situation was a strange and disconcerting one: Far from representing the antithesis of bourgeois values, as she had assumed, certain features of the art world perpetuated these values in a more pronounced and ugly way than anyplace else she knew.

Rick Johnson's story has its own share of bleakness, bitterness, and, perhaps, discoloration. After a stint in the marines, the prospect of becoming an artist seemed "glamorous" and "fascinating" to him. On the first day of school, however, Rick realized that he might have been a bit off in his expectations. "I bought what I thought were the right college clothes: a three-button jacket, a sweater, a real college outfit." Everthing was looking good. But then, he said, "I went to the auditorium and I was the only one who was dressed decently; they were like bums." Given this initial encounter, it is ironic that these were the very people he came to emulate. He hadn't been in any great rush to mature after art school. There was the decision to go to New York, which indicated that he was serious about what he was doing, but he hadn't been one of those who were frantically driven toward success. This was wise; given that he had taken to filmmaking rather than painting, there probably wouldn't be much opportunity for it anyway. So he began humbly, working odd jobs, selling whatever he could at flea markets and the like, and pouring back everything he made into his films. The world of film had been extraordinarily engrossing for a time. As with most art, he said, it had to do with "building whatever monument one builds to oneself, for ultimate recognition, approval, vindication . . . immortality." And he did build some notable monuments: At the height of his success, his films had been shown at the Whitney and reviewed in the *New York Times.* He had still needed to live hand-to-mouth – making money, then films, going back and forth between the two – but this was to be expected; there just weren't as many financial rewards in experimental filmmaking as there were elsewhere.

But things got worse as time went on. "The more serious I became as a filmmaker," he said, "the more dilapidated my life got." Part of the problem was simply a lack of money, particularly since he had a family to support. He recalled an event that summed up his situation all too well. He was out on the street of the city, selling something, and up walked a couple of students who had heard him lecture at their university a few years back. It was shameful and embarrassing: "Here I was the grubby street hustler, and they had seen me at my best." He had thought that being an artist would be exciting and colorful, that it would provide the kind of happy bohemian existence he had heard about. "The life was colorful, all right," he said, "but it was sleeping with bedbugs, driving a cab, working like a slave, hustling, even making porno films." This was a "low ebb," as he put it, and it wasn't too long after this time that he realized that he had better think about doing something else.

In addition to financial problems, there was the problem of being an artist itself. There were so many people involved, he said, that he came to feel out of control of his own destiny: "You're depending on those other people to affirm or negate your existence. . . . You're totally dependent on their approval or disapproval." This was especially so in relation to those people who composed his audience. If they liked his work, he would be "king of the mountain"; if they didn't, he would immediately feel "devastated" and become defensive. Well, he had asked, "'What the hell is that?' If somebody claps their hands, you exist and you deserve to exist and you are going somewhere. And if people are lukewarm, then they are going to erase you from the pages of history. It was just ridiculous," and the result was that he was perpetually a "nervous wreck." The bottom line was, he had been too self-centered as an artist, and it had hurt both himself as well as his family. By no means was he unique either. The entire art community of which he had become a part was composed of people much like himself: "a bunch of neurotics . . . half-crazy."

Things eased up a bit when Rick got a job as a plumber. It was nothing terribly glamorous, but it was good, solid work, and he appreciated it greatly. But shortly thereafter, surprisingly enough, he got offered a teaching job, which, on the surface at least, seemed like an answer to his prayers; he would be able to keep up with his art and make a decent living besides. Wasn't this what he had always wanted? The decision was a difficult one. "The reason most people stay on," he came to believe, "is that they have an investment in it and don't have the courage to give up the investment." As for himself: "I began to realize that if I had the guts, I'd go away from it." Plumbing it was. He went on to explain in greater detail why he elected to leave art. "I said, look at all these people in art. There is this academic world and art world where they're all jerking each other off, neurotic." The plumbers he knew, on the other hand, were "healthy, real, did something that had a real function. It was a concrete world, and at the end of the day you were tired but of sound mind. At the end of the day hanging around artists, I didn't know if I was right or wrong or upside down or inside out." Like a number of others who had had similar complaints, there were no "reference points." Being an artist, he said, "is like anchoring yourself to a cloud"; it had no "solidity" at all. "The real artists," he believed, "produce something concrete, like a plumber does, but only a few artists achieve that. The rest merely purvey bullshit." Furthermore, "few artists aren't corrupted characters; they are fucked up people leading fucked up lives." What it came down to, therefore, was who he respected more, plumbers or artists. And once he was able to frame the issue in this way, his decision was made. "Over there," he reiterated, "it was like a fog world, a ghost world, ghosts upon ghosts. In galleries, there are real people. But they are businessmen," he said, "not artists."

Even when things had gone well, there was no small measure of perversity to the life he had been leading. "I used to be focused," he admitted, "on getting as many of these little ornaments I could get; I'd want all these things, women, clothes." It wasn't only in the reception to his art that he needed to be affirmed; he needed to be affirmed in his social life as well. It was simple in a way: "The more I had, the more confident I was." It was true, he noted, that being an artist had its good points, including the spiritual "unification" it would sometimes provide. But he could get enough of this sort of thing from being a plumber, he felt, that he didn't miss being an artist.

Rick became more bitter and cynical as the interview proceeded. "The world our artists live in," he said, "is an egocentric, self-centered, selfish, almost desperate world. To be an artist is to turn your back on the everyday." The artist was all too often a "champion of egocentricity," who was given to "masturbating on a grand scale" for all to see. It was almost as if this was what artists were supposed to do, as if they were so extraordinary that they weren't to be bothered with the world out there: "It adds up to this sense of exceptionality that we try to hype our lives up with." There were better things to be doing, he felt, than living out mythical narratives of grandeur, as so many did; not only was it philosophically problematic, because it tended to put artists on a pedestal of sorts, but it was empirically false as well. Once one saw just how routine, and in some cases ugly and destructive, the whole scene could be, it was impossible not to feel disillusioned.

There are many reasons Rick elected to leave art. What stands out most, however, are the problems he had with the very role the artist assumed in our society, the shortcomings of which had been evident from the first day he set foot on the campus of art school and met up with so many "bums," eager to put their countercultural dreams in motion. But it was only when he became immersed in the thick of the art world itself, with its strange mixture of self-seeking and self-annihilation, inflation and deflation, immortality and mortality, that he realized how wrong things really were. There was too much of a burden placed upon the shoulders of individuals themselves. Alone as they ultimately were, trying to create the work that would lead to their own affirmation as artists and as people, they could be left feeling that their world was devoid of "reference points" and "solidity"; they were floating in the void, and whatever density would arise would derive from others, only to be exploded once again when they rejected the work. Moreover, it was tremendously difficult to reconcile the all-out involvement that was required in such a singular, self-oriented pursuit, particularly when there existed others who were paying the price for it; it was too easy to feel that people were mere hindrances to one's own grand schemes.

It may seem hypocritical that this man should be so down on his fellow artists. He himself had learned firsthand how difficult it was to keep one's priorities straight; the rules of the game made it so. His anger and indignation were by no means directed at them alone, however. More than anything, I would argue, they were directed at himself, at his having had the need to buy into this game: to be unique and exceptional, to do something more "elevated" than ordinary folks did. People tended to seek the by-products of being an artist more than the processes themselves, he explained at one point, and the consequence was that the art community had far too many people in it for all the wrong reasons. Only when the role of the artist was overhauled, Rick suggested, would there exist the possibility of doing the kind of work and being the kind of person that most people, deep in their hearts, truly desired.

THE ARTIST AMONG OTHERS

Rick's story, like the one before it, is extreme. Rather than thinking of this sort of story in terms of what *did* happen, as a matter of course, or even what *often* happened, perhaps we should think of such stories simply in terms of what *could* happen, particularly if one had elected to become a member of that sort of high-powered community which these people had. How, though, are we to understand what Chris McKay and Rick Johnson have told us? Partly responsible for their respective plights were the mythical images with which they had carried out their activities. Chris, for instance, had spoken about how poverty was frequently mythologized by artists and how destructive the consequences could be. Relatedly, Rick had spoken of the "sense of exceptionality" with which artists tried to "hype" up their lives. Also responsible for their plights, no doubt, was the fact that they had inhabited a world in which there existed scarce resources, which forced artists into competition with one another. Envy was a particularly big problem, one man said; people would sometimes knock down each other's work with the hope of selling their own. In one notable instance of this, another man recounted a time when one of his peers was doing remarkably similar work to what he himself was doing. This peer was apparently more of a salesman, however; he had been busy for some time "getting his image seen out and around by everybody," which was a way of "conditioning people that you would eventually want to be interested in your work." In any case, once this man saw how similar this artist's work was to his own, he became totally preoccupied with the idea of competing with him: "This pervasive one-upmanship," he had to admit, was "just the reality of the field." After his rival's latest show had begun, therefore, he "did some real quick sketch paintings on paper and went around and posted them upon the streets in a few places." This way, he had thought, he might be able to show that he deserved some recognition too. Unfortunately, within 48 hours every one of these was torn down by his "competitors, whoever they are." He couldn't get too angry at this, of course; his own tactics had been much the same. There simply wasn't enough fame and fortune to go around.

Finally, we cannot dissociate the kinds of tactics we have been considering from the "quest for the self," as Bellah (1987) has put it, that has become so much the target of social and cultural criticism over the course of the past couple of decades (see also Bellah et al., 1985; Lasch, 1984; MacIntyre, 1981). Whether the specific issue concerns the perils that have befallen the American family or the difficulties of forging ties that bind in a "community" wracked by competition, greed, and "one-upmanship," one of the root sources adduced is that vision of the self which culminates in our being "arbitrary centers of volition" (Bellah, 1987, p. 372), monads, interested in doing what moves us. "This democratized self," as MacIntyre (1981, p. 30) calls it, "which has no necessary social content and no necessary social identity can then be anything, can assume any role or take any point of view, because it *is* in and for itself nothing." It is no wonder that families and communities are torn apart from this point of view; there may be "nothing" there to hold them together.

The art community could sometimes help bring about a measure of order and coherence to artists' lives and work. As those who found themselves isolated often learned, it was difficult to go it alone. Many seemed to long for the communities to which they had once belonged, shortcomings and all; it was important for them to feel that they were participants in a common project, that they lived and worked among like-minded others who spoke the same language. Even if there were problems, which there no doubt would be, they would at least suffer them together. As we have also seen, however, art communities could work against people's interests, by serving to magnify some of the problems that were inherent in becoming artists. At an extreme, in fact, there seemed to be a tendency within these communities for individuals and their respective plights to feed off one another and become mutually reinforced and perpetuated. It may not be quite right to say that these communities were entirely without "bonds"; something was holding them more or less together. But this something, rather than being in the nature of a shared structure of values, beliefs, and ideals, could instead be in the nature of a shared sense of anomie and alienation, the bonds in question being precisely of the sort from which there emerges the desire to escape.

So it was that even the best-known and best-rewarded artists could grow tired of the scene and begin to think of ways in

123

which they might escape. They wanted to return to being occupied with their art itself rather than preoccupied with all the
intrigues, games, and ploys in which they had found themselves. "I'm in hiding here because I can't stand most of it anymore," Jim Cronin said of his (custom-built) getaway in the
Hamptons. "I mean I can't complain: I've got a nice house, I
have lots of shows, I have four pages on a curriculum vita. If I
want to buy myself a car, I can go to the bank today and do it.
But I don't know if the rewards are commensurate with how I
feel most of the time: If you're miserable, it's not worth it."
There wasn't one single day in his life, he swore, that he didn't
think about selling the house and "forgetting it all." He wasn't
alone either, apparently; "a lot of people at similar points in
their careers would tell you the same sort of stuff. They're not
unappreciative, they've made money, but they don't know
what the fuck they're doing."

Jim and his friends would go to an exhibit like the Whitney
Biennial, where he himself had shown several paintings, and
ask, "'What does it mean?' and 'Is it any good?' and 'Is the
fourth floor better than the third floor?'" The whole thing was
nerve-wracking. In addition, they came to realize that it was a
"very, very dangerous business" they had become involved in,
with their lives continuing to fluctuate in true "schizophrenic"
fashion "between fear and shame and gloating and power."
This was a life, he said, "for somebody who has to go from
being a saint to a salesman, from a priest to a pimp; it's a quick
change act," in which nearly everything that happened was
subordinated, ultimately, to someone's "business problems."

What Jim suggests, and what is implied in much of what others have said as well, is that perhaps the most salient problem
for artists living and working in the company of others, particularly those others who are part of the same communities as
they are, was that the demands of the field were often thoroughly antithetical to the formation of just those ties that many
sought. The climate within which these people lived and
worked was not simply unconducive to the growth of community, in other words, but actively retarded it, precisely by
ensuring that its members would be pitted against one another

124

for their very survival. For some, the effects on their art were minimal. They would simply try as best they could to make sure that the work got done; the intrigues could come in the off hours. For others, however – including, of course, those who stopped doing art altogether – the space of creativity was anything but immune.

Many of the ideas discussed in this chapter are tied to commitment and how it is best maintained in the midst of different social environments. Within the context of both close interpersonal relations as well as family, the main task for many of these artists was to effect a suitable reconciliation between their own demands and desires and those of others. For many, this proved to be difficult to do. In the case of men especially, there was sometimes commitment to one's art at all costs, which in certain respects seemed to be exactly what was needed in order to make it; it was either all or nothing. The image here is a familiar one: The true artist must be unswervingly dedicated and wholly consumed, living, ultimately, for art alone. The only problem, of course, was when there were others involved.

Now some might believe that the problem at hand is an irreconcilable one; you can either have a great life, one man had said, or great art, but not both. To the extent that this is true, there is but one solution: Forget about everything but the art itself. Some people did exactly this. For most others, however, there emerged the need to establish a balance, between commitment to oneself and one's work and to those others who had entered the picture. And this balance, far from immediately becoming the kiss of death to one's artistic activities, seemed to be what allowed them to continue productively. In part, this was simply because guilt sometimes had to be assuaged; if it was difficult to go on knowing that others were paying the price, adjustments would have to be made. There were also those, however, who came to believe that it was useful to be taken "out of oneself," that a more fully rounded existence was not only compatible with creating art but positively generative of it. The point to be emphasized here is not that one can "have it all." Nor is it that one must be committed to others in order to create; artists have gone it alone and done just fine. The point is

125

that those who have elected to be with others would probably do best to be cognizant of them as they move forward with their own personal and artistic commitments.

For women, this task of establishing a suitable balance between commitment to oneself and one's art and commitment to others often assumed a rather different form. Abiding by their own sense of responsibility to and for others, they and their art could get lost in the shuffle; there were too many other things that had to be done, some felt, for them to become involved in as "frivolous" a pursuit as making art. In several cases, in fact, they were told as much, by their mates and their children: A woman's place was in the home, not the studio. What many needed to do, therefore, was figure out how to include themselves – guilt-free – within the orbit of their own commitments and responsibilities, how to clear a space for their own personal and artistic desires. Without this, the result could be a lingering and painful sense of self-betrayal and loss over the opportunities that had been forfeited.

In framing these problems as I have, I do not mean to suggest that they are fully or best handled by will alone. In addition to individuals deciding for themselves to rework their commitments – which, of course, presumes that certain dilemmas are there to begin with – it is important to imagine ways these dilemmas might be minimized or prevented. If, for instance, gender roles continue to be transformed, some of the differences that we have observed may diminish; men will be on fewer heroic quests and women will find a more substantial place for their own interests and desires. Relatedly, if images of artistic success and the paths required to attain it were to change, then the "all or nothing" ethos might diminish as well. More fundamentally still, if the structure of the art market itself was to change, so too might the very nature of one's aspirations and commitments. Perhaps the creation of art would no longer be constructed as a singular pursuit and artistic success a race to the finish, but something else altogether, something more integrated into the fabric of life. We ought not to hold our breath until these things happen, of course, for they may never.

But unless we begin to imagine how to move beyond a reliance on sovereign acts of will, all will remain essentially intact.

Problems related to the art communities of which people were a part exemplify this point well. One of the possible ways of handling these problems would simply be to encourage artists to be aware of them and to resist becoming compatriots in their own mutual destruction. Let's be good to one another, they might say, rather than bad. Let's be cooperative rather than competitive. Let's have a true community rather than a false one. These sorts of changes of mind would undoubtedly have some effect. At the very least, they might help people to feel that they weren't hurting their friends and neighbors. To the extent that the inner workings of these communities are inseparable from the inner workings of the field of art itself, however, we can expect that many of the problems at hand will remain: There is just so much resistance to be mustered in the face of an apparatus that is in large measure responsible for one's sustenance and well-being. It is not enough, therefore, to chide artists for their selfishness or egocentricity, deserving though some of them may be, and nor is it enough to plead with them to rid themselves of these ugly traits, desirable though it may be; without going so far as to deny free will, it amounts in the end to blaming the victim. Perhaps we will better understand why this is so when we explore in greater detail the nature of the field within which these people have tried to carry out their artistic activities.

Chapter 4

Creativity and the market

ART AND PROSPERITY

Although a significant portion of this chapter is, as the title suggests, about the relationship of creativity and the art market, it is more generally about what we have called the "field" of art, which here refers to the productive and organizational dimensions of the art worlds of which these aspiring artists became a part. As Becker (1982) has pointed out, it is important in this context to speak of art worlds rather than an art world, taken as a singular, unified entity, the most basic reason being that there is not one but many such worlds. Moreover, these art worlds frequently operate in very different ways, making different demands and presenting different challenges to those who wish to enter. This does not mean that the notion of *a* singular art world is irrelevant; as many artists readily testify, the presence of this world is in fact highly relevant, and entry into it a much-sought-after goal. We will nevertheless try to keep in mind the plurality of art worlds as we proceed, if only as a reminder that other goals do indeed exist.

Several other things may be worth keeping in mind as well. As Douglas Davis (1988) has recently argued, in a special issue of *Art in America* devoted to economic aspects of the contemporary art scene, the market is unquestionably here to stay: "Given artists may fade and the market itself may rise or fall with the state of the economy, but the art marketing system now in place is anchored in the center, not on the margins of society, and therefore is secure" (p. 23). Not only have art works become more and more commodified, Davis adds, but the very notion of what art is is in the process of changing: "The precious but fragile notion that art is 'above' the world, an ideal once nourished in countless poems, classroom lectures and aging textbooks in which art is considered useless and beautiful, like a flower in a field, may be about to crack" (p. 21). More severely still, writes Lucy Lippard (1984, p. 6), "the history of a work of art once it gets out of the studio is far more closely entwined with the actions of a discriminatory, martial government and the capitalist system that supports it than it was the ideas and aims of the artist who made it." Indeed, the only corrective some might wish to add to Lippard's contention is, again, that we need not wait until art gets out of the studio to see these actions at work; they are often right there from the very start of the process of creation.

With these kinds of sentiments in mind, some have come to consider the art "game," as Wraight (1965) has put it, to be a "vast confidence trick," the most fundamental objective being to produce "a luxury commodity for which a market is deliberately created and maintained by financially interested parties who are neither more or less noble than the operators of any other legal sort of market" (p. 14). What this means, Wraight believes – and keep in mind that he was writing this more than 25 years ago – is that buying pictures for love "is virtually a thing of the past." What it also means is that, "even in the booming art market of today there is room for only a limited number of artists to be successful, and of this limited number most will sooner or later have to become unsuccessful in order to make room for the new successes" (p. 45). It comes as no great surprise, therefore, that we have come to witness the emergence of the "instant artist," who "straight from school is encouraged by the commercial setup to regard himself as a finished artist, to splurge his immature libido across a series of outsize canvases in the hope that they will attract attention to him" (p. 197). It also comes as no surprise that many people, artists included, have come to watch the market like hawks, in the hope that they might gain entry, and that there exist lists of forecasts for those ranging from the "rich" to the "hard-up":

129

anything that might increase one's chances, either as producers or consumers, at making a score.

There is no small amount of cynicism in these ideas. The very notion that the art market may be one great big game, having little to do with with the intrinsic value of the works that circulate through it, is enough to give us serious pause. It may also be wrong, at least in part. As Harold Rosenberg (1965, p. 390), for instance, argued at approximately the same time that Wraight was seeking to expose this "vast confidence trick" being played, "The outstanding characteristic of the American Art Establishment," secure though it might have appeared, was its "shakiness." It was true, Rosenberg noted, that many people did live "with eyes and ears permanently cocked for trends," but it was also true, he believed, that "no dealer, curator, buyer or critic can be depended upon to produce a reputation that is more than a momentary flurry, nor can any existing combination of these." The market did have its share of games and ploys, in other words, but to claim that it consisted of nothing but these was too extreme and jaded a point of view; the work still mattered. The problem, however, was that aspiring artists, unable to predict with any certainty which kinds of work would have currency next, would no doubt experience anxiety in dealing with the market; in part, it was out of their control. The goal for many, therefore, was to attend to what was *in* their control, which would at least better their chances at meeting with success. The question was how to do so without sacrificing or compromising one's own creativity.

One could, of course, simply do the work, forgetting about market realities completely, and then do what was needed to get it seen and, hopefully, sold. Some people did this. It was more likely, however, that these market realities would come on the scene well before this, even if unconsciously. Why "unconsciously"? It was generally rare for these people to be self-consciously calculating in relation to the market, particularly early on in their careers; there was enough idealism and enough of a sense of art's "preciousness" that entrepreneurial strategies made manifest in the work itself tended to be avoided. It was troubling enough, as we shall see, to think strategically after the work was done; to do so in the midst of it would have been an act of betrayal. A number of people did eventually realize, however, that, although their initial motives did *seem* to be pure, they really were not. Only when they could see the extent to which market realities had permeated the space of creativity could they take measures to open it up.

But first things first. Before inquiring into the process to which I have just referred, it may be useful to return to the earlier stages of these artists' careers and see what kinds of issues they had to face as they tried to carve suitable paths for themselves. We begin with a very basic concern: what exactly to do, besides create art, to ensure one's prosperity. This proved to be an extremely important concern for these artists, for unless one was independently wealthy, to continue doing art on anything approaching a regular basis required either a steady job with flexible enough hours to permit one to do art in one's free time, a job in which art was actually a part of one's ongoing responsibilities, or the good fortune of making enough money from one's art alone to support oneself comfortably. Achieving this last end, I should emphasize, was very rare for the individuals in this group, with fewer than five being able to do so over the course of the years. Many tried to show and sell their work, including those with steady jobs, but they usually learned quickly that there wasn't much money to be had. What many also learned was that their desire to make money from their work, even their ability to do so, could sometimes tarnish the process of creation itself: Even in their own eyes, it could become a commodity, given up to someone else. Again, though, these sorts of problems often came later on in these artists' careers. Let us see what happened earlier.

"PLANS"

Teaching was by far the most frequently selected occupation. It was variously described as "the best way to eat," "a good way to have a steady income," "the cushiest job you could do or get," and so on. If the desire was to move beyond "the freak thing," living hand-to-mouth bohemian-style, teaching seemed to provide the security many were looking for. For some, it was "the only pathway to stay related with art and make a living." Or, to put a slightly different spin on the matter, "Teaching art," one woman said, "tends to be the next best thing to doing it." Thus "The Plan," as one man had called it: to be a teacher, to have a studio, to make art, and to have them all work together harmoniously. Security and harmony were not the only motivations to teach. One African-American artist, for instance, had wanted to teach for its own sake, for the service he would be providing his community; it was very much a "mission" for him. Another man had at one time "made a covenant with God to devote a great deal of [his] talent and time to instructional, didactic kinds of work, in the same vein as Michelangelo." There were others too who approached the prospect of teaching with the same sort of missionary zeal. By and large, however, it seemed mainly like a good way to get things going, vocationally, financially, and artistically.

For several people, it actually did work out like this, their teaching and their art running nicely in parallel with one another, a relationship of mutual benefit. Many others, however, found that The Plan "doesn't work." Nearly two-thirds of those who had been teachers during their careers reported serious difficulties either in their job or in their art. Also telling is the fact that only half of this group has remained teaching, the other half having elected to move on to different things. One of the main factors was the time and energy that went into teaching, which took away from art itself. As several people emphasized, teaching had diminished their contact with art to an even greater degree than might have been the case had they chosen an unrelated occupation. The fact that they had to *talk* about art so much, at the expense of actually doing it, was just salt in the wound. One woman cited an old saying in this context: " 'Those who can, do. Those who can't, teach.' " Teaching was apparently close to art in some ways, but very distant in others.

What he liked to do most, one man told us earlier, was "make stuff," which he had not done much of as a teacher. Another man taught high school for a year and, in addition to feeling that he was not making enough money, he felt a lack of progress. After he turned to printing, he came to the conclusion that he related better to machines than to people. Teaching high school art was about as close as he got to being an artist, said a man who had become a salesman, but it didn't work out as he had thought it would. The biggest problem for him came to be boredom. For a number of years, he had been able to devise enough challenges for himself to continue, but he eventually lost the will to do this; the range of schemes he was able to come up with was too limited. For those who continued to enjoy teaching, meanwhile, there often existed the desire to cut back. She "can feel the words not wanting to come out," said one woman. Even though he was fairly happy, added one man, it would still be preferable "to be totally free of having to earn a living." Again, "Nothing replaces doing it." The woman who reached this conclusion had taught art for some time at a major university and had found that there was so much history and theory that the art part of it was barely recognizable.

Another woman had intended to teach as a "backup." When she started teaching at the college level, however, "it just became, really, my life." Overall, this situation seemed to work out fairly well for her. But there still persisted a "conflict between teaching and making art." The reason for this, she explained, was that teaching was a concrete responsibility, one she had to fulfill for her livelihood: "The thing I make money at I'll be dutiful about." But she was "not always that dutiful about art." Her conflict, therefore, was always won by teaching; it seemed to have become a foregone conclusion. But it was a conclusion that was no less hard to endure: She felt that she was being cheated. There were other problems too. Younger teachers were on the rise, and she, rather than being revered for her longevity and commitment, was sometimes condemned for it. She also felt that teaching was too much like "social work," that she was spending too much time taking care of people. Finally, given all of its demands and responsibilities, teaching presented too good an excuse to avoid her own rhythm of working on her art; its regimen served as a defense against her meeting herself and her own creative capacities – or incapacities – head on. She not only felt cheated, then; she felt that she was using teaching as a vehicle for avoiding what she ought to have been doing.

This could be both disturbing, personally, and worrisome, from a career perspective. As several others noted, college art teachers, like most types of college teachers, faced considerable pressure to come up with new and creative things, particularly during sabbaticals and the like. No one had the luxury of waiting for the muse if they were on the payroll, one woman said; there was the need to produce. You always have to be in shows, added one man, "restock" your vita, and so on. The authorities want to know, "'What have you done this year?'" And if you haven't done much, he said, "you get all these funny looks." As another man put it, "The university depends on you to do what you might call relevant art research." Teaching, he went on to say, is a professional position, and "when you're in a professional position, you have to maintain production." Artist or not, "you have to justify your existence for the university." One woman was told that if she wanted to be kept on full-time, she had better "diversify" and do it quickly; if she persisted in doing the same basic thing over and over again, her hours would be cut short. Another person, now that he had left academics, felt that the pressure to create, to offer up new and improved products every year, had diminished greatly. This man had finally secured the will and the opportunity to follow through on something at his own pace; there was an image he wanted to repeat to see how many times he could make it work. Like a number of others, he found that his creativity developed best when he was free from the pressure to create, free enough to work on a single project if he wished rather than move on for the sake of proving to his colleagues that he had an evolving, innovative research program.

What made things more difficult still was that despite the demand for progressive change, it was also imperative that one's art never be too different from year to year. The model here is not unlike that of the scientific research program: There had to be some rhyme and reason to what an artist did; one couldn't be all over the map. This was a prominent theme, I might note, not only for teachers but for many of those who were involved in showing and selling their work. The only difference is that whereas demand for what might be called "innovative variations on the same" was largely a function of the need for testimony among the former that there was indeed a mindful project in the making, in the latter case the demand came from dealers, curators, and collectors, all of whom had a vested interest in keeping things more or less continuous and predictable. In anticipation of later discussion, let us simply note how that the ideology at work here is pervasive in the academy: Even as it is imperative that we do not repeat ourselves from one activity to another, lest those in control of our destinies suppose that the wellsprings of our creativity are running dry, it is also imperative that we do not stray too far from our projects or research programs; only then will we be able to demonstrate that our works – and, by extension, our*selves* – possess some semblance of unity, integrity, and direction.

A further problem, tied more to teaching itself, was that students, fellow teachers, and administrators often seemed to lack a serious commitment to artistic pursuits. Students often "meddle" in art, one man said; they didn't realize that "it's not easy." This man wasn't even sure he wanted to teach but wound up having a job offered to him that was too good to turn down. The place where he taught, however, was not really an art school, the result being that students came in through the "back door," tried to be artists for a while, and then left, usually to do something else altogether. Another person, teaching at the high school level, never liked the fact that "art was considered a frill for the kids," more a "time to goof around" than anything else. The students were often unimaginative, lazy, and destructive, complained yet another. Art was simply unimportant to them. But she was quick to add that there were more people at fault than students themselves. In recent years, she said, art had become less important than computers. She thus felt like a "missionary," trying to ensure a complete education in the face of a creeping, technologically founded incompleteness. To make things even more difficult,

135

administrators had begun to try to fill teaching positions with people with bachelor's degrees rather than master's so they could pay less. Because the attitude toward the arts had become less favorable, she believed, the money was going elsewhere, mainly into more scientific endeavors. As for herself, in the role of art teacher, "you're just a work object," she felt, meeting the needs of the bureaucracy at the expense of the students' needs as well her own. "Society's going to pay for it," she swore.

Another woman agreed that teaching art was not nearly as esteemed as it had been when she began. On top of the fact that guidance counselors steered students away from art, pointing them in the direction of more practical things, she also felt that she was little more than a largely silent witness to the simultaneous demise of art and the rise of science and technology. "You don't feel any recognition," she said; she was getting tired of constantly "doing battle." Like some of the others, there was the feeling that more time was being spent on behalf of the "mission," the attempt to resurrect the arts as a serious and worthwhile pursuit, than actually teaching and doing it. In short, what had originally been conceived as a means to the end of doing their art in a context of security and understanding had for many become an end in itself. This particular "plan" was therefore not quite so foolproof as it had initially appeared.

Next to teaching, commercial art was the most frequently chosen professional occupation for the individuals in the present group, with approximately one-fifth of them having done a commercial stint at some point during their careers. As we have already seen, some of these people came to realize that they needed some form of hands-on creative work, and they became determined to secure it, whatever the cost. Although most of them knew from the start that commercial art would be a very different pursuit than fine art, much less inner-directed and intrinsically motivated, it had still appeared to be one of the best plans available; they would be doing creative things and making some money besides. Moreover, if all went well, perhaps they eventually would be able to leave it behind and return to those pursuits that truly moved them. The idea, said one woman, "was to make a decent salary and perhaps from there be able some day to just paint." The plan was a straightforward one, added another woman. "At first, you're interested in getting a job; you have to live." At that point, she emphasized, "You're not working as an artist to satisfy yourself; you're working as an artist to satisfy your employer." Again, though, if all went according to plan, "hopefully you could quit that place one day and make a living at what you're interested in."

Even while some of these people were still in art school, however, they could see how difficult it would be to carry this plan through. For one, there was something taboo about going commercial, however sensible and lucrative it might have seemed; not only was it different than pursuing fine art, but its rationale, many felt, was entirely antithetical to what art was all about. For those who attempted to mix the two, therefore, perhaps by doing one by day and the other by night, there could be an immediate blot on one's name. One man, for instance, had felt "snubbed" by many of his peers, rejected for his impurity; in their eyes, he was nothing more than an accessory to exactly the sort of mentality they were trying to counteract. "I heard a lot of the hustler feedback," he said; "anybody that's an ad man," he had learned, "is not a real artist."

It therefore became necessary, as another man put it, to "rationalize" the commercial work; because most people had continued to abide by the "cultural myth" of fine art purity, it was difficult to avoid being put on the defensive. Recall, in addition, the man who realized that in some people's eyes he was "just an asshole who advertises a product." There was also the man who would "torment" himself for doing commercial art and who finally gave up fine art altogether, just so he could live with himself; it was better than going back and forth. One major problem for some of those who elected to do commercial art, therefore, was the criticism they might have received or the shame they might have felt over having sold out. It wasn't enough that what they were doing was hands-on or that it was creative or that it really was a lot like art: It was a far cry from the real thing.

The second major problem tied to the practice of commercial art was that by and large tasks were oriented toward the execution side of the creative process; the problems to be solved were usually determined by someone else, someone, perhaps, who had never been seen before, face-to-face. One man who had done some work as a publisher, for instance, recalled how alienated he had become from all the bureaucratic types with whom he had been forced to associate. It was just a business, he said, and the whole thing became false. He was producing something that had no meaning for him at all; it was just one "bum product" after another. "They had nothing to do with me as a person," he explained, and "I wasn't able to get to a point where I could become an art producer, so to speak." He therefore became involved in printing, which, though more mechanical, involved less compromise than the "idiot work" he had done earlier.

The reverse side of this issue is that for those in the position of coming up with ideas, there could be the frustration of not being able to carry them through. After being trained in furniture design, one man had been offered a job for a lot of money with a prestigious firm. He felt that he had needed something more "manually challenging," though; "it was obvious that it wasn't right." Many of his friends thought he was insane not to take the job; it could have launched him into just that state of financial independence so many desired. But he simply "disliked the idea of sitting at a drawing board designing something that someone else was going to make"; it was too much of a tease. Another man hated his job doing commercial art due to its bearing no relationship whatsoever to his fine art as well as to the tremendous pressure he was under. "Some of the people are really rotten, the way they treat you," he said, and the result was that he would often get "extremely nervous," even to the point where he was unable to swallow his food. He had choked in a restaurant a while back and attributed the incident to his work, to the tension he had to endure trying to meet everyone's demands. He would also get so tense sometimes that he would grind his teeth and his nerves would begin to irritate him so that he would lose hearing and sight on one side of his face. His was obviously an extreme case; most others' problems weren't quite so visceral. He was firmly convinced, nonetheless, that commercial work was not only alienating; it had rendered him half senseless.

One final problem should be mentioned before we consider fine art pursuits. Given that the sale of products was the ultimate objective, there often emerged the need for commercial artists to establish uniform, readily identifiable images. His work was fairly satisfying in terms of problem-solving, one man said, and he enjoyed the precision that went into it, but it could also get extremely restrictive at times, as if everything he did was simply a variation on a set theme. He saw the fine art that he continued to do as a reaction to this regimentation. The irony this man had come to feel, however, was that the situation of fine art was not really as different from that of commercial art as he had been led to believe. With this in mind, it may not come as a surprise that many of the problems that were reported by commercial artists were also reported by fine artists. The only difference was that they came as much more of a shock and were, as a rule, much more difficult to withstand: Little did many of them know that the world of fine art had itself become so commercialized that they would face many of the same creative dilemmas and handicaps as the "ad man" peers that they had once shunned. Rather than diving headlong into these dilemmas and handicaps, though, we shall now consider what might arguably be considered a success story, of an ad man turned fine artist. This will help to clarify further some of the issues presently being considered.

HUSTLING THROUGH THE ART WORLD

After a traveling fellowship subsequent to finishing art school, Skip Thomford had gotten a job at an advertising agency, where there had been big accounts, a big budget, lots of experimentation, and lots of fun. Later on, he got another job as art director of an agency and, after that, decided to create his own agency with a friend, which brought him sufficient financial resources that, by the late 1960s it was time to do some art. At the time we spoke to him, he was a member of an important art community in Chicago, filled with filmmakers, painters, photographers, and so on, he was living in a big loft and had a house in the country besides, and, except for the fact that he and his wife had divorced, all was basically well. By conventional standards, then, Skip was indeed one of the success stories in the group, one of the few, in fact, who was able to live well exclusively from the sale of his work.

Interestingly enough, he hadn't even been a fine art major in art school; he had been an advertising major, and had every intention of continuing in advertising for his career. He did feel that he "outpainted" just about everybody back then, including his allegedly superior fine artist peers, but it was in commercial work, he thought, that he would make his mark. The kind of work that he had done when he was in advertising, he said, very much remained with him. Specifically, he had wanted his art to come out of a "future, technological realm" rather than out of the "classic forms"; he wanted his art to partake of the energy, vitality, and ability to captivate the viewer that he had tried to include in his commercial work. Nevertheless, something about commercial work had bothered him. He had found it frustrating, he said, to try to make art out of objects that were never going to really be art. He simply did not like the idea of creating commodities, and he found that his interest in becoming a fine artist was stronger than he had supposed.

He had no regrets about having done commercial work, however, for it was his success in commercial art that had allowed him to move on. What he had learned most of all, Skip suggested, was the meaning of humility, which many of his peers did not have. "It was always worth it to me in my self-education," he said, "to take that place in the pecking order where you humbled yourself: 'I know nothing and I need to learn and I'm going to keep my mouth shut, take whatever abuse I have to take, and it will be worth it in the long run.'"

Particularly since he had a wife and baby to care for back then, there just wasn't much time for "the bohemian bit." His earliest job, he went on to say, was as a delivery boy, which would help him to get his foot in the door: "I wanted to meet people," he admitted, and "I didn't want to go breathe garlic on them and tell them I'm an artist and that I was creative." Others were unwilling to do this sort of thing; they saw themselves as too special to prostrate themselves in order to succeed. And again, they apparently resented him greatly for what he had done. "Years ago, when I was doing this," he said, "it was a real put-down." He was the "hustler," and most people wanted to have nothing to do with him.

Many of them had gone off to teach. They had believed, he said, that teaching was a purer way of earning a living than advertising was, less tainted by ugly commercial consider-ations, and requiring less in the way of bowing to the powers that be. But they paid the price as well, some of them even going so far as to seek his counsel regarding how they might get back on artistic track: "I can't tell you how many of them have come back and wanted me to help them put their portfolio together so they could go down and be able to get a job." The sad thing was, he had to turn some of them away: "It's too late now; they blew it way back." A lot of people had the spirit, he said, but not the "muscles"; they just didn't know what it took to succeed. It was "like a crying reincarnation," as he put it, "coming out of people who want to be something that they might have been."

Skip had "always been a kid on the other side of the tracks." When he got to art school, with his "Iowa kid work ethic," he didn't know anything about Jews or blacks or Latinos; he had never even eaten Chinese food. But there he was, suddenly, in the middle of the big city with all of these progressive artists, supposedly in the know: "There's always been this snotty, big, educational-institutional system that walks around pooh-poohing [certain kinds of] art that always made me sick to my stomach." He would much prefer to see "the real childlike gen-uine emotional response from people who don't know shit about art." This was why he never "buttered up" to those who

141

were thought to have cornered the market on what it meant to be a true artist and create true art, why he hadn't "played up to that museum-curator-critic art success story that a lot of artists have gone and made." It was that "high-blown institutional attitude" that he hated most; "all the intellectuals," he said, "have fucked up pretty many areas of the art process." His own attitude was different. "I want to create pieces of art that I can sell thousands and thousands of times to thousands and thousands of people," where the power of the work would be generated "over and over again," where it would be removed from the threat of becoming another precious object on somebody's wall. He also spoke of the desirability of public, free exposure to his art; whatever it took to counteract the "intellectual museum university structure."

An example of what he was talking about was when one of the ironworkers who had helped him with his last piece drove 50 miles home one night and came back with his family, who had gotten all dressed up, so he could show them the fruits of his efforts. It was this sort of thing, Skip said, that made it all worthwhile. The piece was for a big company, and he had very much hoped that the people who had commissioned the work would like it as well. But what he had received from this ironworker's returning with his family after a long, hard day "was as big a compliment and felt as good to me as the president, the owner of the company, paying me a compliment." To be able to "show everybody from the working craftsman to blue-collar workers in Detroit that I could build something as an artist that was not just a piece of shit, that they'd be proud of . . . then I was really accomplishing something." Skip went on to speak of the shoddiness of a lot of contemporary art. People were too often lazy, he felt; they wouldn't put the needed time into their work, the consequence being that it would be of lesser quality than it ought to have been. His work, on the other hand, was built to last, and would endure, as he himself would, for a long time to come. The goal was simple in this respect. What he wanted was "a respect that will come long after I'm gone." As for who would be doing the respecting, he said that he didn't care if it was the "art elite"; he was more interested in having those who appreciated quality workmanship respect his work, those who could see just how caring and masterful and meticulous he was. He was not only an artist, he said, but an engineer; he had even proved the ironworkers wrong on occasion concerning issues of balance and the like. It was important that people see this side of his work.

Skip also wanted to expose some of the myths that existed about artists and what they did, particularly that art was fun and games or blissful catharsis or some such thing. He was the one we encountered earlier who had insisted on presenting himself to others as the "small businessman" he was. The same sorts of myths were operative in conjunction with recognition as well: "You figure you get some recognition . . . and the phone's going to ring off the hook and you're going to be set." As he himself learned, however, "it doesn't work that way; it's a slow, seeping process," requiring persistence and hard work. The recognition he had initially received, he continued, had rendered him complacent about his future; it "made me want to be passive and think that I'd finally hit it, made it, and that I had the answers." But it wasn't so; showing was hard work and demanded much more than waiting for the phone to ring, mainly because the art market was so ruthless. "The whole gallery structure has not treated artists like natural resources," he said. Instead, "they try to strip the mine bare as fast as they can." They had no desire to see to his preservation merely because he had gained some recognition; there were plenty of others who could replace him. Getting into the gallery system had been especially difficult early on, he added. He hadn't been able to get people to come and take a look at his work; they were interested instead in his reputation or "where I come from or where I went to school or what I did to somebody else or who I punched out or who I fucked" and so on. Moreover, there was tremendous pressure on his own part to succeed in the appropriate way: "that New York thing – got to go to New York, got to do it right . . . have a legit gallery . . . get in the right collections . . . be seen in the right places . . . go to the right openings . . . talk to the right people . . . have the right people write recommendations for you." This had become less important to him as time went on; he had decided that he just didn't need to have his name in *Art in America* every week. But getting himself a measure of recognition had been difficult, and remained so: If the work was no longer up to par or if others came along who could do better for a gallery, he could quickly be forgotten.

One further problem Skip mentioned in conjunction with the gallery system was that for the most part it was conservative, particularly when times got tight economically. "You go into the gallery now and they can't afford to turn the gallery over to an experimental idea that doesn't have any sellable commodity. We live in a capitalistic democracy . . . and to survive you have to know that and deal with that and get it to a [point] where you can stretch it and get some of that." He remained a realist in this respect. Whereas other artists had found this situation to be cause for frustration and angst, for him it was simply a fact of artistic life: Business was business.

Let me try to bring together what appear to be the most salient contours of this man's history, as he related it to us. Unlike most of the others being considered, who had begun as fine art majors and who had aspired from the start to be fine artists, this man had begun in advertising, which immediately resulted in his being considered an inferior brand of artist; in many people's eyes, he was a hustler. It was precisely these people's tendency toward being purists and toward romanticizing the artist that had prevented them from succeeding in their own endeavors; they had failed to see that compromises would have to be made. Eventually, he noted, many of them were able to see this; disenchanted with their teaching jobs, some of them had returned to their former adversary for help, only to learn that they had gotten too far derailed. In this respect, then, Skip's background in advertising had served him well. He had taken his commercial savvy and brought it to fine art, where it was applied with considerable success.

With regard to the art he eventually did, the story continued in much the same fashion. As Rick suggested, the kind of work that he did as a fine artist wasn't all that different from what he had been doing in advertising. He had taken to working on large sculptures that required technical expertise, so he would draw up plans as he had earlier and then go on to execute these plans with the help of ironworkers and the like. The main difference between the two lines of work had to do with the destination of the object: Whereas the commercial art object had to be designed explicitly for the sale of some commodity, the fine art object would only be contemplated and appreciated. And it was this that he came to want most of all.

As for who would be doing the contemplating and the appreciating, his hope was that he could help to bring art out of the rarefied atmosphere of the museum, with all its snobbery and elitism, in order to allow everyday people the chance to see what art could be and do. He even spoke at one point of wanting his work to give an "American spirit" to art, which for him meant democratizing it, making it accessible not only to those allegedly in the know but to those masses of others who might benefit in some way. In line with these ideas was Skip's insistence that his work be sturdy, that it be built to last; given all of the shoddily made, impermanent, perishable objects that artists often created, his conviction was that art should have sufficient durability and quality that it could be appreciated for the long haul. In effect, he suggested, there was too much contemporary art that, by virtue of both its shoddiness and its complicity in the latest aesthetic whims, succumbed to a kind of planned obsolescence; it was fine for the moment but would be forgotten when the next whim came along.

It might be noted that some of Skip's work was shown not at art museums, but at places like the Museum of Science and Industry in Chicago. This was fine: As long as there were people who would enjoy his work, where it was shown was of little consequence. It might also be noted that many other artists might have bristled at doing this sort of thing; if their art wasn't shown in those places consensually regarded as the right ones, they would be better off not showing at all. It figures that this man's work would wind up in a science museum, they might have said; he was always more of a technician than an artist anyway. But these concerns were simply not his. There was only one right place to show his work, and that where the greatest number of people possible might see and enjoy it.

Finally, Skip's perspective on the gallery system was essentially a pragmatic one. Galleries were first and foremost businesses, and consequently, if one wanted to participate, it would be necessary to play their game. What this meant, mostly, was ceaseless hard work. Not even artists like himself could rest easy with their recognition, for they themselves were little more than commodities in the eyes of dealers and owners. But there was nary a hint of lament on his part about this situation: If there was any desire at all to reap the material rewards of being an artist, then there was little reason to cry over the fact that this was a business. This man was unique in this respect. Not only did he refrain from launching into the sorts of tirades against the market that others often did, but there was no evidence of guilt over his participation in this structure and no evidence that he felt compromised either. Since he had never aspired toward the more bohemian side of being an artist, with its countercultural visions of free expression and so on, there was nothing at all to be compromised. Even the resistance on the part of galleries to experimental ideas was nothing to fret over; it would have been foolish for them to carry out their business any other way. If one wanted to innovate, then it would be necessary to do so from the inside; one would have to stretch the boundaries of acceptability slowly and methodically and ensure these galleries that whatever risks might be incurred would likely pay off in the end. This is exactly what he had done.

What are we to make of Skip's story? For those among us who are purists, it may be that what he has done will be distasteful and offensive. Our response, in short, may not be unlike what his peers had said many years back, that he was indeed an "ad man," and that he would never be a true artist. Moreover, he might be taken to task for his art itself; rather than the romantic entanglement with the muse that we hear so much about, he seemed calculated and cold in a way, more of a technician than some might desire. His wish to disseminate his art to the masses may be considered laudable, but even here, it could be argued, perhaps he had merely sold out. Perhaps, that is, he had taken to doing work that was so bereft of conventional aesthetic aims that he had indeed compromised the mission. Finally, in conjunction with Skip's perspective on the market, it might be held that types like him prevented the market from becoming more accommodating and humane, for instead of challenging the notion that artists were to be treated as commodities, he accepted the situation as it was, adapting to it as best he could. It was only through the frustration and angst and guilt referred to earlier that artists could change the status quo and thereby construct more optimal conditions within which to create, some might feel; anyone who did anything less could only be called a traitor to the cause.

But then there is the proverbial other hand. Hadn't he been a realist when it had come to forging a career? Hadn't he been insightful enough to reject some of the mythical images under which others had been operating, which allowed him to be humble enough to succeed? Hadn't he rejected many of the bourgeois trappings of the contemporary art world and chosen instead to work for exactly those people whom many disdained for their crude and uncultured philistinism? And finally, hadn't he been able in the end to secure an appropriate place for himself within the gallery system, occupying just that sort of inside track that would allow him gradually to innovate as he desired? Aside from his messy divorce, he seemed quite content, with both his creative activities as well as the compensation he received for them. What more could one ask for? Whether we choose to indict this man or hold him up as a model to emulate, it may be useful to keep his story in mind as we proceed.

Things didn't work out quite so positively for most others. The following case, extreme in its own right, may in fact help us to see that humility and a willingness to adapt to the demands of the art world may have yielded decidedly less salutary outcomes. When I spoke to Colin Lowell at his loft in SoHo, he was a bit down and out. After art school and then graduate school, Colin and his wife lived in New Mexico. But New York, they

147

decided, was the place to be. He had been disappointed with what he found there, he recalled; it was more conservative than he had supposed it would be. But he was nonetheless ready and raring to go. Like Skip, he began in humble fashion; he worked in a gallery for some time as "the back room nigger," as he put it, carrying out a variety of menial tasks. At one point, he had two other jobs as well. Eventually, he was fortunate enough to get a teaching job at a local community college. It was nothing to write home about, but it was good, he said; at least he didn't have to be a "nigger" anymore. He had assumed, then, that he had done the right things to get his foot in the door of the art world.

In addition to a number of stints as a visiting artist, he had many one-man shows (14, by his count) and had been a part of several group shows as well, at galleries ranging from the likes of Betty Parsons's to Leo Castelli's. Given that these galleries were considered to be the premier galleries of the New York art world, he had clearly become a success, which was exactly what he and his art school peers had expected. Even back in school, he said, he had been considered a "New York artist"; he was one of the ones whom people could easily imagine becoming part of that scene.

What was this scene like? "It's like an open-ended Borscht circuit," he said; it was filled with upper-class people, the elite, hobnobbing with one another, gossiping over the latest cultural developments. There were glamorous international shows too, and lots of glitzy parties, peopled by important decision makers, many of whom would "gawk in front of a painting with cocktails." He was the man who had talked about "the hero thing" in this context, like he had wanted to be "the court painter of the Kennedys." It's not that he was a careerist, he went on to qualify. Not only had he never fully understood the commercial aspect of being an artist, but he remained firm in his belief that he never succumbed to changing his work so as to meet audience demand; he had never been a glory-seeker who would sell his very soul to hit it big. But he had not been anonymous either: You didn't come to New York, he said, to be anonymous.

There was also something very exciting about this scene. "When you go to an opening," he said, "you think the best thing that's going to happen is you're going to walk in there and everybody's going to fall on the floor," so taken would they be on sighting the artist. "A few shows that I had," he continued, "the gallery director would call me up, say around three in the afternoon, after the show had been hung, and say, 'We're all anxious for you to get here. We've just sold four of your pictures.' Things like that are nice," he admitted; "they make you feel very good." There was also the other side, however: "So what," he might have said, "so they sold four paintings. . . . Why don't they buy them all? And what if they didn't buy any of them? And so you start questioning these things, and then you try to be loose and try to be social." It wasn't easy.

It should be added that Colin was one of the fortunate few who actually had some good things to say about gallery people, particularly Betty Parsons. He might have been something of a Jackson Pollock in her eyes, he said; she liked the way he talked, his ideas, his "word." As a result, she gave him lots of space to develop. It was very intense back then, he felt; many of his fellow artists were envious and tried to knock him down. They wanted a piece of the pie, too. What was interesting, though, and important for his own creativity, was that Parsons wouldn't push too much business his way. He was promising and would undoubtedly come to success – she wouldn't have taken him under her wing otherwise – but her own feeling was that young artists needed to wait and let their talents mature before they got caught up in the business end of things; it was important that they not forge ahead too quickly or whatever they might have had would be jeopardized. The fact that Colin had remained loyal to Parsons even when other galleries were interested had gotten his wife somewhat annoyed; if other people were knocking at his door, with money virtually in hand, then he ought to have answered, she felt. But he wouldn't do it. It was almost like he was her captive, he said. The other thing his wife might have resented was the fact that, by his own account, his relationship with Parsons was almost a kind of "romance." After her death, he said, one of his dreams "was to

exhume her, to restore her as the queen of the art world again."
She had apparently given this man's life a point of contact and
orientation that he would lose after she was gone.

Just when things had gotten reasonably secure financially,
with his teaching job and his art going well, Colin's wife
decided that she could quit her own job as a teacher. But then,
unfortunately, he got fired, the sales of his paintings hit something of a dry spell, and their security was lost. They even had
to go on welfare for some time to make ends meet. It was
around this time, he said, that with his welfare grant of 55 dollars in hand, he pretended that he was a black man. "So for
about twenty-seven bucks," he recalled, "I bought a two-piece
white polyester suit, got a white straw hat, got some white
high-heeled shoes." From a junkie in the street, he bought a
pinky ring too, for 8 dollars, and they went to the welfare center
with a deck of cards and began playing "with two other black
guys." That night he went to a party, filled with art world people, "just back from Barbados or wherever," and given how
tacky he looked, no one would speak to him. He really must
have been at his wit's end, he said, crazy; they were tough
times.

When his wife left him not too long thereafter, Colin was
going to buy a book on suicide but bought a Henry Miller novel
instead, and before he knew it was drinking Pernod; there were
other alternatives to dying. By the time the next show came
along, however, the consequences of which were some un-
equivocally bad reviews, he contemplated suicide once more
and eventually became hospitalized on account of his profound and lingering depression. His wife had really been "on
his ass" to make it. For the most part, he admitted, she had been
extremely positive and encouraging about his work. But when
both he and his work began to take a serious tailspin, it was
time for her to move on. He had come to be somewhat relieved
about her departure, he suggested. He was with someone else
now, a woman who was a "gift," as he put it, who was able to
skip the "muse routine." The result was that he had finally gotten over his depression and was ready to live again and do

some painting. But there was still a bitter taste in his mouth from all the pain and suffering he had endured.

In addition to his own personal problems, he continued, there was something thoroughly unhealthy about the whole New York art scene. He again referred to the problem of careerism in this context: "I see artists that are so career conscious," he said, "that they could be working for Breast of Chicken tuna fish – [like a] company man." He himself had tried to avoid this sort of thing, as he noted earlier, but there were no illusions about the fact that on some level he had been a part of it and still was. He began to be wistful at this point in our conversation. Sometimes he wished that he could have a place in the country, with a little house and some land. For better or worse, however, he was in too deep by this time to flee. "I used to think that society respected the artist," he continued; "that's when I was a student in art school, studying art history." But as concerns the present situation in art, "I don't know how that could be." His whole life, he said, wound up being "a downhill trip where I picked up a wife and three kids." Sure, he had done some good work and had gotten some recognition for it, but given the sorry way his life turned out, he couldn't help but feel that he would have been better off doing something else entirely. "Art doesn't mean or stand for anything," he complained. "Art world people are in it for the clothes and the parties, they are shallow and superficial, and, above all, love and do not share the money." The whole thing "stinks," he said. It's "too decadent," and he would be perfectly happy if all of these people were "put on a small island and blown up."

If only he was off in Vermont or someplace like it, away from all the "pollution, violence, racial tension, dog shit, noise, status seekers, opportunists, amoral art politics." In the end, Colin said, "there are no rewards, it doesn't pay, and the people in it are usually dumb and sleazy." With all the "poverty, unfulfilled dreams, hardships, and handicaps," he had written to us, a short while before I met with him, he really felt that he had made the wrong career choice. The fact was, he had "wound up with nothing," and not only had he suffered, but his family had too. He wished that he could have provided for them better than he had. Things were, however, looking a bit better lately. Colin was doing construction work, which was demeaning, he felt, but good. He would rather be home painting, of course, and he still did occasionally, but with a family to support, he was so worried about money that he could no longer afford to do so on a regular basis. Emotionally, things were better as well, particularly in virtue of his new mate; the relationship had proved to be therapeutic for him. And there was always his past, which, as his vita testified, had really been pretty good – "almost success," as he put it. There was an impressive record of shows, a Ford Foundation fellowship, a stay at the Mac-Dowall colony, and so forth. He had no problem admitting that, however wrong they might have seemed to him now, most of the choices he had made were his own. No one had forced him to live in a loft in New York and be an artist and become a member of this strange inbred community, filled with disappointed people like himself; he had done what he wanted. Had he known the consequences of these choices, however, he surely would have done things differently.

I find myself feeling uncertain about how to respond to this man's story. I liked him, he was easy to talk to, he was warm to his little boy, and there were times during our conversation when I truly felt sorry for him and especially his family, who, with the exception of his wife perhaps, had been innocent bystanders. His oldest boy wanted to go to art school, but it was unclear whether there would be sufficient funds for him to do so. Now there are too many people in the world who are starving and diseased and so on for me to become too despondent over this boy's not being able to go to art school. And there are too many black men and women – *real* black men and women – for me to be overly sympathetic to this man's rather bizarre welfare masquerade; had they known the circumstances that had led him to come their way, with his deck of cards in hand, my guess is that they might not have been quite as interested in playing. For all of these qualifications, though, there was no doubt but that this man's pain was real. And by and large, no one likes to see decent people in pain.

152

But couldn't it also be said that this man's own bloated expectations and desires led to his downfall? Hadn't he elected to attend all those glitzy parties? And hadn't he probably been downright friendly to all those stupid, shallow, superficial, sleazy people who would stand there with their fancy drinks, gawking at his paintings? If he wasn't the kind of fellow he was, it might be argued, he wouldn't have gotten himself into this mess; he might indeed have run off to Vermont and lived happily among the maple trees, painting bucolic scenes of a way of life that still seemed to haunt the collective memory. But this wasn't the way it turned out.

What was it, then, that had happened? Why such bitterness and venom? Part of it, I would offer, was likely directed at himself, for having become a part of the whole scene. Here he was, a man who had actually been involved in street events and radical politics back in the 1960s, sipping cocktails with the enemy; here he was waiting for phone calls from his dealers, with baited breath, with the hope that he would again be validated by the objects he created; here he was with a family, who was paying the price for his own egoistic dreams. But then there was the allure of the scene itself: the grandeur, the early apprenticeship with Betty Parsons, the delirious mixture of excitement and fear and resentment when a new show was about to open, the write-ups, the parties, the heartfelt talks, the drinks, the wonderful decadence, the beautiful cheapness of the whole thing. How could a young man like himself, eager to become an artist, possibly resist this? It was a great big male fantasy, much of it: the roguish hero, spewing forth grand but inelegant abstract paintings so that he would be etched in the memories of those who aspired to know the real thing. Even the suicidal tendencies fit the script; he was, after all, following in the footsteps of Pollock and all the others for whom life had ended abruptly and, even in the case of "accidents" perhaps, by their own dirtied hands.

Once he was in, there was no getting out; his life had taken the form of a modern mythic tragedy, the end of which was all but determined from the very beginning, from the moment he set his eyes on the variously dazzling and dreary sights of the big city, which would continue to hold him, like a prisoner, until he could no longer see beyond. He wished he hadn't bought into this myth, he had told us; he wished that he could have been better able to differentiate his real desires, which were to do good works of art, from those more manufactured desires to be in the limelight. He had been so self-conscious about everything, he also said; if only he could have ignored all of those things that interfered with his authenticity and his integrity, as an artist and as a man. He was speaking from hindsight, of course, from the terrible wisdom of his own knowledge of the consequences. At the time it could often be "wonderful," he admitted. This was precisely what kept him going. But it was also what kept him from seeing how pernicious the entire situation was: He had been blinded by the light, and only later on, after he regained some semblance of vision, could he see what had happened.

"All of this," said another artist, "takes a massive effort," and was involved "with the rhythms of manipulating people, materials, money, just about every social aspect you can think of." Others agreed. Marsha Riddell, whose husband had been instrumental in getting her to face squarely the business end of art, noted that it took an enormous effort to "peddle yourself." She found much of this out during some work as a critic, when she began to realize how "political" it all was, "how knowing people, going to all the openings, being very evident, very visible, how it could really help you be successful." She was straightforward about the nature and intensity of the pursuit: "If you want to show, you've got to peddle," she said, "and it's a full-time job." It was extremely important to be gregarious and visible, added Jim Cronin. You would have the right people come over to your studio to see your work. You would see a hundred shows on a Saturday and by the end of the day, "you'd be so tired you couldn't walk." In addition to whatever else people might have thought it was, "art is a business. And you must pursue that business. Otherwise, nobody's going to know about you." You "have to get out there on the pavement" and be "terribly aggressive," others said; unless you are a "social beast," this woman came to believe, it was "naïve" to think you could make it. Another woman was glad that she and her husband, also an artist, "ended up meeting the right people." They had been active in the community for a long time and these people had become willing to help them. She too believed that, "A lot of it is making the right contacts, knowing the right people, and doing the right things."

With these stark admissions in mind, it may not be surprising that a number of the people with whom we spoke reached the conclusion that artistic success had less to do with talent than with manipulation, financial and otherwise, notoriety, or, as Samuel Palesky had put it, "supreme pushiness." It might also have angered these people to "see much lesser artists succeed in the marketplace." There was no doubt about it: "The public is blind!" this man exclaimed. There were too many people, added another man, who tended to "confuse being a good artist with being a successful, salable artist." In any case, it was a terrific mistake, apparently, to suppose that one could simply be discovered. There simply was no place in the art world for the "shrinking violet," one woman realized.

We can also see why Marsha Riddell, who had been told "to get out and face the market and deal with the market and not be used by the market," was glad her husband had been so heavy-handed with her. The fact was, you could be "enormously abused," particularly by those with big investments. "I can't tell you the number of times I've been screwed by galleries," she said. "They just treat you like dirt." Most dealers were "just awful," she continued. "They're crooks, they're terrible crooks," and they were able to be that way, she believed, "because there is nothing to prevent them from being that way." It was like this "in any area of life where there is no structure," where people were so "unprotected." They lead you on, she said; "they watch you, they come back, they diddle with you. You don't have a foot to stand on for your demands." This, in a nutshell, was why one needed to "learn to be tough." It all boiled down to power, she had concluded. "You're treated like a child," she said, "because there's nothing that can help you be anything but totally at their mercy" – until, that is, "you have a big name. Then you can start."

Jim Cronin concurred: "Artists are set upon by people who for their own personal or monetary or career professional reasons are constantly picking one over. You feel like the day after Thanksgiving," he said; "your life feels like leftover turkey." There were of course certain decisions that could be made, like "how much you want to give in, how much of an elitist you are, how much power you've got, and how much you want to live," but they were extremely difficult and painful. And just in case people thought that success would immediately result in artists being able to call their own shots, this man knew that it wasn't quite so easy. Appearances notwithstanding, he said, there were very few artists who were really free. Artists like Jasper Johns and Willem De Kooning had freedom because of the tremendous power they had gained through the years. In fact, he went on to say, the only way for artists to be able to create freely was if their own wealth exceeded that of the people who marketed their work; it was that simple. What freedom required, in short, was power and money. This was why it was so difficult to avoid becoming a "business partner," as Jim put it, in the art world. He related a story in this context. His brother, apparently, had once accused him of making far too much money, to which he promptly responded "that the stakes were not the money but that the work survived. I couldn't help but make the money," he had said, "because I was in cahoots with the people. If I didn't take it," he went on to say, "they'd manipulate the shit out of me, which they do anyway." But "if you don't accept these responsibilities, then they're going to screw you." This, again, was "why you have a Jasper Johns who can tell Leo Castelli to go fuck himself basically: Leo needs him more than Jasper needs Leo. And when you think of the power of Castelli, that's quite an accomplishment, because everybody else is trying to get a piece of his action."

What was so sad, added another man, was that there were so many artists, particularly in New York, who were sitting on the doorsteps of galleries and who would do anything, "who would literally sweep the floors and wash them every day for nothing," to get a show. The whole thing proved to be too much for some people. "I could schlep my slides around and be one of those little twits who gets rejected time and time again, and maybe accepted for a show by some obscure gallery," said one man, but he found the prospect too "humiliating." Others wished that they had the nerve and the aggressiveness to get out there and hustle but weren't willing to "prostitute" themselves. Even though she thought she would be "rich and famous," said Ellen Beaudoin, it apparently wasn't meant to be. She should have gone to more openings, she said, and she also should have learned more about the business end of things. But she was still "kind of stymied" by all this. She could, of course, have turned to one of the so-called vanity galleries to show her work, in which artists paid for an exhibit, but she just didn't like the idea; it was too crude and commercial. But neither, Ellen said, did she like the idea of "having to sell yourself." In part, she felt that she wasn't ready to do this. But the bottom line was that she was afraid. "Any time I get a rejection I don't want to try again," she admitted. "It crushes." And even though "I've learned a little bit more that you have to depersonalize it," she apparently wasn't able to do this to the extent that was necessary. Even if she had been in shows, things might not have been much better. "The trouble is, you can be in shows and most people aren't even aware of it." As for the idea of proceeding gradually, perhaps by trying to gain a measure of local recognition, that was certainly feasible, but it was nowhere near enough. Hence her all too stable position on the "lower rungs" of the art world ladder. By no means had she lost hope: "It'll come," she believed. "I know that." But it would undoubtedly be a good long while before this would happen.

It was perhaps with these sorts of ideas in mind that Ellen had recently taken to signing her paintings with her initials instead of her name. Some of her friends, she noted, had been critical of this practice, feeling that she was "hiding." But she was convinced that prejudice against women artists was so pronounced that, in order to get a fair shake, it was necessary to resort to tactics like these. Interestingly enough, when she did more craft-oriented work, she had no reluctance to signing her name; this sort of work was what women were *supposed* to do, so it wasn't any problem. But with fine art, it was an entirely different story. Even though some of her friends deplored what she was doing, there was at least one who knew where she was coming from. This woman's own husband had apparently suggested at one point that she sign *his* name to her paintings rather her own. She chose not to do this for obvious reasons, but the idea behind this tactic was much the same: Other things being equal, a man would have a better chance at becoming recognized than a woman.

It would still be crushing, of course, if the work continued to be rejected – maybe even more so, in fact, because it could no longer be blamed on her being identified as a woman – but she was willing to go ahead with these tactics and see if anything changed. Given the fact that she refused to go for vanity galleries, and given as well that she had no desire at all to sell herself, this was the least she could do to try to improve her situation. Ellen had experienced rejection not only as an attack on her work but on her person, which was being rendered inadequate by those – mainly men – who were in power. I am not about to claim that there weren't men who experienced similar responses to rejection, for there were. But given that most of them had been socialized into adopting a somewhat more competitive and aggressive mode of acting in the world than women had, they generally seemed less adversely affected by the forces at hand. For women, however, hustling and peddling could mean carrying out activities that they experienced as antithetical to their very being as well as laying themselves on the line in the process of doing so, toward the end of their own possible annihilation. This is another reason for why there were fewer success stories, conventionally defined, among women artists in the present group: In more ways than one, they had been forced to enter a man's world.

SHOWING AND SELLING WORKS OF ART

What made things more difficult still, for men and women alike, was that the business end of things and the art end of things could become all but impossible to disentangle. Consider the following two cases, the first of a man who elected to remain in art and the second of a man who elected to leave. At one time, a number of years back, there was every indication that Peter Trantino was headed for success. Having had his work reviewed in the likes of *Artforum* and *Art in America,* having had important gallery connections in Europe, and having made a good deal of money from his work, he had not only believed he would become famous – which he still did believe, actually – but rich as well. Early on especially, he said, he had tended to go where the money was, his motivations in the art world avowedly being "economic more than anything else." Part of this, he went on to explain, had been a function of his youth, his attempt at becoming recognized as an artist being a "major drive." Peter had been a "hot shot," he had won scholarships and prizes and, overall, loved that "celebrity" aspect. Only now, as he gazed back, could he see that some of his motivations were rather "cheap," having less to do with the art itself than with the trappings of being a young artist. Of one series of works, for instance, he admitted that the rationale behind them wasn't really artistic at all: "I became identified with it, so I kept doing it until I got tired." Perhaps if he hadn't been a university teacher, anxious to get tenure and to ensure his future, his motivations might have been purer than they were. But there was always the need to keep on producing and showing, to let those in control of his destiny know that his work was indeed valid and important. Apparently, however, they were unconvinced: After some 7 years on the job, he was denied tenure.

Despite the fact that Peter had been greatly disappointed by this decision, there were some salutary consequences. For one, there was a change of scene; he and his family moved from up north to New Mexico, where the environment was astounding and where he was incited to do a very different kind of work. New Mexico, he felt, took him away from the trendy audiences for whom he had painted before. He would even go to craft galleries rather than art galleries to try to sell his work; he was "no longer afraid of being decorative and craftsy." As for the work itself, it too changed significantly. He was the man who had moved from "sensory bombardment" to a more contemplative kind of art, that seemed to mesh better with where he was. He also found that he had more freedom once he left academics. There was less pressure to produce and to prove that he was capable of perpetual innovation; he could take more time to experiment, to let the work itself, rather than outside authorities, determine what changes were in order. He still wanted to make some money, so there remained pressure to produce, but his goal was simply to break even, to receive the remuneration he deserved, nothing more. Finally, Peter had come to have a more personal definition of success, one that was less tied to those cheap motivations he used to have. He too had never been much of a careerist, he believed, which was probably the biggest reason why he didn't get tenure. But he was even less of one now. Because he was earning his money mainly through a steady job in geologic illustration, career concerns were less at the forefront of his life. In short, some good had come from the transition he had been forced to make.

There were some not so good things, however, as well. He found, for instance, that he had trouble selling his work. He spoke of one show in Florida, for instance, that had been something of a failure, and he had taken it to heart: "That no one in this hick town wanted them hurt my feelings." Even when he did get good feedback, Peter continued, it didn't really help. As he had learned repeatedly, you "can't take all those good feelings at face value," for they may well culminate in nothing at all. As things stood at the time this man spoke with us, in fact, he had stepped back from showing his work; he was just too unsure about its worth and validity. Confidence "comes from people's responses," and if these weren't forthcoming, it was difficult to move ahead with conviction. Furthermore, even though money was no longer as primary a concern as it had been, he found that he couldn't quite shake the idea of its importance, if only as a means of signifying that he was indeed a good artist. When money becomes doubtful, he said, it makes the inner process itself difficult.

Peter was suffering from a loss of faith in his art. There were some artists who could gather faith exclusively from their art itself; they would go ahead and do what they felt was good and right, and if others didn't like it, then it was too bad for them. In his own case, however, he had been used to recognition and had come to think of it as a kind of yardstick of his worth as an artist. He was candid in this respect: The fact that even those people in hick towns didn't want his work drained him of self-respect. Now some might find it problematic that he continued to define his own worth as an artist through recognition and money; he was doing his work for the wrong reasons, they might say. My own sense, however, is that this was not the case. As he himself admitted, there had indeed been times when his work had been done for the wrong reasons, but he looked back on these times with disdain; it seemed hard for him to believe that he had gotten so sidetracked from artistic concerns. In any case, no longer was he painting for the sake of money; he was painting for the sake of art. But the fact still remained that without the sort of confirmation that money brought, he was left feeling uncertain about who and what he was as an artist.

Perhaps if he had never been successful, if he had never experienced certainty and conviction, things would not have seemed so bleak. With all of his customary markers stripped away, however, and with a belief that recognition, signified especially in the form of money, was still very much "the name of the game," he had come to inhabit a kind of artistic void, filled with fear and anxiety about his prospects for the future. Perhaps eventually he would divest himself of these needs, and learn better to be on his own, doing his art. But this would take a great deal of time and patience: It isn't easy to leap over one's past and carry out one's activities in the world in an entirely new way. Meanwhile, all he could do was continue hoping that someone, anyone, would find some worth in what he was doing; only then would he be able to move forward.

Ned Cranston's story was quite different. He had just grown tired of the struggle. Ned had taught for a while in the Midwest. He had enjoyed the teaching, had done lots of painting, and had been selling his work on a regular basis to highly respectable places. Upon learning that his teaching contract would not be renewed, however, he had been terribly disappointed: "I had all this time finally that I really wanted to have to spend on the work, and here it was taken away from me." All was not lost, though. Good galleries, in both Chicago and New York, had still been interested in his work and, with this in mind, it seemed as if the time might be ripe for a break. So off to New York he went, with his family. He felt a bit strange about this move; it was tough to say why he left Chicago, where success had been imminent. But New York being what it was, he decided to give it a go; after all, it was what he had always wanted.

After he arrived, painting took something of a back seat. He had gotten a loft, which needed a great deal of work, he was doing construction work 3 days a week in order to put food on the table, and although he spent a fair amount of time painting, the whole experience proved overwhelming. Not too long thereafter, in fact, he began working 12 to 14 hours a day, mainly for the sake of making ends meet. Not surprisingly, there was virtually no painting during this period of time, which amounted to about a year. More distressing, though, was the fact that even after this difficult first year had passed, he not only had trouble coming up with ideas for his art but became less interested in doing so. He had become burned out, he said, and, for the most part, he has felt this way ever since that fateful time. For a brief while, he noted, his experiments with drugs opened things up a bit, as did meditation. "It was like I was working along [before then] not even thinking about what was happening." But his occasional attempts to rekindle his former passion failed.

The last serious bit of art Ned did – it was at the time he had become involved with meditation – was when he got up each and every morning and methodically poured paint on his canvases. The process, he said, was very different than what had gone in his earlier work. That work had involved a thought process, representing an attempt to imitate a look that he liked. Pouring, however, had nothing to do with imitating; it was a question of interaction, at the moment. This went on for some 6 months, and then, there was nothing. He had always had the idea that he would get back someday, maybe when things settled down more. The idea recurred still, in fact, but far less frequently than it used to. Perhaps, he said, it takes as long to get rid of something as it took to put it in there. After doing a little recreational drawing and painting, for instance, he would say to himself, " 'Well, maybe this isn't such a bad idea. . . . Maybe I should do some large canvases, see if I can get a show somewhere, market them.' But as soon as that idea occurs and then I have to go out and act on it, I lose interest . . . [which] takes all the enjoyment out of it." It was better, he decided, not to think these thoughts at all. If he could do this, art could be just what it was, an end in itself, pleasurable and fun, without any strings attached. This was what he wanted most of all anyway; he wasn't cut out to be a professional artist, doing all those things, aside from the art itself, that had to be done.

What Ned had come to feel was most enjoyable – and it might be noted here that much of his art work had once consisted of hard-edged, geometric, color-field-type paintings – was building, the physical process of making things. He had begun working with architects, and had therefore taken to executing their ideas instead of his own. He preferred doing this; there was a sense in which it was purer and freer. When he was conceiving the work, on his own, the possibilities became too great; there were too many different ways to go, too many choices that had to be made. And it was something of a relief not to have to do this anymore. Before he started pouring, Ned went on to say, there always had to be an idea of what he wanted to do: "I wanted total control at that point," and the ironic result was that "the actual process often got in the way." It was almost as if he had tried to dominate the work, to force it in a particular direction, which couldn't help but distort the integrity of the activity; conception had gotten in the way of execution.

As of late, however, there was no desire to labor through this kind of process, trying to figure how to actualize the ideas in his mind; he only wanted to do the work. Ned had grown tired of all the ups and downs, the intense involvement, the struggle. It was true enough: He might never be as deeply satisfied as when he was painting, but he was willing to give it up if it meant being comfortable. He wanted contentment, he said, "levelness," nothing more; it was a good trade-off. His entire life had become much more "inward" lately: Rather than forcing the various issues you confront in your life, "you try to be like a witness to all that's taking place," to keep an "objective attitude" toward everything you do and everyone you're with, including family; it effects a certain clarity in consciousness, he said, and ensures that his involvement with the world will never get so strong and passionate as to become disabling, as it had.

In lieu of his art, then, there was life itself. There was something going on in each encounter with the world, he explained, and if you were an objective enough witness, it would be possible to eliminate problems and develop those features which aim at understanding. He has continued with meditation, which he does no matter how he feels, the reason being that he had become firmly convinced that how he felt sometimes had little to do with who he really was. He seemed to feel a bit strange, if not disappointed, about the way things had turned out. He had thought he would become a painter and make a living at it. But he also had the sense, after all was said and done, that he really didn't make the choices that had culminated in his present existence; they were made for him. He has woven these beliefs, it seems, into a philosophy, a way of looking at the world. He would attempt to refrain from exercising "preferences" for one thing over another, for all they do is "interfere"; one had to just let things happen as they would and hope for the best.

But what was it, we must finally ask, that led to this man's falling away from art? My own sense was that art had simply lost its charm for him. In reading this sort of case history, brief though it is, some readers may feel that perhaps this man wasn't an artist to begin with; perhaps he didn't have the drive or the fervor or the confidence to stick with it. This may have been true on some level. Others might attribute his demise to the countless responsibilities that burned him out, leaving him little desire and little energy to take to his art. There is likely some truth to this as well. But the bottom line, in my own estimation, is that art came to represent for him just that sort of strenuous, ego-involved project that was an anathema to his innermost desires, which were simply to *be*.

Even when he was involved with painting, he had wanted things to be simple. There had been the desire ultimately to extinguish his own ego, his own ideas, his own preferences, which would pave the way for the most authentic and immediate artistic encounter possible. What he seemed to realize, however, was that no matter how pure and unsullied this encounter might become, no matter how emptied of laborious decisions, there would still remain the task of doing something with these paintings; they would have to be taken out into the public realm, such that he would again have to become ego-involved to ensure their proper destiny. And once these sorts of ideas entered his mind, he told us, his creative activities would suffer; they would suddenly become tarnished by the intimation that, at some point, he would have to become invested in something other than art itself. It was too much trouble; it was too topsy-turvy, too cluttered with motives, too far away from his main interests, which were to do things, physical things, that were enjoyable. Along these lines, his work in construction proved to be most appropriate. In that context, he could meet these interests, but without incurring the same cost that would exist if he were to do art.

Is his story to be regarded as a tragedy? I would have to say no; he wasn't one to cry over lost opportunities, nor did he feel that he had made serious mistakes. Furthermore, he seemed to have grown content with his situation. He knew that he had relinquished some of the highs of painting, but that was all right; one couldn't expect rapture without pain, and he had already had enough of that. Subjectively, then, all was basically well. On a somewhat more objective plane of interpretation, though, there was indeed something sorry about Ned's case. For what he showed us, I would suggest, is that for those whose primary allegiance was to art itself, it might have been extraordinarily difficult to keep their activities protected from the myriad forces that threatened to interfere. I am not just talking about external forces either, such as the need to become involved with the art market; I am talking in addition about those desires for fulfillment, acceptance, and recognition that can transform even the purest of artistic motives into something else, into a means to some other end. Let me also add that there is significantly more going on here than the mere victory of extrinsic over intrinsic motivation, as if his desire for "rewards" was at the heart of things. What this man had gotten caught up in was nothing less than what Weber called the process of "rationalization" itself, a process wherein even one's innermost desires became entangled with the alienated appeal of calculatedness and instrumentality. What Ned came to reject, therefore, were certain salient features of Western modernity itself, with its refusal to let things be. It was better, he decided, to become entranced in the simple clarity of his meditative world, even if it meant the end of much that he had formerly held dear.

If in the previous man's case capital served as the needed yardstick against which to measure his worth as an artist, in Ned's case it served as a reminder that other-than-artistic motives could quickly, and destructively, tarnish the creative process itself. Again, I would not want to reduce his creative difficulties to the deformative power of capital alone; it wasn't the prospect of making money per se that he found so troubling, but the prospect of having to *do* something with his art, to use it as a vehicle, as a means, to achieve recognition. When the desire crept into his mind to have a show or to market his art, it would immediately become part of a project, of his own professional "becoming." And it was exactly this, he came to feel, that he did not want. For one, he no longer had any interest in going this route again; it was difficult and unsettling enough the first time. For another, this desire had always seemed to implicate itself into what began innocently. His art would suddenly become other than what it was, or at least what he wanted it to be; it would enter into a calculus and thereby lose whatever simple integrity it might have had.

In each of these cases different motives became entangled with one another, such that each man's creative activities suffered; they were undermined, precisely by the existence of desires to take their work into the public realm and have it be

166

recognized officially by others. These kinds of desires permeated the minds of many, particularly early on in their careers, when their developing identities needed to be affirmed by others. With Dennis Mackenzie's first show, a part of him "suddenly burst into being." He had worked at a feverish pitch from that point on, he said, because he had "suddenly realized that all this work did have a reason," that it was finally "amounting to something." Notice what is being said here. Only when he had this first show did the work acquire a reason: No longer an end in itself, it too had suddenly become something other than what it was; it had a rationale for being.

Dennis wasn't one to complain much about this state of affairs. He had had lots of shows since that time and was generally pleased to have fared well. He had worked "hard and honestly," he said, and for the most part it had paid off nicely. It had never been easy, he emphasized. He recounted, for instance, the problem of "stopping everything for an exhibition and the other person" – namely, his ex-wife – "not understanding that," and even went so far as to describe the path of the artist as a "hell road," demanding a great deal of time, energy, and single-mindedness. Perhaps this was why his marriage was such an "absolute and utter disaster." But there was no point in grieving too much about the personal liabilities of doing what he had done; they were merely "the price of success." There was, however, a further price to success. Despite the fact of his having "burst" into being, when you begin to sell your work, he said, you become "the ultimate seducer. . . . You're constantly producing an item and attempting to seduce buyers into liking it enough to part with their money for it." To a certain degree, this was perfectly justifiable; he had as much right to make money as anyone else. But it left him feeling somewhat uncomfortable. What made him more uncomfortable was that his work had come to be in a price range "that the average person can't afford." There were days, he went on to say, when he felt that he was "only producing things for the elitist rich," and this made him feel that, ultimately, much of what he was doing was essentially "meaningless." Years ago, Dennis said, he was "one of those people who was putting daisies down the end of the rifle barrels of National Guardsmen in Berkeley." He had moved to Canada for draft-related reasons and, like so many others, seemed to have prided himself on his antibourgeois leanings. He had therefore come to find it very difficult to "rationalize" doing what he was, particularly "when there are people in the world starving."

Dennis believed that being an artist was overrated. He didn't think that artists had any more important role to play in society than plumbers had. Rick Johnson, who had actually become a plumber, would certainly have agreed. He also would have agreed with the need to "wipe out the snob appeal" associated with art: Not only did it serve to romanticize and inflate the role of the artist, but it led to feelings of guilt as well, particularly over the fact of catering exclusively to the haves rather than the have-nots. Now again, there was a sense in which Dennis was pleased with his success; part of him had been affirmed by the good fortune that had come his way. At the same time, however, he said that some of the very things that had made him so successful also tended to make him miserable. There was a strong likelihood that, sooner or later, he would give it all up. Knowing what its destiny was, he simply couldn't enjoy his work as much as he once had. Here, then, was yet another way in which capital could intrude on the space of creativity: In producing commodities for the contemplative satisfaction of the elite – which had at one time been the very goal he had sought to attain – it had become difficult for this man to live with himself and to create work that he felt was valid and real. Beauty was great, and he no doubt wished that everyone could be exposed to it, but it did not quite measure up to food, clothing, and shelter. For all of his love of the objects he created and for all of his success, he found that he had gone over the top, and was descending from the hard-earned peaks of his good fortune into the valleys of shame and guilt. Unless he found a more suitable way of living with these emotions, he would have to move on to something else.

There is a contradiction at work here that we need to pursue further. You have got to be concerned with establishing yourself, said one woman. "After you've been in school for so long,

that's the next step." It was extremely important, added another, "seeing that I could be successful." She too, it seems, had
burst into being. Showing and selling their work remained important for many people. Although it could certainly be
depressing when things didn't go as well as they might have
liked, it could also be "thrilling" and "exciting." Even in those
cases where there might not have been a "burning desire" to
shoot for the top, it could nonetheless be "ego feeding" to be
offered money for the objects one created. Showing one's work
could be important in other ways too. "One of the great values
of showing," explained Leah Tormey, a well-known woman
artist, "is that it's quite possible to become very involved in
your life and in your thinking and in the little world that you
construct in the studio," and "that world," she believed, "needs
to be tested." The entire process, she went on to say, is "a very
mixed blessing and it's extremely painful," but the fact of the
matter was, "we all want it." Things had changed for her recently, however. "Everyone I know wants money," she admitted, and there was also a strong desire for most, herself
included, to be "on top of the heap." But she had also "put
something else first," namely, her art itself. Along with several
others in the group, critical acclaim and monetary reward were
perfectly acceptable, but only, she emphasized, if they were the
by-products of her artistic activities rather than interwoven
with these activities themselves. There were many artists, Leah
noted, who proceeded quite differently. Like her own earlier
self, they were "task-oriented," and were willing to do anything and everything that was needed to establish themselves
in the art world. She had been fortunate to no longer have to
operate in this mode. But she no longer wanted to either. She
simply was not interested in "the current mode of success," for
it was antithetical to, and destructive of, the very process of
creating works of art. Her most basic goal in this context, then,
was to try to make sure that the art continued to come first,
which could happen, she believed, only if one did not actively
seek success. She was apparently much better at doing this
than many others.

Another well-known woman artist told a similar story. There

could be "enormous pleasure," she said, when success came her way, and she "would absolutely love to be famous." She was well aware of "all sorts of defense mechanisms that are built up to say it really doesn't matter," but "particularly in the United States," she believed, "the world accepts you for what you make, not what you do." There was no denying it: The worth of a work depended in significant part on "how much money you get for it." She even went on to admit that she relied on money in certain respects for her own motivation; showing and selling work, she said, "speeds up your process of creation." She nonetheless insisted that none of her work had ever been done *for* money, nor would it be. She too had been witness to the destructive effects that befell those who entered, wittingly or unwittingly, into this sort of calculus.

Some people never went the route we have been discussing. In line with some of the problems related earlier, they might have felt that they were not up to the challenge of showing and selling their work. Some were also uninterested in doing so. Recall the woman who was never "of a mind" to go out into the market with her work, never saw it as being important outside herself, who disliked when there were "hooks" on those things she had lovingly created. She had called herself a "closet artist," and was doing what she could to remain that way; only then would she keep her work pure. Again, there may be some defenses at work in these cases. The woman who eventually got "enormous pleasure" out of showing her work had been afraid when she was younger. "I didn't know where I was going with it yet," she said, "and I'd be too offended by criticism." Because "the hardest thing for an artist to face is rejection," she added, it was preferable back then to keep to herself. "When you really know where you're going," on the other hand, "the criticism doesn't bother you." It didn't bother *her* at any rate. Rejection still "crushes," another woman told us. Not selling her work led to a feeling of "desperation," added yet another. This woman's main problem, she admitted, was that she still lacked the aggressiveness and the self-confidence to make things happen; she wouldn't want to be so defensive as to deny this. But there was more to it, she insisted, than her insecurity alone: Once money entered the picture, a substantial portion of her own self departed. The experiential and artistic sacrifices that trying to show and sell her work entailed for her were enough to make her ambivalent about the entire process.

"There's not really a detached interest ever," another woman complained; "it's a manipulative interest," one she had elected to do without. The contradiction at hand comes to the fore once again: She really wouldn't mind recognition, this woman went on to explain, but she found that it had inhibited her, that it destroyed something all of a sudden; it was enjoyable until the point at which she became objectified, packaged into someone who deserved something in return for what she had created. At this point she would retreat, into a world more fully her own. We might recall yet again the filmmaker-turned-plumber in this context as well, how perverse it had been when he was depending on others to affirm or negate his very existence. He would be "king of the mountain" one day, only to suffer the threat of his being erased from the art history books the very next. And it was only when he became aware of how thoroughly and perniciously this situation had crept into his very being that he was able to call a halt to it. Let us explore further how others have managed to achieve a comparable awareness and thereby free themselves from their own captivity.

ALIENATION AND DESOCIALIZATION

Although several people told how showing and selling their work had become more of a focus for them, usually as a function of their burgeoning confidence, for many others the importance of these activities frequently diminished over time. In the process of becoming more aware of their motivations, they became better able to see them for what they were; the realization that they had been operating under extrinsic rather than intrinsic directives became tantamount to their recognition of the coercive power of the conditions through which they had been living. Their own alienation was therefore the initial moment in their own desocialization.

Finding the muse

Maria Dell had done some work early on that she came to realize was "great for corporate art," but not so great for her. Her geometric, hard-edged paintings, in particular had really been "kind of superficial"; it was "safe, contemporary, design-y art," that pleased everyone and moved no one, and she had eventually grown "tired of everything being so pure and clean and sweet." She therefore started to include imagery in her art, especially fairy-tale imagery. "There's a lot of waiting involved with the women in fairy tales," she explained; "the feminine is the part that has to learn to be patient." What was it she was waiting for? For none other than Prince Charming, she said, her "animus," as Jung called it, that masculine side of her own existence which had been submerged under the purity and cleanliness of her corporate creations.

She had tried too hard to be accepted and acceptable, it seemed; she had desperately wanted people to like her work, and so set out to do exactly that kind of work for which acceptability was all but guaranteed. She had also "thought it was terribly important to be in a gallery." But the work that she had created failed to evoke anything. Maria spoke humbly about how things had been: "I don't know how my old work could have evoked any kind of an emotional reaction." Now that she had stopped aggressively pursuing recognition, however, and had chosen to deal with "something way down inside," people had become interested. It used to be that she would be "turned to tears" by others' remarks, she added, but "it just doesn't matter" anymore. If things happened to advance her career, fine; there was no reason to shun success. But art had to issue from inner demands, she learned, not outer ones, for there was no way to create when one's primary concern was to be acceptable.

Consider as well the following case. Upon arriving at art school, all fired up and ready to go, Donna Streeter met with the first of a series of profound disappointments. What had happened, as she told it, was that her introductory drawing teacher, upon seeing her work and her own commitment to it, told her she should go back to her home in Wisconsin and forget about being an artist. Not only was she merely "playing

172

around" with art, but she was a small-town girl who didn't really know how to deal with the big city. So off to Wisconsin she went, where she "stewed" for a semester. It was true; she simply hadn't realized all the work that went into being an artist. The question then was whether art was important enough for her to try to return to school. She found that it was, so back to art school she went.

It was still tremendously difficult for her. If people weren't stable and secure, Donna said, they could easily be destroyed. She knew: She had apparently been one of them. There was a time when she had construed art as a life or death situation, claiming that if she couldn't work she would have to kill herself, which, in fact, she tried to do. She also had a nervous breakdown at one point, which testified further to her psychological fragility. What made things more difficult still was that there would be these "massive critiques" at art school, where people would feel as if their very selves were on the line. In her own case, this feeling had been especially salient. What she had to do, therefore, as nothing less than a survival strategy, was take whatever measures were needed to ensure that these critiques would come out well. And this meant doing the sort of work that was in vogue, mainly in the tradition of Abstract Expressionism.

When she was out of school, Donna would often do quite different things, such as traditional landscapes. These, she felt, were actually more consonant with who she was, particularly given her small-town Wisconsin background. When she was in school, however, her strategy had been to try to gain the recognition, as an artist and as a person, she so desired. "I used to try to please everybody," she said. "I went through my De Kooning phase, I went through my Max Ernst phase," and so on. As for the result of this strategy, it did indeed work on some level; as time wore on, she gradually became better integrated into art school life. At the same time, however, it had become clear that, rather than bolstering her art or her sense of self, she had actually been in the process of annihilating both: The identity that had been created was not really hers. One scenario said it well. Her instructors, knowing what sort of work had currency at the time, had told her that her paintings needed to become larger, a directive with which she complied. But once her paintings got to be 6 feet by 6 feet, she found that she had no control of her images anymore; she would be climbing around awkwardly, trying to do work that she really had no business doing. So she eventually called a halt to this strategy, armed with the realization that, although it had served its purpose, her art and her sense of self were still suffering.

At this point, therefore, the attempt was to do her own work rather than somebody else's, work that "was mine, totally mine." Her strategy, in other words, was to do the exact opposite of what she had been doing previously. "I didn't have any influences at that point at all," she said. But this strategy proved to be problematic as well, and for fairly obvious reasons. By trying to create art devoid of the influence of others, and by trying so very hard to move into her own personal interior, she had begun doing art that was so autistically self-enclosed that no one quite knew what she doing, including, on some level, herself. Her images at that time "were so away from everybody else," Donna said, "people didn't know what to do." This was especially true of her male teachers. Because her images were "women's images," it was that much more difficult for them to understand what they – and she – were about. In any event, this latter strategy had not improved things much. Despite the fact that she had tried to move inside herself, there had been little that was truly internal; she had simply become engaged in a kind of artistic reaction-formation, substituting what appeared to be radical innovation for the slavish imitation to which she had succumbed earlier, the result being much the same.

Donna finally gave up painting altogether, even going so far as to give her paints away. She had felt painting leave her, she said; there were no more ideas. Turning instead to prints, she described the incredible feeling she had of beginning anew; she would "wipe the slate clean, start all over again." What also helped were her travels to Mexico and Egypt, where, among other things, she had experienced the strength of women's mythological images along with wonderful new landscapes, which apparently rekindled her desire to deal artistically with the natural world. From prints, she began to create elaborate collages, filled with things like spines and bones and stones, which were designed to incorporate her mythological interests into the texture of her work. "I just pick up things," she said. And even though this work was by no means for an "everyday" kind of audience – people had to have an affinity for the mythological to appreciate her work – she found that these later efforts, which abided by the objects she encountered rather than her own radical ideas, were more readily appreciated than anything else she had ever done. She found this strange in some ways: Although her work was more personal than it had ever been, "people are really responding to it." It used to be that Donna didn't feel she fit in anywhere. But now, she said, "I feel like I fit in. It's okay: My selfhood fits into this whole thing."

Upon doing work that was truly internal rather than merely an oppositional response to her former imitativeness, Donna had finally managed to do some things that others could appreciate. In addition to personalizing her work, it had also become feminized over the course of time. It was about the earth and nurturing and birth, about the "organic metamorphoses" that transpired in the world. Indeed, not only was the work about these metamorphoses, but it exemplified them as well. Men, she said, tended to get into a style and repeat it ad infinitum. Women, on the other hand, were constantly inward-looking; they were constantly "mutating," organically, like the earth itself. The only problem with these mutations, of course, was that there would inevitably be those who were put off by them, those who felt that this mode of creating compromised the work by making it too heterogeneous and disunified. But this, she came to feel, was their problem; they were the ones whose work was compromised, not hers. Donna went on to relate a brief story in this context. People had once told her she painted like a man. She had protested at the time, but continued; her desire to belong had been too pressing back then for her to proceed in any other way. But now the situation was different. She was comfortable with who she was, as an artist and as a person, and there was no reason to bend to the will of those who were supposedly in power any longer. Donna and some of her friends eventually gathered further comfort and security in the face of their opposition by becoming members of a large group of women artists in Chicago who networked with one another. "It used to be," she explained, "that women were afraid of doing [this] because they wanted to be identified with male art all the time. And so, if they identified with other women artists, they'd say, 'Oh well, I'll never get my credentials.'" But it had become time to challenge this fear and to mobilize, to achieve that sense of community and solidarity which might allow them to move ahead with their work more surely.

This woman, like so many others, had to become desocialized – and *re*socialized – in order to create with integrity. Upon entering art school with her small-town naïveté, only to be sent back home where she would ask whether she was truly committed to being an artist, she had realized that she would have to proceed very differently if she and her work were to be accepted. On returning to art school for the second time, therefore, she began doing work that, while alien to her innermost concerns, helped her to gather the acceptability she desired. What had happened subsequently, though, was that her own alienation became palpable enough to incite her to move inward; she would do her own work, she had said, and no one else's. But many of the problems she had faced earlier wound up remaining intact. She hadn't really moved inward at all; she had simply acted in opposition to her former desire to please by doing work that would never be confused with any other's, the result being that she had once again fallen short of the mark of doing work that was authentically hers. It was only when she traveled abroad that she was finally able to hit her stride as an artist. Her art had simultaneously become personalized and universalized: The depth she had found within was precisely the vehicle for her capacity to express and communicate, to raise her personal concerns beyond the idiosyncratic. Finally, in addition to being affirmed by the critical recognition she received, she was affirmed as well by the community of women artists with which she had become associated. Indeed, this too raised her concerns beyond her own singular self. For in becoming a member of an organic social body of like-minded others, whose primary interest was to create a measure of resistance to the largely male-dominated status quo, she was able to move into the world knowing that she and her art were legitimate.

Others told similar stories. Leah Tormey, for instance, who had earlier spoken of her rejection of "the current mode of success," had at one time been "madly" involved in its pursuit. She had been a member of a select group of artists who shared many of her ideas and ideals, and it had been "a lovely way to begin showing. It was very low pressure, we were full of piss and vinegar, thought we were the hottest shit on earth." But "by the time it became more serious," she continued, "which began with the selling and the commercial galleries, and who got galleries and who didn't," she had begun to feel a little sad: "I recognized that something of the joy of the work was over." Things had quickly gotten competitive and rather ugly, too weird too fast. A further factor responsible for diminishing this woman's joy was the fact that however much she may have benefited from her association with this group of artists, she found that she just wasn't into the kind of art that was being done, filled as it was with a kind of boisterous imagery, reflective of that piss and vinegar they were all about; it was fun and it was a great way to begin, but there were other things that commanded her attention more. So it was, she said, that "I began working against everything I learned in school." She was interested in creating her own art and her own artistic identity, one that was more in line with who she was, and this meant that she would have to abandon some of the old ways and take off on her own. Her move to New York was intrumental in this context. Chicago had started "closing in" on her, she said, leaving her with the feeling that her artistic options were limited somehow, so it was time to move on. Moving to New York, she felt, "was probably the first decision I was conscious of that was clearly for the development of my work." Many more were to follow.

Among the most important of Leah's subsequent decisions was whether she would remain an artist. Having rejected the

imagistic art she had created earlier, and having immersed herself afterward in exploring how paintings were constructed,
she found that her work got more and more "reductive" and
formal. Another way she described this process was as one of
"elimination." She would continue removing from her work
that which was unnecessary or extraneous, until finally she
would be able to determine what paintings required for their
very existence. What had happened, however, is that her work
gradually became so reductive, so thoroughly purged of ines-
sentials, that it reached a point of no return; if she kept on going
in this direction, there would soon be nothing at all. She therefore had to decide whether there was enough in painting to
sustain her in the long run, whether she really loved it, whether
there was any justifiable reason to go on. For all of the existential puzzlement that these questions entailed, the answers, she
found, were rather simple: She was an artist and would need to
figure out some way of reconnecting herself to the fullness of
art for her future to be viable.

"It became a process," Leah explained, "of accepting the tradition of painting and introducing additive thinking." The first
of her new works, apparently, "looked almost as reductive as
the work which preceded it." Manifestly, therefore, it was
difficult to detect the revolution she had undergone. But "there
was a different construct underlying it." Her previous work,
she went on to say, had been about perceptual issues; they were
paintings that "the eye scanned in a certain way." But she had
gradually come to feel that there was something "manipulative" about these paintings: Rather than moving a whole human being, they coerced an organ, the eye, into responding
predictably. They were therefore pale substitutes for true art,
which did significantly more. In addition, Leah also grew less
interested in playing out "issues" in her work. It used to be
much more important to her "to have a kind of intellectual control" over her painting, to be "capable of addressing certain issues," so that "if someone said that this was a particular critical
issue in the air at that moment, in some way or other the painting dealt with that, whether by ignoring it or tackling it or

working against it." In this respect, her work had been as much a symbol of her own knowledge and awareness as a demonstration of her creativity. But all this had finally faded, she said: "I just don't care about those issues anymore. . . . I think part of becoming more comfortable with your own choices and just part of getting older," she explained, is "less of a need to answer to the world."

Her foremost desire was simply "to do a really good painting," and this, she had learned, was only possible once one identified one's other-than-artistic motives and cleared them away. The entire process hadn't been easy, she emphasized, because it had been one of "giving up" certain modes of acting and creating that had become deeply ingrained in her. If she was really serious about doing a good painting, however, this was what had to be done. Her work would henceforth be "operatic"; it would be "inclusive of everything I know that seems appropriate for that painting." The main goal was therefore to have each painting be true itself and nothing else, to be "more or less its own entity," which meant that it could no longer be subservient to some art world idea about the proper way to proceed.

One of the things Leah learned through this process was that she was "still a romantic," and that she wanted her work to be expressive in some fashion. Even in that "tight, tough analytical period," when she had been so concerned with reducing her paintings to their barest essentials, this desire had been there. As of now, she went on to say, "I think that work with content that is strictly formal is very boring, and I do think the formalist dialogue has dominated the art world since [art critic] Clement Greenberg; it has often dictated the terminology through which one thinks about painting. But it's not enough." Indeed, in her "heart of hearts," she admitted, she was most comfortable with work by people like the Abstract Expressionists, who at least had been expressively engaged with what they were doing. She was not especially interested in "that form of male heroic" which often accompanied their work, but there was nonetheless a great deal to be said about their passion and their commitment, their refusal to efface their own subjectivity in the name of an idea.

There was some cost to this "operatic" way of proceeding, and it is one that we will learn a good deal more about in the next chapter. In striving to have each painting be "true to itself," it would inevitably be the case that "less gets carried over" from work to work, thereby rendering her own artistic identity less manifestly continuous than it would have been if she had continued to work serially. Once again, though, if she wanted to be true to her work – rather than to her own identity or, more concretely, to her own dealer – there was no other way. A further cost, which we will be taking up in greater detail later on, had to do with the anxiety and doubt that these sorts of paintings entailed. "There are always points," she said, "when it seems to be going well and I think I'm this great genius and everything's wonderful and I'm in love with myself and the painting and the world and everything else. There are other points," however, "when I hate myself, the painting, the world, everything else, that kind of emotional reaction to the work." Any work that is "truly large," Leah went on, "that is not task-oriented – which my work was for a couple of years – just includes the whole hubris and everything else." Doubt, she went on to say, "is simply a part of it on one level"; it is an intrinsic facet of the "twentieth-century condition." There was no way of ever really knowing whether the work was good or not; the criteria were too ambiguous and ephemeral. The task, therefore, was "to always measure your feeling against what you really do in the world," difficult though it may be. As this woman well knew, "It's very easy to give more credibility to doubt than one ought to." The only saving grace was this "connection that periodically gets made between the material, the person doing it, and the thing being done, where it all fuses." It was this, above all else, that rendered bearable her own doubt and gave her the feeling that she was indeed successful.

It was not an easy way of life. "There is an interdependence with the world that there isn't in a more protected kind of position; you're more dependent on the world's good opinion."

There simply wasn't much in the way of "cushioning," Leah added. "We're organizing our own lives to some extent with a minimum of rules, and that's very scary stuff." Furthermore, she felt, "We're not wanted particularly." Artists were often seen as little more than society's "irritants," and as such, it had sometimes been difficult to move on feeling that what she was doing with her life was worthwhile. There was a time a while back, in fact, when she herself had become convinced that artists were basically "superfluous and useless," particularly because what they did had so little "utilitarian value." But this was a mistake, she suggested, which derived from employing the wrong standards. Even through all the hardship and anxiety and doubt, she said, "We are not alienated workers."

At the same time, Leah refused to romanticize art's possibilities. Avant-garde thinking was over, she believed; "it had its historical moment." Consequently, she said, "I think that we are not going to alter and affect society the way the Constructivists and the Purists and the Cubists all felt." More generally, the problem of "social impotence" loomed large. All this meant, however, was that it was time to reassess art's priorities. In the end, she felt, art was only impotent to the extent that people believed it to be – to the extent, that is, that artists capitulated to those utilitarian values currently being employed and applied them, erroneously, to their own work. What was of the utmost necessity, therefore, was to refuse to buy into the culture's current point of view; it was imperative for artists not to succumb to an ethic of worthlessness by coming to believe in it. But there was really only one way for people to have faith in the worth of their own work. And this was for them to do the sort of work that, in their own "heart of hearts," they knew was real. Anything less would come back to haunt them, by transforming them into yet another crop of alienated workers, producing means to some exterior ends. This alienation would in turn echo throughout the art world, leaving these people, quite rightly perhaps, with the sense that creating art was just another job, and not an especially useful one at that. If only they could re-collect those dimensions of their own being that been submerged under the trappings of the art world – and of our own culture more generally – they might finally succeed in doing something meaningful and important.

PRODUCTION AND CREATION

We have witnessed the transition in this chapter from what might be called "external hustling" to "internal hustling": from the observable tactics often consciously employed by these artists in order to make their way into the art world to those less observable – and perhaps less conscious – tactics employed in order to gain recognition. It should be reiterated that for some the desire for recognition seemed to bear little relationship to the desire for capital per se. The payoff for them may have simply been in being seen or in being on the cutting edge of new and exciting art world developments or in finally forging an identity for themselves after so many years of false starts. For others, however, there emerged the realization that their motivations might not have been as pure as they had once assumed. Whether in the form of fame or fortune, it was not unusual for these artists to eventually see that they had become sidetracked, alienated from their true desires. The result for some was a renewed commitment to their art: Now that they knew what their desires were, they could go on to actualize them. The result for others was leaving art. The result for others still can only be called confusion.

Consider one final case. Art had been mainly for himself, Jason Bird said, until he began selling his work. At that point, its entire rationale became transformed. "I continued to learn about nature," he said, "but my view of my art work came from a different point." The transformation was quite simple, actually: "I painted products," he said. "I was producing a product that was for sale." It's not that he had never sold work previously, he clarified, for he had, "but that was not the intent behind doing it." Now, however, it was. He used to not even finish some of his paintings, he went on to say. After getting what he wanted out of the process of painting itself, he would walk away and do something else. But he no longer had the luxury of doing this: "The way I've been looking at my art work now is different because I've been forced to look at it differently. I've now looked at it as a way of making a living, and now the need to finish something exists because, unless it's finished, it doesn't fulfill that requirement." There still remained some artistry involved in what he was doing, and there were times, he said, when he wished he could have some of his paintings back. But by and large, he said, "None of my work is that precious that I'm not willing to give it up." If he missed a given work enough, he said, he could always do it over again.

Jason had few qualms about his situation: "I've accepted it as part of the reality of why I'm doing it" and "I don't have to make excuses for it or be ashamed." What it all came down to, he felt, was time: "People are paid and rewarded based on time; that's really all there is. What they do with their time determines their value." As concerned the content of his work, the story was much the same. There would sometimes be a demand for a certain type of work, for instance, and he would have to figure out a way to meet that demand. "If it's something that can fit [this demand]," he said, "fine"; there would obviously be no conflict. But there was little conflict in the absence of fit either. He would simply ask, " 'What do I have to do to get it to fit?' " Whatever people wanted was what he would do. He hadn't thought that things would turn out the way they did. In truth, he said, "I thought I would be able to sit back and do my art work and there would be a ready market for it." But this wasn't meant to be; and there was no reason to be so proud and pure that he would wait until other people's tastes accommodated to his own. Because there was money at stake, he would have to do the accommodating himself and paint those products that could readily be consumed. When asked if he ever painted only for himself, in which case he might be able to create things closer to his heart, he said that he used to do this but not anymore. The reason was again simple: "In order to justify the time spent on it," particularly given his own dire financial straits, "I had to get something in return," which essentially meant that his hobby days had officially ended. However enjoyable the process of creation might be, therefore, it was no longer enough to sustain him: It had become a means, through and through.

Perhaps he was justified in adopting the perspective he had. If you are going to face the hardship of having to deform your own artistic activities in order to earn a living, he seemed to say, there is little reason to flagellate yourself on top of it. There is of course no denying that this man was a more willing accomplice in these matters than most others, or at least than most others admitted, and in this sense there is not much point in getting overly saddened by his situation. One might even argue in this context that if artists could begin to think of themselves as he did – as producers rather than as creators, as people in a particular line of work rather than as artists, bathed in an aura of originality and purity – they would be better off. They would get rid of their guilt and shame once and for all, they would bring to an abrupt halt their own alienation, and rather than lamenting the big, bad system of which they had become a part, they would simply *capitalize* on it, milk it for all it was worth. In part, therefore, the issue boils down to where our own commitments lie. If we think that art and creativity are nothing special but have only been made so by virtue of being juxtaposed against the artlessness of so much of American life, then perhaps this man is the one to emulate; he knows what he's doing, he gets some enjoyment out of it, and he's making a decent living. If, on the other hand, we are interested instead in seeing creativity as something other than producing products, then perhaps we will find his brief story more troubling.

I am not sure if Vasquez (1973, p. 200) is correct when he writes, "Artistic labor can only safeguard its creative and free essence by remaining an unproductive activity from an economic point of view, that is, by extricating itself from the fundamental law of capitalist production." There has been enough written about some of the liabilities of art in socialist countries to suggest that its "creative and free essence" may not be all that attainable there either. Moreover, this notion of a creative and free essence may itself be an idealization, derived from a fundamentally romantic notion of what art and artistic activity are. It is nonetheless safe to say that for many of the artists in the present group there was often exacted a serious price in their lives and in their art for attempting to create within the present system. The result was that the process of artistic creation, rather than being a haven for those wishing to escape the terrible lures of the bourgeoisie, was often just the opposite. In the next chapter, when we inquire more fully into problems tied to the domain of art itself, we shall find still more evidence for this lamentable irony.

Chapter 5

The dream of artistic freedom

THE RHETORIC OF PLURALITY

As I acknowledged in the introductory chapter of this book, much of what the artists in the present group indicated about the inner workings of the domain of art came as something of a surprise. Partly this had to do with my own naïveté about the contemporary art scene; although I certainly had a serious interest in art prior to that time, I was hardly well schooled in its subtleties and complexities. This surprise, however, also had to do with the fact that a significant portion of the literature I had read in order to learn more about what was happening presented a picture of the situation of contemporary art that frequently ran counter to what I eventually heard from artists themselves.

Of the 1960s, for instance, Adams (1978, p. 7) has written, "Never before had there been such tolerance or such great variation both in style and in what was admissible art practice"; there was at this time, Kostelanetz (1980, p. 19) adds, "unprecedented permissiveness" in what could be considered art and in the actual creation of works of art themselves. This basic state of affairs was seen by some to extend in the 1970s as well, another writer (Robins, 1984) dubbing the era the "pluralist" era, one in which art had become nonsuccessive, nonheroic, and populist – quite the opposite, for this woman, of what modernism had been all about. As still another writer (Smagula, 1983) has framed it, gazing now in the art of the 1980s: "We face the most pluralistic, complex, and contradictory era the world has

186

ever known," the situation of contemporary painting consisting "mainly of individuals embarked on personal journeys of artistic self-discovery and fulfillment" (p. 40). As for the result of these journeys, Smagula goes on to write, it was an incipient realization of "the dream of artistic freedom" (p. 98). Now for him, I should note, these sorts of trends signified the rebirth of modernism, not its demise; they told of a resurfacing of the profoundly individualistic vigor that had earlier been witnessed during the heyday of the avant-garde. The basic premise is nonetheless the same: Artists, by virtue of their living and working in an artistic climate virtually unmatched in its degree of pluralism and freedom, were finally getting some much-needed breathing room.

Needless to say perhaps, not everyone embraced this state of affairs as wholeheartedly as these writers. Referring again to the 1960s, for instance, Canaday (1969, p. 23) writes: "Becoming an abstract painter is like entering the monastery of an order where the indulgence of any private mania becomes the insignia of acceptance into the brotherhood, where the degree of extremity in the indulgence is likely to be the measure of merit as applied by an international coterie of critics and award-giving juries." Right away, then, we see being posited what some have come to regard as the underside of a pluralistic and free art world: the primacy of a narcissistic brand of individualistic, essentially private self-indulgence (see also Gablik, 1984). Or, as Harries (1968) came to think of the matter, much of contemporary art was about the idealization of freedom, which, while certainly having its good points, could also serve to undermine both creativity itself and art's communicative potential.

There were other problems as well. "With avant-gardism," Greenberg (1973, p. 435) was to write, "the shocking, scandalizing, startling, the mystifying and confounding, became embraced as ends in themselves and no longer regretted as initial side-effects that would wear off with familiarity." And what this led to ultimately, Greenberg maintained, was the "standardization of the unconventional," which in turn cut off exactly those artistic possibilities that many had assumed would emerge. "This rapid domestication of the outrageous," adds

Steinberg (1966, p. 210), "is the most characteristic failure of our artistic life, and the time lag between shock received and thanks returned gets progressively shorter": The *enfant terrible* could become an elder statesman in virtually no time at all. And lest we suppose that the concern with the "new" was a purely artistic one, it had become "the daily concern of vast bureaucratic enterprises" whose prosperity depended on keeping consumers supplied with "a steady flow of compelling but perishable goods" (Kramer, 1973, p. 4; see also Jameson, 1983). All told, then, alongside those who maintained that we were in the midst of witnessing a new artistic dawn, there were some who were profoundly suspicious about what seemed to be going on in the art world: The much-touted pluralism and freedom that had come to permeate the rhetoric of contemporary art were not the panacea others believed them to be.

Also implied in some of these statements is that, appearances notwithstanding, there might not have been quite so much freedom as many were contending. If the situation at hand led to the standardization of the conventional, the domestication of the outrageous, and so on – if, in other words, the end result was indeed *un*freedom – how could freedom itself be responsible? How could freedom lead to unfreedom? From this perspective, therefore, it wasn't quite right to say that freedom had the potential to yield undesirable effects, or that there could be too much of it, or that it could get out of hand. It was more appropriate to say that what was being observed was not freedom at all save in the most crudely defined, negative sense – that is, as the absence of external constraints. Another implication, of course, is that pluralism and freedom may not be quite so connected with one another as is sometimes supposed. Despite the pervasiveness in recent years of what I am here calling the rhetoric of plurality and despite the frequent tendency to place the rhetoric of freedom alongside it, my own conviction, based on the information we shall be discussing shortly, is that the situation of contemporary art has led many aspiring artists to be particularly unfree to create meaningful works of art. Indeed, they have been unfree in at least four distinct ways.

First, as has already been suggested, a pluralistic artistic domain can apparently create a situation wherein certain artistic "strategies" are required as a means of carving out differentiable artistic identities. More crudely put, a pluralistic artistic domain may require of its members that they create works – and selves – that are sufficiently distinct from other works and other selves that there exists the possibility of gathering attention and recognition. At an extreme, in fact, artists may have felt the need to devise "brand images," as it were, to cordon themselves off from the teeming masses of others equally bent on making a name for themselves: In lieu of a cohesive tradition outside of themselves, there emerged the need to fashion a tradition of one's own, a tradition of the self, as I called it earlier. This is not *necessarily* a problem, it should be emphasized, especially if this tradition of the self is an organic and authentic one, based fundamentally on one's own emerging artistic project, as it was for some. If, on the other hand, this tradition is a self-consciously constructed one, designed for the sake of preserving one's own existence vis-à-vis the market, the consequences might be much severer.

The second way in which artists may have been unfree is related to the first. Exciting and challenging as it might have been to fashion a tradition of one's own, in principle at any rate, a number of artists in the group arrived at the realization that it would have been preferable for there to exist more of a foundation on which to create, that it was difficult and painful to be left to one's own artistic devices. The problem was not only the proverbial dizziness of freedom either, the vertigo that the existentialists, among others, frequently considered to be part and parcel of living in a world where the existence of God was suspect. The problem was also that it was difficult to know, with any certainty and conviction, what constituted a valid contribution to the domain and what did not. The very pluralistic nature of the art world, in other words – which de facto entailed the destructuring and "de-definition" of the domain of art itself (see Rosenberg, 1972) – led to the creation not only of what Rosenberg referred to as "anxious objects," which could either be masterpieces or pieces of junk, but of anxious artists as well, who could be profoundly unsure about who they were and what they were doing.

The third dimension of unfreedom we will be considering is quite different from the previous two. As Gilbert-Rolfe (1981, p. 210) has noted, for instance, "The kinds of pluralism which ones sees most often in art magazines, and in the policies of museums, have in common a bias against certain kinds of art, and of art criticism, so strong as to give pluralism as we currently encounter it the aim of repressive dogma." In some sense, this perspective was in fact borne out by many of the artists from whom we shall hear: women's art, black art, political art, and religious art, among others, often did not quite seem to fit the bill. The implication I would prefer to draw from this lack of fit, however, is not that "the kinds of pluralism one sees" are biased. It is rather that the domain of art was not nearly so pluralistic as the rhetoric of plurality seemed to suggest. Now there is no denying that the art world became *more* pluralistic than it had been; with the advent of Abstract Expressionism, Pop Art, Conceptual Art, and nonrepresentational art more generally, artistic possibilities did indeed expand. As those who were excluded from this supposedly pluralistic scene were quick to learn, however, there were still some quite definite rules in operation, not the least of which included the one that said that one ought to be doing art that was radically innovative, that made a bona fide contribution to this "free" art world. In short, while I wouldn't go so far as to claim that pluralism was an illusion or that the rhetoric bore no relation whatsoever to the reality, suffice it to say that the domain of art could be decidedly less invitational than one might have hoped.

Finally, many artists came to feel they were unfree because they felt themselves to have become so hermetically sealed within their own self-constructed artistic enclosures that they were unable to speak to anyone except either their fellow artists, critics, or themselves. In some cases, in fact, they may not, by their own admission, have even spoken to themselves; they might instead have come up with work that, by virtue of its profound arcaneness, was inaccessible even to them. What they might have come to realize, therefore, in yet another way, was that traditions of the self could lead to a condition of incommunicability, to a situation where one felt prevented from doing work that was truly meaningful. They were therefore unfree, we might simply say, to become engaged with others. And this, many came to feel, had to change if art was to have any effect on the wider world.

In place of any further introductory comments, it will be useful to see what artists themselves have had to say about these issues. We begin by turning once more to the most prominent artist in the group, who will be providing us with a kind of map of each of the four dimensions of unfreedom just enumerated.

POSTMODERNISM

Jim Cronin was a painter in his mid-40s at the time we spoke, who divided his time between New York City and his home in the Hamptons on Long Island. As noted earlier, he was the most successful artist of the entire group being considered, in terms of both art world recognition and money. By his own account, however, he was not quite a "superstar." In any case, after art school Jim landed a good teaching job in the Midwest, which had worked out well for a couple of years. The problem, however, was that it was too comfortable: He was the man, you may recall, who knew that he had to get to New York and who had in fact orchestrated his departure from the very start by bringing in visiting artists. So off to New York he went, anxious to hit his stride, which he did. With the exception of a number of visiting artist stints throughout the years, he was able to live, well, from the sale of his work alone.

Success aside for the time being, Jim was remarkably cynical about what it meant to be an artist and to create art. Foremost among the problems he had come to face was "the problem of having to do something new all the time." It was a "pluralistic time in the art world," he explained, which was unquestionably positive on some level. "People wanted a pluralistic art world," he said, "because philosophically it exists." But the difficulty for people like himself, he went on to say, is that "a pluralistic art world, although it exists philosophically in reality, makes marketing difficult. So I think what we're in now is a period of high marketing: You need to have a monotheistic thing on the surface for business reasons." Right away, then, we see one of the contradictions just previewed at work. On the one hand, there is this notion of pluralism, which ordinarily calls up the idea of freedom, a climate of unfettered creative expression, and so forth. On the other hand, however, there is the idea that precisely because of this pluralism, there was the need to establish a "monotheistic thing" in one's work so as to be able both to construct a unified artistic identity and to differentiate oneself from those seeking to do the same.

Along these lines, Jim felt that "the problem of painting – the dilemma of survival in painting – is that paintings, like people, have skins. Painting is like your handprints," as he put it, "this record of your life being different than mine." Your work must "go out into the world as this thing, that has this face to it," for without this face, he suggested, there would be no possibility of even entering the competition. What made this situation so difficult was that "you can't even make judgments" about what will be deemed valid and important and what will not: "You measure in degrees why one travels and another one doesn't. It's like Sebastian Coe and Steve Ovett running in the fifteen hundred meters: The difference between the winner and the loser is measured in milliseconds. And I think that that's a lot of what the dilemma of being an artist is." Many artists' response to this situation was to be as outlandish as they possibly could: "Generally," he said, "it's got to be something awful," particularly in the case of big exhibits. "You have to put something out there that attracts their attention because they're zombies."

What was it like, more concretely, to participate in this sort of competition? And what exactly could be done, other than "awful" work, to ensure that one would become a winner rather than a loser? Among other things, there was the need to know exactly who the audience was: "You're fighting for a very limited attention span with a highly jaded, supercritical, fickle audience and you have to 'curate' those decisions." In other words, there was the need to keep a kind of vigilance over his audience's ever-changing tastes and to make his artistic decisions as consonant with them as he possibly could; otherwise, they would take their support elsewhere. More specifically, what you do when making these sorts of decisions, he explained, is "you look back on what you've done and you want to make a move in your work; you try to maintain some sort of linear relationship . . . you can take from your past to make the future." Jim was at a distinct advantage over younger artists in this respect. In a sense, he had already created enough of his own tradition to allow him to move forward; he would extend this tradition in some way by drawing on his corpus of past work and establishing some measure of continuity between the old and the new. There was no great mystery about this process. "This is not Versace," he said, referring to the famous designer. "This is Robert Hall," the popular New York clothier: "It's on the racks, like small, medium, and large. These are made to order."

Were there other ways of dealing with this dilemma? "I once had a notion," he said, "that I wanted to do a painting of myself where I'd put the paint on the bathroom scale for structure, and then I'd paint on it until it weighed as much as I did; and then I [would be] stuck with this damn thing until the day I died. . . . The only dilemma, then, would be either painting it heavier or reducing it somehow." This way, he explained, there would be "a lifelong commitment to a single problem, where it's you but not you, where all of those things are in balance." This hypothetical project, in short, would allow for the required continuity and would provide an easy forum for making artistic decisions; he would always know, ahead of time, what the next move was, and the next after that too. Moreover, he would be able to do it all without really disclosing anything about himself, personally; there would simply be the project itself, working out its own destiny, in line with his diet. But this was entirely too facile a solution to his dilemma. For the time being, all he could do was "try to have the things make some sort of connection from one group of objects to the next."

Again, he could accept this situation philosophically: "Every-

193

thing is in transition," and art merely "mirrors that transition." Experientially, however, there was something uncomfortable about proceeding in this way, for there were times, he admitted, when he felt that the only thing he really made was transitional work. Except for the skin it possessed, he suggested that his work was without a true center and identity; it was all change and difference, with each painting playing off what preceded it rather than standing on its own. He seemed to wish that the situation could be otherwise. Jim knew all about the fabled freedom of this pluralistic art world, which would allegedly allow artists to create from their hearts, but appearances notwithstanding, he felt that there were very few artists who were truly free. Artists like Jasper Johns and Willem DeKooning had it, he had said earlier, because of the money they had and the power they wielded on account of it; they were the superstars, not him. The issue of audience came up in this context once more. "New York has no memory," he said. It is "the most vicious, fickle place in the world; they'll forget you in two years" – unless, of course, you take measures, serious measures, to ensure that you will have a chance to endure. Look, he said to me at one point, "I'm not a foot doctor. I mean, there's a market out there: People got bad feet." But the situation he was in, as an artist, "all changes." The only key to staying power, therefore, was to do exactly what he had done concerning the maintenance of his own artistic identity, which was to create a kind of mock developmental path designed essentially to provide for his own – and his audience's own – perpetuity. They wanted him to develop, it seemed; they wanted to see signs of his own growth as an artist; they wanted to see a history that looked like it was really going somewhere. By and large, he had been able to meet these demands. But he was also starting to feel that perhaps this was being done at his own peril.

Things hadn't always been so linear and continuous. Back in 1969, Jim did a painting that had in it a multiplicity of different styles, "like a Sears catalogue," from which he continued to draw ideas for his present work. But ultimately, he saw this painting as "an existential problem that failed." This is because "the notion of painting every day a different style is ultimately as confining as trying to develop one style: because the limitation is you. So the only way you could beat that problem is you become a stylistic entrepreneur, and the only way to create that is to hire people to paint for you, thus becoming, in a sense, a patron of your own art." This idea interested him. But at the same time, he acknowledged that ideas like these represented a "nihilistic attitude" toward society. He found a tendency in himself to go back and forth between philosophical beliefs, between what is meaningless and what is meaningful. Like a number of others, he found himself suspended in this in-between space, "balancing the tightrope between nonobjective art, conceptual art, and figuration . . . like the Walendas." It was a dizzying one: "I sometimes think," he continued, "that with the death of modernism, in a sense, what I'm doing is *performing* the notion of painting, that all of this is a highly realistic theater that comes with real painting and real pleasure, but possibly that's what some of us are doing: talking about the end and not the beginning of an art form."

Alongside the market-based problems he referred to, Jim experienced a sense of profound uncertainty not only about the validity of contemporary artistic creation in general but about his own art as well. Now philosophically speaking, he suggested, there was no reason to lament this state of affairs; much of contemporary art was precisely about this uncertainty. Much of it, in fact, sought to cast its own validity into question, in true deconstructive form; it was as much about simulation and theater and unreality as it was about anything else. But at the very same time that he could affirm these ideas philosophically, he also seemed haunted by the death of those other ideas – like the real and the true and the beautiful – that he himself was dedicated to killing. People on tightropes, we can probably assume, fear what lurks beneath them; they are all too aware that their performance may suddenly be brought to an abrupt halt. Jim's fear, therefore, was that somehow this theater that came with real painting and real pleasure was about to shut down. As of now, he suggested, there still remained a connection to the real, to a realm of experience and expression beyond the merely theatrical, but it was a fragile and tenuous one, a mocking one, threatening to be severed at any moment. In addition to being fearful and uncomfortable at the prospect of this happening, my own sense was that he felt ashamed of the fact that he himself had become an actor in this performance; he had bought into the role and had learned how to play it successfully. And while there was some consolation in the fact of his being aware of it at least, which many others were not, there wasn't much.

He referred, for instance, to the burgeoning of the corporate art market during the late 1970s and how all of a sudden there was a great deal of money available to buy paintings in a certain price range. The result, he said, was that there arose a crop of young artists coming out of a number of specific graduate schools who could do "a good New York painting" and would get paid handsomely in return. What was strange, though, was that, "You talk to some of the people, and they seem to have no cognizance of their own corporate existence in relationship to this garbage that they make." He had apparently gotten to know many of them during his various visiting artist jobs; he had gotten to see their artistic bankruptcy firsthand. And all he could say in this context was, "I thank God that I don't have to go [to these schools] three days a week and look at this stuff, because . . . when you start to feel responsible for that stuff and you know that it's literally impossible to make anything good and you know who that audience is out there and what goes on in that art world, you'd come home in tears every day."

He swung in another, but related, direction. "I try to make paintings that border on expressionism but are controlled." He referred to these paintings in terms of "repressionism," and they have to do with repressing certain images, "never getting too loose with the paint, but understanding what paint can do. A lot of people," he believed, "never learn anything from the paint because they're so involved with a didactic idea about history or philosophy." But the problem was that without this knowledge of what paint could do, without attention to the "skin" of the work, the "magic" that paintings can hold cannot

196

be "released." He spoke, for instance, about Magritte and Rousseau in this context, how certain of their works remained for him "very intense abstract realities." Other paintings did this too: They were able to be present "in an existential sense of, like, a *thing*." From simulation and theater, therefore, from painting one step removed from the real, this man could still speak, cogently, about magic, intensity, and the thing-ness of objects. He felt that he, unlike many others, recognized "the importance of trying to control the paint and understand what it does."

He could not find much solace in this, however, and needed to return to the question of why, despite his avowed connected-ness to the medium, his life and work were so dreadfully un-comfortable. "Maybe," he mused, "it's that artists can only make these . . . fake careers, that painting is so bankrupt that your whole career becomes an intellectual construction. It's such an unmeaningful art in this century," he said, that perhaps the only thing people like himself were really doing was "con-structing a life that has documentation." Painting didn't look too good, he reiterated; its virtue seemed to be its stupidity. One of the only things that was interesting about it, in fact, was "the intellectual arguments that people who are equipped can make about its death" – or, if not its death, "its existence as a vehicle for criticism and writing." Along the lines being drawn here, perhaps what he was doing in his art was ultimately a mere means to the destructive ends of others, of these critic-parasites, who fed off his own dilemmas and the pain and anx-iety they entailed.

But he could not fully believe this. He went on to recall a painting he did, back around 1975, that had found its way into a major museum. It was a giant painting of dinosaurs, elegant and colorful, living in the scene of a time "before man existed . . . almost a perfect world. The painting rejoiced in its big, dumb shapes – a twenty-foot long brontosaurus, painted light pink," for instance. This painting, he felt, provided "a kind of lesson about ourselves." It exemplified "the language of the dumb shape," as he described it, "the language of visual stu-

pidity." But it was nonetheless "elegant, I mean beautiful looking." It may have been my own imagination, but his voice
seemed to be cracking as he spoke, wavering over this stupid
beauty that he knew was somehow both possible and impossible. There was wonder in his voice as well as a great sense of
loss, together, in the same words. Juxtaposed against his still-
impassioned relationship to art – or at least to the idea of art –
the world he had come to inhabit by virtue of his success
seemed cheap and ugly.

I was a bit afraid to ask him, after all that he had been telling
me, but did he have any advice for those setting out to become
artists? "Most of the time you should have a big hand over your
mouth," he answered. "Off at art schools, they should hand out
in a freshman kit a big stone hand to remind you to keep your
mouth shut and not do any backbiting. You should just shut
up," he said, "because most of the things you say are going to
come back to haunt you." Be prepared, he would tell them; if
they were interested in becoming artists of the sort he had become, their entire lives would change in ways that they hadn't
dreamed possible.

In the midst of what would seem to be a pluralistic art world,
free of the dogmas of tradition, there would be the need for
them to establish an unequivocal front, a "monotheistic" brand
image, in order that they might differentiate themselves from
the rest of the field and thus be able to enter the race with a
chance of winning. Many, it might be noted, thought that once
they were in the race, perhaps by having gained some measure
of notoriety from their work, they would be able to become
freer in their artistic processes; they would have acquired the
requisite power to create as they wished. To this extent, lin-
earity, serial thinking, whatever we choose to call it, might have
been seen as a necessary evil, that could be left behind in due
time. In principle, they might have been quite right: "With
power comes that kind of freedom for an artist." What they
didn't realize, however, was just how much power was required. Even with this man's sales well into six figures for the
year, he felt completely manipulated and unfree. And it would

no doubt remain this way too, unless he managed to become a Jasper Johns or a De Kooning. The reason was simple: "The people from the art world don't like artists who have freedom." The fact of the matter was, the notoriety this man had received, far from liberating him, actually seemed to further the need for repetition, for devising variations on already established themes: You had to keep going with what worked.

He might also tell those starting out that in addition to marketing issues and the like, the very nature of their art itself would become problematic. In the eyes of critics for instance, Jim's art appeared to be one of liberation, a kind of joyous, madcap dance through the heterogeneous sensibility of the postmodern way, with its refusal to get too hung up on all of those pressing questions about the real and the true; it sought to loosen the hold of the somber, deeply felt passions that had been tied to much of the art of the past. In lighter moments, I would guess that he himself could experience this loosening; perhaps in these moments he could see in his work some evidence for a new and compelling way of looking at things. But as was the case with his career more generally, there was something about the work he had chosen to do that simply was not quite right: Something was being denied in his own performance of painting. However acceptable the philosophical discourse surrounding his work might have been, it just did not mesh with his innermost sense of what painting could be. He was therefore left hovering, precariously perched on this strange tightrope, like the Walendas, trying to figure out for himself whether what he was doing was real or whether, instead, it was one great big perverse charade. It was strange that he should get paid so much, given such profound uncertainty; for some reason, people had assumed that he knew where he stood. In any case, aspiring artists might wish to know about this as well, if only to prepare themselves for what was to follow.

Finally, they might also want to know about what sort of life they were destined to lead if they went this man's way. There would be adulation and glory, and then shame and guilt; there would be a sense of beauty and fulfillment and then nostalgia and grief; there would be, in short, a kind of "schizophrenia," as he put it, that would be pervaded in turn by uncertainty about which end on this continuum of existential flips was really real. *Was* painting meaningful or was it not? *Was* there an obdurate reality to things or was everything ultimately a construction? *Was* he a real artist or was he an impostor? *Was* any of this truly worthwhile or was it a complete waste of time? These were the questions they might have to ask, and not only in moments of reverie either.

Although Jim's situation could arguably be called an extreme one, founded on his own relatively unique position in the New York art world, he was by no means alone in his perspective on the problems at hand. In addition to the problems already enumerated, most of which have been tied less to the domain of art as such than to its various trappings, we see here that the domain itself could be extremely troubling for some artists. Now I say "domain itself," which refers to the specifically aesthetic sphere of artistic operations, mainly because it does indeed exist on some level; there were, and are, certain principles of artistic activity that exist in and for themselves, as a function of extant beliefs, values, and ideals concerning what art is or ought to be. Some of this man's artistic difficulties were undoubtedly tied to this very sphere: the "meaninglessness" and "stupidity" of contemporary painting, the feeling of it being simulated rather than real, and so on. What we also see in this case, however, is that even if the domain of art may be said to exist autonomously in principle, the practical situation may be quite different, with the domain "itself" being virtually inseparable from the dynamic constellation of forces within which it is enmeshed. Indeed, perhaps the most salient problem of all for this man was precisely this: the conflation of the domain with everything else that went on in the art world, and the consequent impossibility of doing anything that felt real and authentic. Let us now proceed more systematically through some of the issues Jim has enumerated for us, beginning with the problem of artistic uniformity.

PLURALITY AND UNIFORMITY

The problem at hand is not an especially new one. Hauser (1979, p. 508), for instance, has suggested that "the specialization of painters in particular genres is one of the most important results of the trade in works of art to develop since the end of the Renaissance," and it arose, he argues, because "art dealers are constantly demanding the same sort of work by their suppliers, ones which have shown themselves to be the most economically viable." Cork (1979, p. 66), more recently, has offered a similar perspective: "How tempting it must be, once a dealer has established his protégé by publicizing a particular brand image, for the artist to repeat himself over and over again, secure in the knowledge that clients are queuing up for examples of one set style!" So it is, Michels (1983, p. 5) adds, in her book *How to survive and prosper as an artist*, that there have come to exist so many "Little Johnny One Notes, churning out whatever made money in the past, in fear that venturing in a new direction will bring them back to Poverty City."

Two qualifications ought to be presented here. The first is that however long-standing this movement toward artistic specialization may be, there is reason to assume that it has become more pronounced in recent years in line with the increasing pluralization of the art world. Foster (1985, p. 15) puts the matter well: "Posed as a freedom to choose, the pluralist position plays right into the ideology of the free market." Indeed, he suggests, in trying to gauge the nature of the relationship between pluralism and marketing, it becomes unclear which comes first: whether pluralism creates "high-marketing" conditions, as Jim had put it, or high-marketing conditions create pluralism. There is of course a third alternative, namely that the two go hand in hand, as part of a total package, with causality thus being more "structural" than linear. The point in any case is that recent changes in the domain of art have been accompanied by certain distinct changes in marketing strategies that have constricted the space of creativity precisely by requiring that artists not stray too far from their own self-constructed niches.

As an aside, and by way of foreshadowing an issue to be taken up later in this chapter, the space of communication may be constricted in turn. For pluralism, Foster (1985, p. 31) adds, can lead "not to a sharpened awareness of difference," one of its putative ideals, "but to a stagnant condition of indiscrimination – not to resistance," in other words, "but to retrenchment." For all of its worth as idea and ideal, pluralism, as Said (1985) agrees, leads to "the neutralization of dissent" and thus, ultimately, to incommunicability: The din of Different voices culminates in the white noise of the Same, which amounts in the end to silence.

The second qualification is that this movement toward "specialization," rather than being limited to those who have *already* proved their worth in relation to the market, has also appeared regularly in the case of those *wishing* to do so. "I do think there is something, some kind of very deep core to artists," said one woman, "and that one thing may be very similar that they're trying to express in each piece." This seemed to be so, she added, "particularly the more successful they are." On the basis of what she has said thus far, one might simply conclude that these artists' success was in fact a function of their depth, of that "one thing" which continued to haunt them enough to spur them to create. Her point, however, was that "one of the keys to success is you have to have a style; you do have to have your image and there has to be some consistency in that." Otherwise, dealers especially will complain, "'Here you're doing this. Here you're doing that. We don't know who you are.'" One's own artistic autonomy and individuality, therefore, was for her nothing short of a precondition for entry into the art world. You "should" be able to do things in the same artistic style in order to claim it as "yours," added another woman, particularly in places like New York, added yet another, "where they want you to stay in one style." Again, without this, there would, and could, be nothing.

One dimension of her own maturation as an artist, said one woman, had to do with the fact that formerly she had been reluctant to show if she "didn't have a body of work that looked similar." She had tried to move ahead too early, she came to feel, and had been "forced into stylistic dead ends." It was more important to make the work good, she reiterated, than to do what was necessary to show it. Turning to some of the problems associated with her own education in art, particularly in graduate school, there was the idea that you were an "embryonic professional artist," who would "have a body of work that appears to be one central thematic objectives-and-goals kind of thing." You were supposedly working through a thesis, she said, focusing on that single problem or issue that would lead to the establishment of an identity. But the consequence of this, she felt, was that the space of one's creativity would become constricted and the work itself artificial and contrived. "Instead of that person spending that time investigating all of the different things there are in the world to investigate visually, they spend that time trying to make a meaningful, slick presentation." And what happened after that, she continued, was that people either stopped working because there was so little motivation to continue exploring different artistic avenues or they became afraid to go back and learn something new. You have to be in New York if you're going to be a real artist, or you have to be in the Whitney, people told her. She herself had these concerns for a time. But once she asked herself honestly whether any of these concerns made the work any better, she knew that she would have to change her ways. She simply couldn't be bothered any longer with whether she was in the mainstream. "I realized," she said, "that I wasn't giving full play to what I really wanted to do because I was afraid of the criticism." It was fun while it lasted, she admitted. She had enjoyed the sense of community and oppositionality that had been a part of her earlier ways. But none of it had helped her work in the least.

Another woman summarized this situation neatly. She "hadn't really set on a style," so her work, she believed, was "hard to sell." Consequently, she tried to "get" a style. "Once you get a style, though" – a "trademark," as she referred to it elsewhere – "you stop growing." More severely still, if he had to do a stylized series of work, which is "what most people in New York are doing," added another artist, he'd "have a heart attack after the third one, or go blind." Despite his reticence, this man continued to recognize the need to establish a measure of continuity in his work; he needed to get something going, he said, so that afterward he would have something to build on. "Then," he explained, "I can start innovating and maybe go off in a whole different direction." Once he acquired a relatively uniform and secure artistic identity, in other words, he would free himself to do as he wished. If we judge by what has been said thus far, however, particularly by the man with whom we began this chapter, he may have been wrong about this: Unless he was virtually catapulted to stardom, to a position of such power that he could call all his own shots, it would be unlikely that he would emerge as free as he had assumed. As one man, with a kind of behaviorist view on the matter had put it, you continue with what is reinforced; you're not going to go off on a tangent if what you do is successful.

Here is the case of another man, who, despite being fairly upbeat about his art, conveys much the same point of view. Michael Castle's foremost ambition had always been to become a painter, and so, even though his father had wanted him to study engineering, off he went to art school. He met with considerable success there, also becoming a member in good standing of the aforementioned group of young painters who became well known for their surreal and sometimes cartoon-like paintings filled with popular images of American culture. He was a bit less involved in this group than some others, since he had begun working full-time as a teacher for local "flunk-outs," but he had gotten a good, solid start. Back then, he said, doing art was terrifically exciting. Art should be convulsive, he thought, shake people up, and this is exactly what he and his friends had dedicated themselves to doing.

On receiving a good job offer in Canada, he moved, continuing to do much the same sort of work he had done back in Chicago. For some time there, he found himself unhappy with what was going on. For one, all everyone seemed to want to do was go to New York and make it, which was all right, but grew tedious. For another, it turned out that the school was mostly oriented toward conceptual art, toward developing a greater awareness of form as well as the flatness of the canvas. This too was all right for a while, and in fact Michael felt that he learned a great deal about the visual dimension of painting. This had been demanded: "If you weren't concerned with that," he said, "you weren't a serious painter." As opposed to what it was like when he was in art school, where the perception was pretty much that he and his friends were "a fluke of the universe," playfully immersed in the latest existential issues, life had become more serious. He had even found himself pondering a number of enduring philosophical issues, concerning whether we perceived meaning in the world or projected meaning onto it; concerning the artificiality of existence; concerning an awareness, as he put it, of the "unreality of reality" and thus the "reality of unreality." The conventions that were inherent in painting were part and parcel of the conventions inherent in the world itself, all of which sometimes made him sad. It seemed that despite these intense epistemological ruminations, he could not quite shake the idea of the really real.

Indeed, however interested he had come to be in these deadly serious issues, he grew to hate all this "formalist crap"; he wanted instead to "just get the message across," like he used to. Although he wasn't a realist philosophically, he explained, experientially he still was. He just wasn't into art about art, like so many other people were; there were too many "removals." The sources, he believed, had to come from somewhere else. So it was that there gradually emerged the desire to do something simple and strong, something that would "knock 'em dead," so "they'd run into the streets, bleed from their ears," blown away by the sheer evocative power of his images. "Close the lines," it would be ordered, "in case there's a riot! People get overexcited." He wanted to affect people; he had never been much of a minimalist and never would be either. Michael instead saw his work as a kind of parade, in which he would use these strange, artificial images to mirror the multiplicity of our existence; it had to do with a "longing for absolute reality or something." There would be something for everybody: "If somebody's interested in patterns, I've got patterns. If somebody's interested in color, I've got color. Whatever."

It's not that he decided to abandon formalist concerns; there was much more of an awareness of mechanics in his recent work, much more finish and control. But he had also needed to get back to the roots of what moved him, some of which had apparently gotten buried along the way. There were too many works, he said, in which people could only get involved initially; they would look at it, they would reflect a bit on the concept behind it, and then they would move on. Not only was there nothing truly generative about these sorts of works, experientially, but precisely by being art about art, they failed to possess any transcendent value. There was too much art that was just a "high-priced form of autograph collecting," devoid of emotion and spirit.

On some level, again, he could accept some of this; he had become sufficiently well versed in the philosophy of the unreal as to doubt whether transcendent value was even possible. After all, if everything we experienced was thoroughly saturated in convention, as it obviously was, didn't this mean that the absolute was ultimately a mere will-o'-the-wisp, and the desire to seek it an untenable kind of nostalgia? Whatever it was, he had decided that he was willing to suffer the philosophical culpability that was entailed in this project of trying to move beyond the confines of the canvas and out into the world. There was no effacing the feelings that he had, particularly the sadness. He could never quite say, of course, what was lost, because that would be to invoke just the sort of absolute presence that he was obliged to cast into suspicion, but he could not help but feel that this great big parade – for all of its heterogeneity and tawdriness, all of its artificiality and ugliness – still partook of something like beauty. Some of his pieces, he said, were like fever dreams; there would be skating, for instance, on smooth, flat ice, through debris and junk. There would be a touch of the sublime, even amid the stupidly banal, the two in a kind of tension, never to be resolved.

It wasn't unlike what it meant to be an artist. On the one hand, there were times when Michael had been convinced that he had painted the "greatest thing that's ever been done"; it would be marvelously new and original, a leap over everything that had come before. Subsequently, there could be utter revulsion and hate, such that he wouldn't be able to look at the work for several years; it would seem cheap and old. Neither one of these stances was quite justified, he suggested; the reality lay somewhere in between. A further problem, however, was this need to maintain his own uniformity and identity as an artist. The problem, again, was that, market conditions being what they were, an artist like himself couldn't really afford to create new and original works all the time. In fact, there was often the need to repeat what he had already done, to satisfy demand. There were times, he qualified, when his creative activities could be inventive throughout; he would be all there, painting away furiously, and the result would be something new and different. But there were also times when he would be forced to fall back on imitating himself, as he put it, his artistic processes becoming mock-creative: rote production in the guise of inspired creation. "Sometimes," he explained, "it's easy to imitate yourself if you've got a certain thing that you do and that people know you for and that you feel comfortable with; it's awfully easy to go on and do some more of that." As for the solution to this problem, it was quite straightforward: "I try to stay inventive within the single style I've developed."

We need not grieve too much over Michael's admission that he had occasionally imitated himself and that he done some paintings that "don't seem very inventive." Even in the best of conditions, there is little reason to expect artists to be blissfully and inventively engaged with their work all the time. Nevertheless, it is clear that Michael was doing more than merely lamenting the ups and downs of the creative process. What he was also lamenting was the fact that his own status in relation to the art world of which he was a part had relegated him to a position in which genuine creativity – however he defined it – was not always possible. Now again, it would be simple enough to argue that the factors responsible for this problem were strictly market-based: Given the demand for the same, and given his need for recognition, money, and so forth, it would be necessary to create variations on a theme. This was undoubtedly operative. In line with this idea, however, there is also the idea that creativity demands a consistent and unified author-creator, an Individual, with an integrated oeuvre of works, able to be identified as his or hers alone. As several others also testified, there was the demand that there existed a project, traceable to a specific point of origin; and what this meant was that no matter how "deconstructive" their work might have been, no matter how much it called into question some of those sacred cows that had characterized artistic creation throughout the centuries, it was no less necessary for this work to keep its ties to a sovereign subject, an identity, with a single style to prove it. Michael's guilt over his occasional lack of inventiveness, therefore, may owe itself not only to the inevitable ups and downs of creating, along with the demands of the market, but to the need for capitulating to an ethic of individual sovereignty that, in a distinct sense, ran counter to the process of creation: In order to produce works of art that were suitable imitations of his previous work – in order, that is, to mock-create – he had to become a mock subject as well; he had to remain who he was thought to be, even if on some level he was someone else entirely.

Is this man to be blamed for his avowed duplicity? Should he have been able to "invent" virtually all the time, demands be damned? Couldn't it be argued that the true vocation of the artist is precisely to *resist* these sorts of demands and be obedient only to his or her authentic desires? My own feeling is that however plausible and compelling these arguments may be, particularly in the case of those artists who knowingly and willingly capitulate to these conditions merely for the sake of fame and fortune, we need to be extremely cautious in framing our expectations. Maybe in epochs past it was easier to adhere to that romantic vision of the artist who would be the conscience of the world, who would resist the lures of commercialism, who would exist as if there *were* no demands being made on his or her artistic activities at all. But to do so now would be to fall prey to an anachronism. My claim here, it should be emphasized, is not that this man was merely an innocent victim, whose creative processes had become deformed by some monolithic machine whose forces were conspiring to shut him

208

down. This would be to effect an untenable split between self and social reality; it would imply that the self existed wholly *apart* from social reality, autonomous and ultimately alone. The irony here is that it was exactly this vision of the self that had to be marketed and sold.

TRADITION, INNOVATION, AND
TRANSCENDENCE

Alongside the problem of artistic uniformity, in several of the cases we have discussed, there was the further problem of feelings of loss and sadness over what art had become; the lingering idea of art's potential wonder and grandeur, juxtaposed against its present calculatedness and complicity in the market, could be extremely painful for some. It was troubling enough to feel that art had become desacralized, that it had become devoid of that sense of spirit that it once seemed to have; it could leave people in a state of mourning or lead them to feel that they had been cheated, by being thrown into as ugly a world as this one. What was also troubling, though, was to be thrown back, inexorably, onto one's own artistic resources: In the apparent absence of the transcendently other, there was a tremendous burden, some felt, placed upon the self.

"It was easier when the focus was just glorifying a deity," said one man in this context. "You had it all spelled out for you." Now, however, said another, artists frequently became victims of "new for the sake of new" and "exploration for the sake of exploration." There was a positive aspect to this situation. It was something of a relief, for instance, one woman said, when the School of the Art Institute began moving from a more or less exclusive focus on Abstract Expressionism to Pop Art; "it meant that there was no terra firma, which meant that you got to do what you wanted to do." When they saw their first Jasper Johns painting, she recalled, the whole school was in an uproar because it seemed to challenge everything the students had been learning. This had been a problem for people, but an exciting one. Now, however, she said, there was a different problem: "Everything is accessible." Much of the excitement has therefore changed into anxiety and frustration. Recall a question that was posed earlier, by a man who had found himself particularly lost in the thickets of modernity: What does the contemporary artist have? The answer, he had said, was that the contemporary artist "doesn't have anything really; he has to find his own way." The problem, he had explained, was precisely that of tradition, "which we don't have now." Note what is implied here: Tradition, rather than being the stifling set of rules and strictures it is sometimes supposed to be, may be precisely the condition through which genuine innovation is possible.

Kurt Wise, an ex-artist who had been a member of the same group of artists as several others we have discussed, seemed to reach a similar conclusion. Members of this group had their own unique style and, as we have already learned, had been successful in getting their work shown and sold. In fact, they had gained more recognition for their work early in their careers than many other artists had ever gained. Nevertheless, there were problems, not the least of which included that of "being so solidified an image" in the eyes of others. For this man at least, the art itself was "too openly, readily identifiable in terms of a type of work." In a sense, he said, he felt that he had been "typecast" back then, and he found that this interfered with his own creative activities; there was too much of a loss of his own identity, as an artist and as a person.

Relatedly, he had also come to feel that "as you progress in terms of working in the world of art or working in the world of *careers* in art, there is a certain sense of professionalism, even a kind of boredom" that could follow; "you lose thoughts as to just why you're doing it and just what kind of personal satisfaction you get out it. You can get wrapped up in the methodologies," he said, and in the "political illusions" that surround it – "the self-realization kind of illusions." The entire process of being an artist and of creating art could gather its own mundane momentum, such that the activity itself could become subordinated to the ideas that were associated with it. He just didn't like some of the "isolating impact" that art had.

"I was constantly getting wrapped up in an internalized process, which really is a kind of interiorized game that has no external rules," the result being that he felt that he had been "cutting himself off" from the world, that he had become secluded in this self-defining, autistic activity that had no rationale other than that which had been constructed out of the esoteric demands of the art world.

Part of the problem, Kurt explained, was that he had expected so much from painting. He had no idea that it would be so isolating and estranging, that he would get so "wrapped up" in the hermetically sealed enclosure of the art world, with its seemingly arbitrary rules and conventions. It had been just the opposite in fact: He had thought art was exactly that domain of activity that moved *beyond* these rules and conventions, that had some sort of transcendent value. As far as he could tell, though, he had been sadly mistaken. "In some ways," he said, "I don't really find painting to be all that elevated a world." There were some people, he continued – for a time he had been one of them – who had thought of painting "as almost this sacred kind of bond to the medium." But it really wasn't this at all. Instead, "it's like consumer goods in a way: It's a marketable kind of commodity, with its own rules and its own little genres and ways of doing things." In this respect, "You're kind of like a little self-employed businessman or something; you worry about all the things in the world and all the things that surround you; you become almost a hermit unto yourself, tremendously self-absorbed, the fact that you just sit there in front of a canvas," trying to figure out what will work. It's not that he was against selling art, he clarified; he had always known that it was a commodity. But he had assumed that what went on in the studio itself would be sufficiently removed from the commodity dimension of art that one's artistic activities themselves would be able to proceed purely, untainted by all that was going on outside of it. And it just wasn't so.

As concerns the art world itself, he simply couldn't find much worth in it. It was an insecure world, he said, filled with people who were constantly on the defensive. He couldn't respect most of them, he said, and he felt that the entire market situation was "all out of kilter." Art education, he went on, had become an industry that had suddenly begun spewing out artists at an astounding rate. But it was too much; it wasn't possible to create that much good art. Kurt realized that the way he was framing these issues sounded a bit reactionary, but his own feeling was that the remarkable influx of new artists into the art world and the changes it brought about, particularly in relation to the commodification of art, "kind of dilutes the process itself, the actual original integrity of the object, the original integrity of the field." The art world had become "inflated" and "magnified" in recent years, to the extent that it had come to appear bigger than life. Appearances aside, however, it was actually "a very small kind of world." It was a destructive one too, because, in addition to the commodification of art itself, artists had become commodities as well: "You're sort of too ornamental to function somehow." The New York art scene, he said, was like Malibu, where people would drive by the homes of the stars – an "East Coast Hollywoodism," as he put it. And then there was the guilt at being a part of this whole scene, particularly insofar as participation in the art world meant massaging "the swollen conscience of the collector by lending that person one's cloak of responsibility and integrity and creativity." For all of its difficulties, school days, he felt, had been much more authentic. It wasn't only the art world that was at fault for these problems, Kurt said; it was our entire society, which had come to appear to him as a "strangely pragmatic, ugly kind of society of certain ways." In a place like Italy, for instance, there was "a certain amount of simple, almost craftlike purpose" on the part of artists. There was also a certain amount of status recognition and veneration, but it didn't have the cheapness that it had here, which tended to turn the artist into "both a personality and a commodity at the same time." Artists there were regular people, with skills and talents, who were respected and loved for their dedication to their craft and their interest in providing worthwhile objects for others to behold.

Why had things become so ugly in our own society? Part of it, again, had to do with the fact there were just too many people, particularly the kind who elected to go to art school, who

were "looking for fulfillment that's not in their world ordinarily." Rather than wanting specifically to create art, Kurt
suggested, they wanted to be certain kinds of people, self-
actualized and special, doing something more meaningful and
important and sacred than the masses. Stated another way,
these were people who seemed to be empty in some fundamental way and who sought to fill themselves up by doing something out of the ordinary. They were not necessarily to be
blamed, of course; their emptiness was that of society itself. But
the consequence was that there were many people doing art
who really ought to have been doing something else.

After several years of teaching, coupled with his diminishing
interest in art, Kurt elected to stop painting altogether. At various times, he had "felt a certain repugnance about it actually,"
and felt that he "really wouldn't ever consider painting again."
Perhaps this was a kind of reaction against some of the things
he had been doing for so long: Better to stop completely, he had
felt, than exert his energy trying to figure out how to make his
own artistic activities more connected and authentic. Yet his
decision to leave was more complex and ambiguous than this
might suggest: "I don't know whether it was a decision on my
part to do other things or whether it was a decision to stop
painting or whether it was a decision to stop isolating myself."
What he did know was that, for the time being at least, painting
was not for him.

Would he ever return? Or was the prospect of painting – or at
least its trappings – so "repugnant" that he was done for good?
He had actually been thinking a lot about painting as of late, he
told me. And interestingly enough, the kinds of paintings he
had been thinking about were not unlike those he did many
years ago, when he was a 1st-year student at art school: "Maybe," he said, "it was like starting over again." As for what kinds
of paintings they were, he described them as trying to picture a
"shimmering fantasy miracle state . . . trying to picture something that had this state in it; that in the actual physical objects,
what was there was just kind of simple and objective, kind of
dumb in some ways, but that somehow the magic of it – or the
relationship of it, the placing of all these things in it – had a kind

213

of transcendence." They were paintings, he felt, that would be able to step out of "all the norm and logic rules somehow," that would transgress the boundaries of socially constructed and socially ratified taste, that would express, through their simplicity and dumbness, the wonder of things.

Kurt's sentiments were not unlike those of several other artists in the group, most of whom had been successful at one point and most of whom had come to feel that they had somehow strayed from art's true aims. In a sense, they might have said, their art had become institutionalized; it had become enmeshed within a highly circumscribed region of artistic beliefs, values, and activities. This, of course, was to be expected in some respects. For the most part, these people were not so naïve as to suppose they could remain immune from this sort of thing, nor did they wish to do so: Belonging to some form of a tradition, they realized, far from impeding their activities, actually served to liberate them. What was this man's problem then? Why had he become so disenchanted with the act of creating? The primary reason, I suggest, was that the various "norm and logic rules" that he found himself following over the years, rather than being experienced as integral parts of a tradition, were instead experienced as self-validating and essentially arbitrary constraints, having nothing to do with a tradition and bearing no relationship to anything outside themselves. They were just rules, someone else's in fact, and not only did they fall short of providing that sort of ground or foundation that rules are often thought to provide, but they actually served to undermine and dilute the process of creation itself; they took him away from what he had thought art was supposed to do.

When Kurt got so far away that he could no longer justify what he was doing, he stopped painting; he would move on to activities that had stronger rationales to them, like building, for instance, which was what he had turned to doing some 6 years back. But he was left with a sense of nostalgic longing for painting. There was still plenty of fine art in him, he said, and some day he would probably see if he could get it out. Even though much of contemporary art had become cheapened and made ugly, at its best art nonetheless created "a different sense of integrity" in people; it allowed them to feel that they were a part of something bigger than themselves, something miraculous and magical, shimmering with the icy energy of the cosmos. It allowed them, in short, to experience themselves as contributing meaningfully to that sort of transcendent vision of things which could take people out of the crudeness and banality of everyday life and hurl them into the beyond.

We might wish to ask how sentiments like these originate. Perhaps they signal a yearning for something that once existed, an oceanic feeling of wholeness, for instance, dating back to the distant reaches of childhood, or a sense of awe before the massive presence of the world. They may also signal a yearning for something that never did exist, an imaginary image of completion, designed to offset the fragmentariness of our existence. There are other possibilities as well. What is most important in any case is the fact that, however repugnant painting had become for Kurt, these sentiments were still alive and kicking, beckoning him to begin again, armed with the innocent integrity that he believed was the hallmark of true creation. The world of art and of American society more generally had done its best to bury whatever authentic artistic desires he might have had and, to some extent, had been successful; it had been a long time since he had done any painting. There was something, however, that had remained, even if dormant, through it all. When the appropriate time came, therefore, he would take this something and run with it, creating works of art that would leap over the rules of the world and sail into the vastness of the heavens.

It was difficult for me to decide where in the book Kurt's story should be told. It is about a great many things, from the mystique and "ornamentality" of the artist to problems inherent in the domain of art itself. What I suggest, in fact, is that this case serves as a bridge between many of the problems we have already encountered, particularly those tied to the relationship of creativity and the market, and those that are, arguably, tied to the specifically aesthetic sphere. In certain respects, the shadow of Weber looms even larger here than that of Marx, for as

215

Weber himself pointed out in *The Protestant ethic and the spirit of capitalism* (1985), the ever-growing significance of capital could not be separated out from the larger process of rationalization that had its sources not only in the changing conditions of labor but in the very ethos that surrounded them: "The problem," he wrote, "is that of the origin of the Western bourgeois class and of its peculiarities, a problem which is certainly closely connected with that of the origin of the capitalistic division of labour, but is not quite the same thing" (p. 24). What this implies is not that the relationship of creativity and the market is to be disregarded or its significance cast into question. On the basis of what has been said in both the present chapter as well as the previous one, there is ample reason to believe that this relationship is in fact highly significant. But we must understand this relationship as itself part of a larger and more all-encompassing package of discourses and forces, many of which have come to acquire their own momentum and their own largely autonomous nexus of operation. Even while the rise of individuality in the West may well have been part and parcel of the rise of capitalism itself, for instance, it has certainly come to possess its own power, which would no doubt continue to persist on some level even if market conditions were to be wholly transformed.

Kurt Wise did indeed have his own creative activities undermined, and some of this could plausibly be attributed to just that commodifying and commercializing process which owes its existence to the power of capital itself. But this process was inseparable, he came to believe, from the "peculiarities," as Weber put it, of the Western bourgeois class, which seemed to have lost any coherent sense of what might exist beyond the mundane calculations of everyday life. If Kurt was disenchanted with anything, therefore, it was with the very life-world he had come to inhabit, as a New Yorker in particular and as an American more generally; there was something cheap and crude about the whole thing, especially, he suggested, if one was an artist. And thus although there had remained a quite definite space in his heart for painting, for what it might yet be, this was neither the time nor the place to resume. The cheapness and crudeness couldn't quite be shaken. He hadn't yet learned to master his own alienation.

FORMS OF ARTISTIC EXCLUSION

On the basis of what has been said thus far in this chapter, it might simply be argued that pluralism has its costs. Some of these costs, such as the need to devise singular artistic identities, were bound up with the market. Others, such as that sort of longing for transcendence we have just observed, were tied to that condition of nonunity which is part of the notion of pluralism itself; to confer primacy on the Many is to detract from the One. From this perspective, then, the pluralistic nature of the art world was real but yielded certain problematic "side effects," as many innovations do. On the face of it, there seems little reason to dispute this contention; the boundaries of the domain had been stretched greatly. But these boundaries, as we will now see, had been stretched in a quite specific direction, with the result that many artists and many kinds of art remained excluded: As those who remained on the margins knew all too well, the reality didn't quite measure up to the rhetoric. From this second perspective, therefore, the domain of art was nowhere near as pluralistic as it had appeared – or, perhaps more appropriately, *pretended* – to be.

Now I am not about to launch into a libertarian attack on the domain of art for being less pluralistic than it ought to be. It should be evident by now that a truly pluralistic art world, if taken to an extreme, would lead to utter anarchy and nihilism: When anything goes, so too does meaning and value. What I am interested in doing instead is inquiring into the specificity of some of the forms of artistic exclusion that have existed in recent years, toward the end of understanding more clearly some of the domain's possible nodes of repression, negation, and denial. One further qualification is in order in this context. Although certain of these excluded populations – women artists, for instance – are amply represented in the present group and thus provide adequate testimony on behalf of the fact of

217

their marginalization, other populations (such as black artists) are not nearly so well represented here. With this in mind, I refrain in the present section from offering definitive generalizations concerning the plight of these latter populations and instead attempt merely to suggest what some of their problems have been.

First, as concerns women artists and more specifically "women's art," a number of people indicated that in addition to those difficulties we have already considered – tied to the image of the artist, to reconciling one's artistic desires with one's family responsibilities, to entering the market, and so forth – there was often outright hostility to the work they were interested in doing. This began as early as art school. Katherine Spector, for instance, gradually came to realize that "a lot of things that I had felt were not proper to do as an artist were what I wanted to do." Most of the instructors, she explained, were into Abstract Expression and Surrealism, but she herself liked to work figuratively. "I had a sort of guilt feeling about it," she said. "That was not done at the time I went to school." Interestingly enough, she continued, these earlier influences, especially that of Surrealism, continued to infiltrate her work even after graduate school. It was strange: Even though she "loathed" this kind of art on some level, there was still the need to work through it somehow. Katherine went on, in fact, to do some works – "cute" works, as she put it – whose primary aim was to poke fun at a couple of notable anti-Communists, including William Buckley and Dale Evans. And they were very successful, finding their way into both galleries and museums. But she had finally been forced to ask herself: "Do you want to be an artist or a rock star?" The answer was straightforward: "If you want to be a rock star, then you go and make cute things, you have a personality and you wear exotic clothes or costumes; you become more important than what you actually do." She came to feel, however, that "there were ethics involved" and that she "had to say 'no'" to this mode of being an artist.

As Katherine went on to explain, "One of the problems in school is that you get a preconceived idea of what art should do." She had been told "that artists should live this type of life-style, that artists should make this type of art," and perhaps most problematically, that "women should not paint flowers because if they do they are castigated." They were of course right on some level, she said; it was true that there were hardly any women in the art books. Mary Cassatt was an exception, she noted, but in general, "God forbid that any of us should ever go out and paint women and children." A fellow artist had once said that her painting had "balls," and she, in turn, had responded very favorably; one of the ideas that had been in circulation back then was that things had to look gutsy. But she was not really an Abstract Expressionist, she realized. What she also realized was just how wrong it was for her own painting – a woman's painting – to be applauded for its mas-culinity. Not only was she informed that "flowers and women and children were revolting," but "you couldn't use feminine color, whatever that was." Her return to figurative work, there-fore, was indeed an act of liberation: from the rules of the art world and, more specifically, from its domination by an essen-tially male mentality. "Degas did it and no one picked on him. Who the hell cares, anyway?" She had to do what was close to her identity, as an artist, as a person, and as a woman.

Consider as well the case of a woman who had recently taken to quilt-making. Back in art school, Ann Magnuson also felt that certain kinds of work were considered problematically "feminine" and were thus rendered taboo by some of her peers. And even though she realized that to capitulate to these taboos was "goofy" and that she didn't necessarily have to "go along with what's current in the art world," it was painful to have been the target of their disdain. "They are a bunch of copycats, a lot of them," she said bitterly. "One person will do something that's really different, and then that's the 'in' thing for the year, and then they'll call themselves the 'Crazyoos' or something, and everybody copies that style." It was "untruthful," she felt, "to what an artist should be doing," which was to create what you feel.

The problem, however, was that there were some serious costs to these heartfelt convictions. For the fact of the matter was, it was only these "in" artists who got any recognition. Quilt-making was a case in point. No matter how excellent this kind of work was, it was still "shunted to the background" in relation to fine art. "Everything that men have done has been art," Katherine complained, "and the things that women have done, which are every bit as much art, have been called fancy-work, crafts, needlework, ladies' hobbies, or whatever." When people heard about quilts, they tended to picture "a little old lady sitting in a rocking chair." But they were just plain wrong, at least about her. She was an artist, interested in creative expression, who happened to be working with fabric. And it was high time that she and her fellow women artists proclaim: " 'This is just as good as Joe Shmoe's painting there, if not better.' " This, indeed, was what seemed to be happening, slowly but surely. Women were becoming less afraid to "come out from the woodwork" and challenge the status quo.

Katherine's own dilemma was a strange and revealing one. Her parents, for instance, used to want to know why she couldn't "do what everybody expected and be a good little girl." In their eyes, she had in fact seemed to be something of a "naughty little girl," particularly since at a young age Katherine (who is white) had taken to painting portraits of blacks, whom her father especially "did not like." They had tried to discourage her from being an artist, telling her that it wasn't something that a girl could succeed at. Others had told her much the same thing: " 'You'll never make it; it's too hard for a woman, and you know you'll want to get married and have a family. You just cannot do that and combine it.' " Her art teachers had offered similar warnings. As for her husband and children, finally, the story was much the same: They were one of the families we encountered earlier, who had done everything in their power to make sure that her artistic interests did not get out of hand. Little wonder that this sort of situation "would squelch your whole artistic background."

In her own case, Ann went on to explain, these people had simply provided fuel for the fire: "The more they told me I couldn't do it, the more I was determined I was going to do it."

Others, however, weren't so lucky. It was "sad that so many women give up" on being artists. Particularly for those who had families, like herself, there was so much sacrifice involved. As she went on to note, "Everybody has an idea of what an artist is or should be, and they expect you to come in with weird clothes and really looking weird and acting a weird part." And if you don't play this part, indeed if you can't afford to play this part due to the fact that you're something else besides – a wife and mother, for instance – "they question whether you're really an artist." Should a woman who was a wife and mother, who made quilts rather than fine art, and who assumed the role of artist almost as if to spite those who told her it was impossible, really be considered a genuine artist, whom others should take seriously? Or was she really just dabbling, in order to inject a measure of integrity into what would otherwise be a "very unsatisfying, repetitive, boring, thankless" existence? It was problematic enough, given Ann's ambitions, that she had to become a homemaker, playing "nursemaid" to her entire family. At the very least, she suggested, she deserved some respect from them when it came time for her to do her own work. But it was exactly this that they would not give her. There she goes, they in effect said, off on her personal odyssey, trying to be what she is manifestly not.

The problems this woman related are intimately connected with one another. Just as she was warned when she was younger that she was stepping into a man's world, and just as she was chided and reduced by her family, particularly her husband, for having the audacity to do something for herself while he was out earning a living, so too was her art itself reduced to something less than what she felt it was; it was women's work, decorative and pretty, but without any genuine artistic validity. Whether she was in the home or out of it, therefore, there was nowhere she could turn to gather the recognition, as a woman and as an artist, she felt that she deserved. It felt good for this woman to come "out of the woodwork," as she had put it; in her own way, she said, she felt that she was a success. Unless both the world of art and her home situation were to change radically, however, it would be extremely difficult to shake her nagging feeling that she was, in the eyes of nearly everyone who mattered, a pale replica of a true artist.

The association of women with crafts is a common one, as is the judgment that the creation of craftwork constitutes an inferior brand of artistry compared with fine art. Not surprisingly, therefore, few men had even entertained the possibility of doing this sort of work. "Craft passing as fine art," as one man succinctly put it, "would always piss me off." In one notable case, however, the decision was in fact to go the route of crafts, even if it meant getting grief from his ostensibly more manly fine artist friends. Dennis Mackenzie, whom we encountered earlier, distinctly remembered "being put down by the sculptors and the painters as being a sort of nonentity." In their eyes, he was "*only* a craftsman, *only* a potter." But this was because of their own snobbery, elitism, and ignorance, he said, for "while the artist was starving on the edge of extinction in his garret, the craftsman was a very respected and a very well-to-do member of the culture." The point in any case is that this man, along with several women in the group, was ostracized for having succumbed to what appeared to be a lesser calling: Pluralism notwithstanding, there was no way they could ever be accorded the status of fine artists.

It was true, one woman admitted, that she would sometimes worry about whether she was being "too charming" or "too saccharine" in her work as a calligrapher; so much of it was so "terribly, terribly sweet and adorable." Moreover, she continued, because "I really follow what the people who come after me are interested in," there was always the threat of becoming too much of a popularizer, thereby compromising her own artistic integrity. In this respect, perhaps some of the criticisms leveled at people like herself were warranted: There was "a delicate line between this kind of thing and crowd pleasing," and she would occasionally experience some guilt over both what she was and wasn't doing in her craft. Once again, however, this was more other people's problem than her own; she had never accepted the idea of "gallery refinement," with its "snob appeal" and its elitism. Ultimately, she said, "I

would rather see people hanging in their homes the most horri-
bly, trashy, slurpy, saccharine kind of art that is personally
meaningful to them than something somebody else has selected and put a stamp on and said, 'This is great art.'" There
may well have been an element of rationalization to this perspective, of course; some of this slurpy, saccharine art was apparently her own. By her own account, nevertheless, she would
rather have done this sort of work, marginal though it was to
the world of fine art, than capitulate to the demands of those in
power.

What seemed to happen more generally, in the case of both
craftspeople such as those from whom we have just heard and
women who had elected to create what they understood to be
"women's art," was that they had to form their own networks
and subcultures. Because there was no way for them to be accommodated into the mainstream, they had in effect to secede
from it, in the hope that they would gather enough power on
their own to thrive. Recall in this context, for instance, the
woman who had eventually found herself as an artist through
the mythological imagery she had discovered abroad in the
course of her travels and who had learned, finally, that she
didn't have to paint like a man to be a true artist. She became
part of a group of fellow women artists – a "caring" group, as
she put it – who had conquered their lingering fear that they
would never get their "credentials" if they weren't "identified
with male art all the time." These women had to regroup, precisely as a means of both resisting what they saw to be a male-
dominated world and gathering the support and care they felt
was necessary to move ahead in their work surely and securely.
As far as they could tell, there was little point in trying to fight a
battle that couldn't be won.

One of the few black artists in the present group articulated a
similar dilemma in his own musings about the relationship of
black art to the mainstream. Allen Powell described himself as
being on a kind of mission: "Instead of going out and worrying
about the art world per se, the thing was to develop the community, the resources you had in the community." The way he
had begun to carry out this mission was to teach in the public

schools. But there, he said, he had to contend not only with racism but with the fact of merely being "tolerated" by the system. The result was that he found this experience too draining and demanding; he knew that he would be embattled – that much was obvious enough – but there was little reason to endure the troubles that had come his way. He therefore decided to move on to college teaching, first down south and then back up north, where he has remained. It has worked out well for him. "The best way to eat being a sculptor," he said, "was to go into education," just as he had, and as of the time we spoke with him, he was "totally satisfied" with both his job and his art.

Most important, the mission remained very much alive. This mission, Allen noted, ran counter to some of what he had been taught at school. There, the big thing was abstraction and more experimental sorts of art, which he quite enjoyed. Nevertheless, he also felt that, for blacks, the "message" was extremely important; there was the need to acquaint black students with the heritage of their own art, their own culture: "'We're going to show you your contribution,'" he had said, and he has always been adamant about doing just that. Maybe for other people, he suggested, there exists the luxury of having their art be about nothing but itself. But as far as he was concerned, "Art has got to say something and mean something." In fact, he went on to say, the task is to "be as as strong and powerful as possible . . . you want to grab them." Only then would it be possible to raise consciousness in the way that was necessary. Black artists simply could not afford to create art for the critic; it was much more important to "educate the people." You have to be a teacher, he believed, and not only in the confines of the classroom.

This too had been a sore spot when he was in art school. "We used to get into large discussions at the Art Institute where the teacher would say, 'I'm creating for the critic, for those people in the know; they have always been the ones who have supported art. And if you are creating for the general public or the middle class or the lower middle class, you're going to be in trouble for the rest of your career. You will literally starve to death.'" The message was all too clear: Capitulate to the demands of the art world or die. There was, of course, a certain commonsense ring to this ethic; he knew what the score was. Furthermore, if his work proved to be acceptable to those "in the know," fine; he had no reason to negate that part of the art scene. But Allen also knew that, being who and what he was, he couldn't "afford," as he again put it, the luxury of sculpting for critics. The mission came first.

After receiving a grant from the National Endowment for the Arts, which allowed him to travel to Africa, he found his art moving still further in the direction of the mission he had set for himself. Indeed, what this trip had apparently done, more than anything, was legitimize this mission; it gave it a kind of substance and rootedness that it had not really had before. There were lots of people who served as role models there, people who never gave up the idea of community, people who were able to move beyond the taboos associated with it. The fact is, he said, there were some who didn't like the idea of saying that they were inspired by others; your inspiration, they told him, should come from you, alone. Pure art, in other words, required a pure creator, one who was untainted by group needs and desires. But the message was more explicit still: There were some, apparently, who felt that it was wrong to be inspired by Africa. That was somebody else's world, they implied, not his; and what's more, once an artist bought into a heritage of this sort, then the art itself would inevitably become somehow secondary to the social concern. But this, Allen felt, was how it had to be. It was true enough, he noted, that the ranks through which his models had moved were vastly different than those customarily associated with the art world; they were doing something else altogether. But what he saw was that they had still been able to make something of themselves, something significantly more important than money and art world recognition. Some of the people at art school felt sorry for him sometimes; they knew the trouble that lay ahead. But he had no choice other than to accept it and deal with it as best he could, with "both feet on the ground." The public image of success, he came to feel, was an "illusion" anyway.

It may be that this man actually fared better in some ways than some of these others, with their taboos and prohibitions. Back at school, he, like all the others, "lived for art, morning, noon, and night; you sleep and dream art." Becoming "selfish," he suggested, was what it was all about. But alongside his mission as well as the family responsibilities that were eventually his to bear, he gradually came to feel that "that's not all there is to life." You have to realize this, he said, for "that's what makes you a better artist." Whereas many of his peers had become trapped through their manic devotion to the muse, he had broken free; and far from calling a halt to his creative activities, these activities had in fact become deepened and enlarged.

The hermetic dimension of much of contemporary artistic creation, he went on to suggest, has exacted a cost not only on those individual artists who refused to step out into the world and be responsible to others, but on American culture itself. "You see so much garbage," he said, that "you get confused; you don't know how to really differentiate what's good from what's bad . . . anything goes." In Africa, however, and even in Europe, he noted, it's very different; rather than art being secluded from the world, it is an integral part of it, and the result is that there is a much healthier atmosphere for artists and surer aesthetic standards for art itself. It was precisely Allen's own marginality vis-à-vis the art world, therefore, that allowed him to understand it in a way that is fundamentally different from those who have been immersed in it. Its foremost problem, he implied, was that rather than being a community, it was a kind of anticommunity, composed of individuals, following their own individual paths; and whatever the manifest appeal of this state of affairs, it was also clear, exactly through the "garbage" that continued to proliferate throughout the land, that something was markedly amiss.

As for the situation of the black artist in America more specifically, his own feeling was that in terms of galleries and the like, they were "in a sense locked out," just as his teachers back in art school had promised. He had gotten a big grant, he had lectured on black art at the Smithsonian and the Field Museum in Chicago, he had a number of one-person shows, and, overall,

226

felt very fortunate, even "blessed," to have gotten as far as he had. But he was not so proud as to forget the plight of the black artist. "The civil rights movement and the events of the sixties helped somewhat," he said, but make no mistake: "It is still a deplorable situation and extremely discouraging." The truth is, "the black artist has been and is still almost completely ignored, as if we did not exist, not even in the art history books." Not unlike those who had elected to create "women's art," therefore, assimilation was simply out of the question; it was a dead end. As for the result: "We are establishing our own criteria and becoming our own critics out of necessity." Allen seemed ambivalent about this situation. On the one hand, it was undoubtedly awkward and uncomfortable to remain on the margins, particularly because he had been put there; his own art, along with that of his fellow black artists, apparently didn't measure up to current standards. The fact that these standards could hardly be ascertained was of no consequence in this context: Even with all the garbage that was in existence, black art was somehow deemed less valuable still. I'm certain the irony of this situation hadn't escaped this man. On the other hand, there was also a sense in which he really wanted no part of the "legitimate" art world anyway; it was counterproductive to the mission and perhaps counterproductive to creative activities more generally, sealed off as it was from the pulse of community life.

How might the situation of contemporary American art right itself? Among other things, Allen implied that we may wish to look at exactly those margins of the art world, like the one he has chosen to inhabit, and see what is going on. In all likelihood, he would say, we won't like what we see; it will be too strange and different. But perhaps it would still be possible to employ our own antipathy, or even repulsion, in the service of returning to the status quo with new eyes, with a new vision of what artistic creation might be like in a community rather than an anticommunity. It wasn't only the fate of the black artist that was at stake, we would have to see, but the fate of art itself.

Let us turn to one final case to round out the picture we have been drawing. Jeffrey Merton was one of those, described earlier, who had gotten into art initially because of "the legacy of the bohemian artist and what that means to society." Like many others, it was not so much art itself that beckoned him as it was the image of the artist, with its intimations of intellectual and spiritual freedom. He would become an integral part of an important community, he thought, filled with people like himself, interested in searching for meaning and bettering the world; they would all show, in and through their freedom, that there was more to life than the bourgeoisie seemed to assume. He would be "starving and fighting hard, doing all sorts of great art that no one was aware of," and thus succeed in actualizing that brand of existential marginality for which artists were noted.

Upon arriving at art school, however, Jeffrey found that the social and cultural climate that existed was not quite what he had expected. He had been one of the few, he recalled, who had a serious interest in nature, both artistically and in relation to ecological concerns. And what had happened, as he told it, was that this brought about an awkward distance between him and his peers. Most of them simply weren't interested in becoming involved in social or cultural or political issues, at least not in their art; instead, and often by their own admission, they saw themselves as purists, creating art for art's sake. "They were always talking about shows," he said, "about developing a style, that kind of career thinking." But this mode of going about one's artistic business was "completely alien" to him; there were other things that were more important.

In any case, after living the life of the bohemian for some years after school, he decided to quit doing art completely; he had just been too frustrated at not being able to afford the needed materials and not having a place to work, and the result was that he did no art at all for approximately 6 years. Instead, he became involved in exploring the wilderness, not only for recreational purposes, but in order to help create an expeditionary hiking trail system that would cut across the whole of North America. Partly, Jeffrey said, he became interested in this because of his love of hiking and his desire to provide good conditions in which to do it. More important, however, was his desire to restrain industry from encroaching any further upon land that ought to have been preserved. His social concerns had therefore remained very much alive even after he abandoned art; and although this project required an incredible amount of work – he would ride buses through America day and night, gathering hundreds of rolls of photographs all along the way – it was exactly the sort of project he had been looking for.

There was again the problem of having virtually no money, and the need, in turn, for picking up odd jobs that would allow him to continue. And the result of this was that, slowly but surely, he began to lose credibility in the eyes of his potential benefactors; the project was interesting and worthwhile enough, but judging from the appearance of this environmental missionary knocking on their doors, some of them apparently decided that their money would be better spent elsewhere. A short while after, he spent some time working on a "pocket survival manual," which, if successful, would give him the money he needed. As it turned out, it gave him more than enough: From the heartland of America he had worked his way to a SoHo loft, where he would return, after his long hiatus, to art. The goal at that point, Jeffrey said, was not unlike the one he had pursued in art school; he would try to unite, as best he could, his artistic interests with his environmental interests. He had to do this, he noted, for there was no way he could have returned to art without having tried to incorporate into it the "human dimension" that was missing from so much of contemporary art. Because he wasn't especially interested in doing paintings whose content was explicitly focused on environmental concerns – even he was too much of a purist to become heavy-handed about all this – what he decided to do was paint whatever he wanted and affix environmentally oriented titles to the resultant works. They would be like "propaganda slogans," as he put it, the primary aim of which was to provide an indictment of the environmental history of Western civilization. The plan was a good one, he thought, because he would be able to meet both his artistic concerns and his social concerns without compromising the integrity of either.

The bottom line, however, was that Jeffrey continued to feel that his own desires as an artist remained vastly different from most of the other artists he knew, particularly while in art school. Reiterating an earlier point, he said, "They all had their heads in the clouds, and all they cared about were these . . . careers; they were thinking of themselves as career artists." He, on the other hand, was into humanity – hence, his decision to stop making "these perfectly useless objects," devoid of practical human import, that all these others continued to make. How strange and ironic this situation was, he mused: The validity of one's art was defined by its uselessness. More troubling still was the fact that "you couldn't deal with nature in any respect." The ultimate goal he set for himself was "meaningful recognition." Art was an eminently social phenomenon, he felt; you're not doing it only for yourself, but for society. It was this belief, above all others, that had gotten him into so much trouble and created so much animosity through the years. Not only had he had the audacity to attach a kind of functionality to art that others believed it ought not to have, but he had rubbed their noses in their own self-involved activities, informing them that their work and perhaps their very selves were all too set apart from life. He spoke further of the "urban art bureaucracy prejudices toward people of rural origin," of the fact that "art dealers shun romanticism," that they reject political content. In short, he felt that he had been up against a structure that was thoroughly opposed to the true mission of art, which was to further the public good through facilitating the expansion of social consciousness.

Jeffrey believed that he was a kind of throwback to earlier times. Like some of the others of whom we have spoken, he had become convinced that modernity ought not to be embraced as unthinkingly and uncritically as it often was; not only had it brought about the alienation of human beings from nature, but it had brought about the alienation of artists from the social whole. Rather than being organically related to the world of which they were a part, they had become so thoroughly absorbed in forging their own private visions and furthering their own professional aims that they had managed to lose a sense of their own civic responsibility. It wasn't simply a question of

230

their being afraid to bite the hand that fed them either, though that was sometimes operative. Rather, their very own desires, he felt, had become complicitous with the fabric of bourgeois social and economic life to such a great extent that they were unable even to fathom the idea that artists might be responsible to more than themselves. *He* was the one who had com-promised, they had told him; he was the one who had insisted that art had to be a means to an end other than itself, that it had to serve a function, that it had to be mindful of the problems of the day. However noble his aims might have been, they were simply not artistic ones; they were social, cultural, and political. And in this respect, they had suggested, he himself had become complicitous in exactly that sort of means–end thinking that they sought to transcend.

The foremost problem Jeffrey faced in his art, therefore, was how to reconcile these two seemingly opposed ideas. Although he had no problem at all rejecting the careerism of his peers, initially at least, he also knew that art and propaganda were two quite different things; he knew enough, that is, about the desirability of autonomous art objects that he himself had no wish to bastardize them by turning them into merely function-al things. By his own account, this was why he elected to paint largely autonomous works of art with "slogans" for titles; at the very least, his viewers might be provoked to think about something other than the formal dynamics of the work itself. But he also must have realized that this "solution" hardly got to the core of the issues with which he was concerned. It was bet-ter than remaining silent about the state of the world, to be sure, but it was still a gesture, in the service not so much of uniting art and social life but of reminding people of the split. By no means am I faulting him for this; he had done what he felt he could. Whether it proved to be enough to assuage his social conscience, I can't say.

The more general problem to be considered in this context was that some artists experienced a profound contradiction be-tween what they thought creating art would be about and what it was. Jeffrey was a product of the 1960s, of a time when the bohemianism he spoke of was very much in the air. As such, it had seemed to him that art was about the most sensible thing one could do; it was countercultural, and could infuse new life blood into a society that had been ravaged by war and by the battle for civil rights by pointing the way toward a new vision of America. There was no more appropriate group of people to further the project of awakening social consciousness than artists, who could articulate, for the masses, their own communitarian yearnings. What he had apparently encountered, however, was an art world that, for all of its manifestly revolutionary motives, had become co-opted by exactly that bourgeois ethic – with its endless cycles of production and consumption, its fantasies of personal fulfillment, its dreams of individual freedom and self-realization – which it had originally, among some quarters at least, sought to indict. The whole thing was shocking and disappointing. He had therefore been left with the feeling that the art world had forsaken both its own true mission and, more specifically, people like himself, who in virtue of their idealism and their romanticism had been deemed hopelessly retrogressive. Rather than abandoning his project, however, he would keep at it and, if all went well, become a kind of midwife of his peers' lost souls.

I have provided but a sample of forms of artistic exclusion. Other forms, it should be noted, were referred to as well, ranging from ethnic art to religious art to art that sought to embody the potential beauty of identical objects, particularly as exemplified in the mass-production assembly line. It can also be said, convincingly I think, that representational art in general tended to be excluded from the domain, with the result that some of those who continued to pursue this path were deemed "outcasts" or "stupid," old-fashioned romantics who hadn't yet learned that the aim of depicting reality was no longer the thing to do. The School of the Art Institute had prided itself on being experimental, one woman had explained; "that's what was accepted. It was assumed that if you did representational work you were kind of out of it." This ethic apparently extended beyond the School of the Art Institute as well. When he went on to graduate school, for instance, one man wound up doing a lot of nonobjective work in sculpture because it was "thrust" upon him. "I had to do it," he said; it was "insisted" that he get away from doing representational work. There was also the woman, discussed in Chapter 2, who had tried desperately to become more modern and abstract and who would occasionally "revert" to representational work just to make sure that she didn't get completely lost in this new land of unreality she felt she had to create. There were a number of other artists as well who had spoken of a similar "reversion" throughout the course of their careers, if not to representational art then perhaps to expressive art, which, in some quarters, had also become taboo: For all that the "formalist dialogue," as Leah Tormey had put it, had dominated the art world and for all its undeniable value in opening up entirely new modes of creating art, many came to feel that this formalism had gone too far, that it had made reality itself taboo and had succeeded in separating artists from some of the features of the world that continued to move them. It just "wasn't enough," Leah had concluded.

She had been fortunate. Because she had become well con-nected enough in the art world that she could choose to move beyond formalism without suffering too many repercussions, she eventually managed to do work that was closer to her heart. Others, however, never got this far. The man referred to earlier who had been labeled an outcast by his peers had appar-ently experienced himself and his artistic aims as being so much in the wrong that he wasn't able to continue with the confidence and the security that was required in order to make it. There was little desire to adopt this lowly role and be chided for his distinctly unmodern ways; there were less painful ways to live. Note the irony here: A number of people had come to art school with the hope of honing their representational skills – it was often just these skills, in fact, that had led to their decision to become artists in the first place – only to learn that they were obsolete, that something else altogether was being done, for which they were completely unprepared. How strange, they might have thought, that such an open and free artistic climate should have led people to rail against those very skills they had assumed art was all about. How strange that they should be rejected for their philistinism. And how strange, finally, that the viewing public should be led to suppose that artists had all but abandoned this desire to picture the world and had moved on to bigger and better things: If they only knew the secret desires some of these artists harbored.

In bringing this section to a close, I shall suggest that many of the extant rules of artistic creation, which were often masquerading as its objective laws, exerted pressure on many of these artists to create forms of art that were largely alien to their most deeply felt needs and desires. Many of these needs and desires were tied to their respective places in the world, as women, as blacks, as people concerned with the environment or even with the world beyond, and finally, as people connected to a still present but in some instances fading connection to reality. Suffice it to say that some of these needs and desires were not adequately met.

A number of these artists were in fact doubly constrained by what they encountered in the domain of art. Not only may they have had to limit the possible range of their artistic activities in order to meet market needs, as we observed in the correlation of pluralism and the establishment of artistic uniformity, but within the context of this very uniformity there may have been further and quite definite rules concerning what could and could not be done. In short, they might have felt compelled to adopt a uniform style of a quite specific sort: one that was at once male, white, apolitical, and highly abstract. This is a very crude composite portrait, to be sure; we obviously cannot reduce the whole of art during this particular period of time to such a limited inventory of its collective "character." My own conviction, however, is that in terms of both the kinds of art that have been produced and recognized along with the creative processes that have gone into them, there seem to have existed many more constraints on the space of creativity than much of the rhetoric about them would indicate. Seeing the sheer quantity of work hanging in museums and galleries throughout the country, not to mention its striking variety, we could easily be led to the conclusion that this was indeed a period of unparalleled artistic freedom, a true efflorescence of unfettered creativity, both individual and cultural. But we need to be extremely cautious in assuming that proliferation and variety signify artistic freedom. If the people from whom we have been hearing are to be believed, the real situation may actually be rather different.

CREATIVITY AND COMMUNICATION

The dream of artistic freedom was thwarted in yet another and still more pervasive way. I am referring to the fact that the space of creativity was constricted further by that brand of negative freedom integral to contemporary individualism itself. As we have observed on several occasions, for many of the artists studied here – and there is good reason to suppose that they were not alone in their sentiments – it could become disheartening for them to realize that their own unique, personal artistic visions could not easily be shared with "the people." Despite the fact that they may have originally desired to become artists precisely because of their interest in speaking to others, in sharing with them the fruits of their own expressive activities, there was all too often a gap between what was being sent and what was being received: The idiosyncratic and arcane nature of their work, which had issued in line with their apparent "freedom," had seemed to lead to their alienation from much of the viewing public, who were unable to make heads or tails of what they were seeing.

Strangely enough, this situation may even have been true for the artists who were creating these works themselves. Although their work often seemed highly personal and seemed to involve artistic visions that were theirs alone, there were some who gradually came to feel that there was in fact something *im*personal about what they were doing; they had been swept up by an ideology of pure innovation and, of course, by market demands for unique and incomparable works, and in the process had managed to forget what art really meant to them. The manifest personalization of the work therefore served to mask the latent emptiness that had gone into it, the result being that their inability to create found its correlate in the inability to communicate: In sealing themselves shut in their own private worlds, real and deep though they appeared, they cut themselves off from the possibility of speaking to others.

Some of the dynamics at hand could be found early on in their careers. Some, for instance, not long after they left art school, realized that many of the artistic ideas and ideals with which they had been saturated did not extend as far into the outside world as they had thought. They might have been terrifically enthusiastic about their artistic prospects and possibilities, but when it became clear that "absolutely nobody knew what you were talking about," it may have been that "you lost a bit of enthusiasm." The world of art, which had loomed so large for so many years, particularly during school, was suddenly taken down to size. This itself proved puzzling and disconcerting to several people. They may not have been sure whether they were being clear enough in their art or whether they were simply more sophisticated than the average people who came to see it. Her friends just can't understand modern art, one woman complained. Another woman was "too much into art history" to communicate with the general public. As one man concisely put it, it was "literally impossible" for the contemporary artist to do this: The gap that separated the artist from the masses was simply too wide to be bridged.

According to some, this situation may not really have been a matter of choice either. One woman, for instance, talked about how much she enjoyed going to junk shops, like her friends; she preferred the unsophisticated aspect of art over all else. In her heart, in fact, she felt that she had a kind of populist attitude toward art, a desire to bring it back to basics. But she was unable to embrace this attitude fully, she said, no matter how hard she tried: "I can't be unsophisticated," she said.

But there were others, again, who gradually rejected this point of view. Artists had "come through this ritual of art education," said one man; they had become "art-ized," as he put it, the community of artists being nothing short of tribal. And there was the need to break out of this tribe. Let us turn first to the case of a woman whom we met with earlier, Marsha Riddell, who, despite having been a "terrible businesswoman," had become one of the most active and successful artists in the entire group. Perhaps the most significant thing Marsha learned throughout the course of her career was that it was essential that one's art issue from one's heart. Initially, she had done huge welded sculptures, which she had quite liked for a time, but which she ultimately found to be too cold and impersonal. She therefore began working with wood, where the process itself was "totally unpredictable," a "continuous adventure," and where her own creative energies could more fully emerge. What Marsha learned upon making this transition, in fact, was that, however much she had enjoyed working with steel, there had existed some unseen motives in her choice to do so. "I was a woman," she said, and "I was trying to make my way in sculpture as a woman. It was very genuine," she insisted – "I would never say it wasn't honest – but a lot of it," she came to realize, had to do with "proving" herself: "I had to be doing this great, big monumental work." People would sometimes say, " 'Look at this work – How does such a little woman like you do it!?' " Steelyard people would be fascinated and give her the respect she had desired, and convey to her the sense that her work was every bit as valid as that of men. What she found upon turning to wood, however, was that her involvement with the objects she was creating was much more personal, closer to her own identity, her own self.

There was a further realization as well, and this was that she, like several others, had gradually become disillusioned with some of the highly abstract, conceptual art she had been doing. Conceptual art was the exact antithesis of what art should be, she came to feel, and it therefore became important to include some kind of "recognizable image" in her work. For one, the inclusion of imagery was more compatible with her inner artistic desires. Even more important, she had grown tired of making art for other artists and critics, for the elite. She had grown "depressed," as she put it, about the esoteric quality of so much contemporary art, about the dead end of minimalist thinking, about the excess verbiage that often had to accompany her work, and finally, about the self-importance conferred upon critics on account of their having to assume the role of telling everyone what everything meant. It was all too "hypocritical" and "disgusting," she decided. "Art really shouldn't have to be explained; it shouldn't need three paragraphs of explanation for people to enjoy it." She therefore tried to create art that would appeal to more than just a select few; anyone off the street should be able to see what she was trying to do, she felt. Again, wasn't expression and communication the reason why many had become artists in the first place? "Any artist, if they were totally honest, would say that they wanted everybody in the world to love what they did, to understand it." This desire could easily become perverted, of course, as had apparently happened in her own case, but all this meant was that it was that much more necessary to rediscover it and thereby return to the more authentic motives that had initially fueled her art.

Yet some serious problems remained, not the least of which was the fact that, no matter how authentically expressive she could possibly be with her art, the cultural climate artists faced was not a receptive one. "The world accepts you for what you make, not what you do, particularly in the United States." This was why she loved France so much; people there, she said, didn't ask how much she had sold. But here, she went on to say, "the respect for the creative process is nil. They respect you if you make money on it. Period. It's too bad," she said; "it's very unsophisticated, ignorant. It shows a total ignorance of what. creation means. The funny thing about a place like France or Italy," she reiterated, "is that the bus drivers understand what creation means."

Upon initial inspection, it would appear that there is a contradiction in what Marsha has told us. On the one hand, she said that she herself had become disgusted with the esoteric, elitist ways of the contemporary art world and had thus elected to work toward creating art that everyday people would be able to appreciate and enjoy. On the other hand, however, there was a sense in which she seemed to deplore the ignorance of these very same people; they were so uncultured and unsophisticated, with their ugly reverence for the almighty dollar above all else. But these problems are less contradictory than they might seem. For what this woman in effect suggested was that, alongside the esoteric ways of contemporary art – indeed perhaps *because* of these ways – people had become so completely alienated from art's meaning and expressive possibilities that they could only comprehend its value as a function of what it was worth. More simply stated, alienated artists inevitably led to an alienated public, mystified by the workings of a culture that they could not even begin to understand. All this had to change. And the sooner people like herself could identify this distorted situation for what it was, the better.

Consider as well in this context the woman who had once been told that her painting had "balls" and who had elected, eventually, to take what she saw to be a more feminine direction in her art. According to Katherine Spector, this had been an act of liberation, an act of freeing herself both from male artistic consciousness and from her own alienation. Once again, there proved to be a further dimension of liberation involved in this very transition as well: Upon making the transition to a more figurative kind of work, she had broadened her audience considerably. Art in America, it was again lamented, was entirely too elitist. "If you don't understand the language," she said, "then you can't be in the 'in' group. I think that we have done that to the population. I think we make work for each other, and I don't think that is right." It was no wonder that Americans were so "visually poverty-stricken and illiterate." By no means had she become a popularizer, however. She had "no strong emotional statement" to make, she was "not telling a story," she was "not an impassioned maker of images," and she was "not a social protester." She was only an artist, and, she noted, a pretty good one at that. And if someone was a good artist, rather than a slick personality making cute things, as she had been earlier, the audience would expand naturally.

Katherine believed that artists themselves were partially to blame for this situation. Even while recognizing that they were socialized into behaving in these self-destructive ways, they ought to have been able, she believed, to transcend this social-ization and do what they knew was right. For her, it was the alienation of the viewing public that had proved to be most troubling, for there was no good reason for things to be as they were. "I think that we have gotten so elitist and esoteric," she reiterated, after reflecting further on her own education, "that art itself doesn't mean anything to the general public. We have made a mystery around the visual language." And what was so tragic about this, she suggested, was that nobody at all bene-fited. She refused to create work that was only for the "initi-ated." Not only was it decadent, leading to the alienation of artists from the public, but it led to the alienation of artists from themselves and their work as well.

Katherine felt fortunate to have become "politicized" over the course of the years. "I found," she said, "that my privileged status was an accident of birth, that I was imposing standards on others simply because everyone else did." So much of what got produced nowadays was "bank art," as she put it, designed ultimately to enrich the lives of those who were often plenty rich enough already. As for art that related to the human condi-tion, whatever that might conceivably be, it was patently clear that there simply wasn't much of it. Nor could there be: To the extent that artists were busy forging their own identities through their "slick presentations," there would be little op-portunity for them to create work that extended into a region of existence beyond the parochial one they had come to occupy.

Some might applaud, in the name of pluralism perhaps, the proliferation of individual identities, along with the refusal to speak to *the* human condition. Given the idea that there may not really be *a* human condition but only a multiplicity of different constructions of it, with no one more valuable and valid than any other, it might again be held that the prolifera-tion of identities signifies a newfound freedom in the world of art, an emancipation from the fetters of tradition. But if indeed artists' identities have been constructed not so much for the sake of attaining their own personal visions but rather for that of maintaining appearances, if you will, what we have then is

240

little more than mock pluralism: an image of individuality designed as a means of capitulating to the demands of those in power. Stated another way still, it would seem imperative, from this woman's standpoint, not to mistake the *appearance* of freedom for freedom itself. She herself had looked and acted the part for some time; she had constructed herself as an artistic renegade, on the loose, by doing cute and catchy things, which those in the know would be able to identify as original and creative. But upon learning to abide by her art itself, she also learned just how oppressive this earlier state of affairs really was.

As a number of other artists agreed, one of the most important conditions of their own maturation as artists was the capacity to refuse to turn their art – and, by extension, their selves – into the sorts of commodities that would inevitably be consumed by a select few. It is important, I think, not to mistake this process of coming to consciousness for starry-eyed idealism either. Katherine had no particular problem with the idea of selling her work, nor did she decide to run off into the woods with her canvases and paint away, blissfully apart from the bourgeois regime that had so stifled her. What she did have a problem with, however, was the fact that many artists tended to overaccommodate, often unwittingly, to structures of power that served to sap them of their own creativity and their own authentic existence as individuals. Whether artists themselves were to blame, as she believed, remains open to question. There is little reason to assume that people are always endowed with the capacity to see through their own mystification.

Whoever was responsible, it was eminently clear that the world of culture, in Katherine's own eyes at least, had come to a sorry state. Not only was much of so-called high art enshrouded in mystery, but a lot of it was downright "awful." Artists often bored people, she said, and were regarded as unimportant. As for art itself, it was "almost dead." And the only possibility for its resurrection was to resist, strenuously, the reigning ethic and turn instead to what can only be called truly human concerns. Indeed, she suggested, it was only by attend-

241

ing to these concerns – elusive though they may be – that artists could succeed in freeing their own creative energies: The proof was in the practice.

Some artists would have disagreed strongly with this point of view. Artists, like other professionals, may have spent many years mastering their trade, so to speak; no one expects physicists or mathematicians to speak to everyone, the argument might go, and no one should expect artists to do so either. Second, it could be argued that excellence in art is often ahead of its time, that artists, by virtue of either their prophetic insights or their unique ability to grasp that which others cannot, will often have to await the future before their contributions can be adequately acknowledged. Third, the notion of truly human concerns, for many, is itself suspect; whether from the perspective of those antihumanistic advocates of postmodernism who seek to question the primacy of the human subject or that of those more "theological" critics who seek to restore art's lost ties to the sacred, it may be held that it was precisely our long-standing fetish with the "human" that got us into trouble to begin with. Fourth, and perhaps most central, if indeed the masses in this country are as caught up in their own mundane, unartful existence as many seemed to think, then they could be a hopelessly lost cause.

However valid these arguments may be, many of those with whom we spoke felt that the situation of contemporary art had gotten out of hand. In part, this could be tied to the variety of concrete factors we have been considering – to mythical images of the artist, bigger than life itself; to the self-indulgent nature of the pursuit; to the pervasiveness of the market in determining who would be allowed to speak and who would not; and to the strange goings-on in the domain of art itself, which seemed to dictate that the more opaque the work the more valid it was. Implicit in much of what was said, however, was the idea that the situation of contemporary art might itself be regarded as a symptom, of a far larger and more pervasive dis-ease in American life having to do with the utter occlusion not only of visual art in particular but of culture more generally from the fabric of social existence: The relentless ascendancy of the rational and

242

the instrumental, having invaded even those domains that had once been thought to serve as sacred preserves, had apparently led to a situation where creative pursuits had been left gasping for air.

Counterarguments can be made here too. The world of culture, some might say, has simply changed, and in a direction that is, arguably, of more value to the masses than ever before. There are movies and magazines, television and radio, and a whole bunch of other things besides, each of which, in its own way, has brought the much-touted creative dimension to our front doors. Perhaps, then, some of the artists from whom we have heard are merely nostalgic or resentful over the fact that they can no longer acquire as big a piece of the cultural pie as once seemed possible. Perhaps, moreover, it would be preferable, ultimately, to shut the doors of galleries and museums, particularly those that depend on the hard-earned tax dollars of people who have better things to do with their money than fund artists who apparently have little desire to speak to them anyway, and turn our attention and our capital elsewhere. More severely still – and this idea was entertained by several in the group – perhaps what we are witnessing now is a movement toward rendering obsolete so-called high culture itself, the constriction of the space of creativity signifying little more than a historical process that has run its course. For my part, there is something nihilistic about this point of view. It is that much more tragic that this very nihilism has become so integral a part of the mind-sets of many of those studied here.

THE PROBLEM OF MEANING

While several of the people discussed in the previous section had become interested in calling a halt to the incommunicability of their art and had thereby managed to free some of the creative energy that had been blocked by their own self-imposed artistic hermetism, others were much less sanguine about the possibility of moving forward in their artistic and communicative aims. It could be, one man noted, that what we are seeing now is but a "quiet lull until art finds its roots." For him, in other words, there remained the idea that the disunity of the artistic scene and the uneasiness that was part of it was best seen as a liminal stage in an ongoing dialectical process, after which time art would once more be able to rear its proud head for all to see. It was as if hidden beneath the surface of difference and plurality was an origin, a point of common ground, a basic connection to the past, to history, to art's "roots." We might call this the "culture in waiting" thesis. This man actually found it to be a "neat time" in this respect; there was something enjoyable about being in a period of transition, even crisis.

For those who were a bit more cynical, however, these sentiments might have appeared wishful at best. The present in art, many felt, was anything but "neat" and, by all indications, anything but a "lull"; and it was difficult for them to imagine how the most salient features of the production and consumption of art could change in the near future. As we have seen repeatedly, rejection was a prominent theme for some of these people; too much art was esoteric "bullshit," "garbage," "crap." Artists, one woman stated flatly, just can't paint like they used to. And although some of them believed that our culture was "suffering" on account of this situation, for others there was nary a regret. Recall some of what was said earlier in this context: Why should one regret this situation when art was such a "meaningless business" anyway? Art had become "superfluous"; it "probably doesn't mean a whole lot." Was there any reason why it should? Again, maybe this was the end of art. Of painting, for instance, another woman mused, perhaps "they've almost said what could be said with that type of medium."

This woman, it might be noted, was not entirely pleased thinking these thoughts. Having taught at a junior high school ever since art school, the primary difficulty she faced through the years had been the shrinking of both her students' imaginations and art's importance. Too often, she said, students were destructive and lazy and simply didn't care about art. But this was no surprise, for the message they apparently received from most people was that education was more about the mastery of

244

computers than anything else. The result was that she felt like a missionary, one of the few who was still interested in providing a complete, well-rounded education. A further result was that her commitment to teaching was full-time; her own art would have to be placed aside, she felt, until she could dedicate her all, "which means retirement." It was unclear what she would do when she returned, she went on to say. She had been a painter, and for a time she had been tremendously involved emotionally with her work. It was partly the depth of her involvement, in fact, that led her to leave painting behind; it was so demanding and draining. She would therefore have to wait and see what would be appropriate to do.

Reflecting further on the situation of art in present-day society, the problem came down to people's attitudes, their sense of priorities. The arts were virtually being passed over for science, she believed. This was understandable on some level, of course, given that science could prove itself in ways that art could not, but it was still a sad situation: Part of our own humanity was being cut off and repressed. In some sense, this had even happened in her own life. Due to family responsibilities especially, it became clear that something would have to be given up; as far as she was concerned, there was no way that one could be a full-time teacher, a serious artist, and a decent wife and mother at the same time. She had thus been "torn in several directions" for a good while, until, finally, she gave up. By and large, she implied, the outcome was a good one. Not only did her husband and children stop complaining about her involvement, which was apparently seen in much the same way as at the junior high where she taught – as an expendable frill – but her own life became less frazzled and fragmented. This too was at once understandable and sad. It was understandable because giving up art made a lot more sense than giving up her family or her teaching. What was so sad about what had happened was that years ago she had seen art as a creative outlet, a balance to all of the other roles she had to perform. Lately, however, it had become a role in its own right; it had assumed the status of another task, which had to be carried out competently and completely.

There is an ironic twist to this brief story I have just related. Even as this woman deplored the idea of art being relegated to the status of an expendable pursuit, she had made it so in her own life. We ought not necessarily fault her for this, of course; the bottom line was, she was too tired to do the kind of quality work she was interested in doing. Nevertheless, it may be worth noting the different ways in which the expressive realm could yield under the pressure of the instrumental. Whether we are considering the computerization of this woman's junior high or her family's complaints or her own guilt over knowing that there are more productive things to be doing than spewing one's soul on a canvas, the dynamic is much the same. She couldn't be too sad about this situation; if painting had run its course, there were probably better things to be doing anyway. Yet the implication here is actually quite serious: Her junior high students weren't the only ones whose imaginations were dried up.

Some of these same sentiments were echoed by a man whom we heard from earlier, who had become a professor of art at a major university. Fred Woyzek had more or less fallen into teaching, having gotten a position after art school without even looking. In fact, he wasn't sure he even wanted to teach. But he has been doing so since 1970. He seemed moderately pleased with his situation, but by no means ecstatic. He was at a university rather than an art school, and as a result, there were lots of students – too many, he felt – who simply weren't as serious about art as he would have wished, who regarded it as extraneous to life itself. Ironically enough, he himself had gradually fallen prey to these same beliefs. Whereas early in his career there was no question whatsoever about art's seriousness and worth, particularly since he had gained enough recognition that he was able to feel good about things, later, when some of this recognition was on the wane, he began to have some questions about what he was doing. It wasn't that he had stopped showing or that people had stopped responding to his work; he had actually done quite well in this regard. Unfortunately, however, there had not been too many sales recently, and he had taken it to heart: "You wonder," he said: "You're at a certain age and this is what you're doing. Is it really worthwhile," he would ask, "or are you just simply there because you don't have to scrounge around?"

More generally, there was the difficulty of "maintaining the conviction that what I do in my art is valid in spite of others' opinions." Again, when the work wasn't selling or when people were critical of what he was doing, whether for valid reasons or not, he would lose confidence and hope, and begin to question his own worth as an artist. These feelings would be assuaged to some extent when business picked up, but even then, he would still remain unsure about the worth of the entire project with which he was engaged. Why was he an artist anyway? Why was anyone?

Fred was actually well recognized, he emphasized again. He had a fairly regular schedule of exhibitions, he did sell some work occasionally, and he had come close a number of different times to having his work accepted at significant galleries. This last aspect of his success was disappointing, he admitted – "After a while," he said, "you don't even pay attention to it because it's happened so many times that it has not worked out" – but he really couldn't complain about his status; he had a lot more going for him than many others had. Nevertheless, still unsure about the vocation of the artist, he spent no small amount of time "trying to resolve some frustrations about whether or not what you're doing is worthwhile." He recalled an issue in this context that he had spoken about earlier: "I suppose you reach a certain age," he said, "when you look back on your life and say, 'Okay, you're not designing airplanes; you're doing this . . . you're smearing a cloth with paint.' And what do you do? You simply look at it. I mean, is this really a worthwhile activity for an adult person to do?"

There are many reasons for this man's uncertainty and doubt about the validity and worth of the very activity to which he has dedicated his life. He did love painting – there was no questioning that – and when things were going well, he was sometimes able to put aside these concerns and to create with the conviction that often seemed to be missing. Had he been more consistently successful as an artist, therefore, his uncertainty

247

and doubt might never have appeared. I had the feeling when I spoke with him, in fact, that were he to have made a connection with what he considered to be a major gallery, much of his angst would have been forgotten. As things presently stood, however, his own feeling was that, by utilitarian standards – that is, those standards that insisted on one's doing things that could justifiably be called worthwhile – he had fallen short of making the sorts of contributions to the world he had hoped to make. His biggest problem, in other words, was that he was haunted by the feeling that what he was doing was, in the general scheme of things, essentially useless.

Despite the fact that art has continued to be defined and constituted in fundamentally nonutilitarian, nonfunctional terms – so much so, as we observed earlier, that those whose work exhibited shades of functionality could be castigated by others for their having abandoned art's true mission – it is clear that there are some who have become uncomfortable with this situation. There were so many things to be done in the world, Fred seemed to say, so many projects, so many ends to be realized, yet there he was, like a child almost, dedicating himself to an activity the only end of which was contemplation – and not nearly as much as he would have liked. Should a grown man, living in a society where almost everyone seemed to be performing some service or other, really be spending his time "smearing a cloth with paint"? At other periods of history or in other cultures, I'm sure he knew, these sorts of questions might not have even arisen. Rather than being seen as a frill, as it tended to now, art was seen as integral to life, and artists could carry out their work knowing that they were making a valuable contribution to the world. There was no need to justify and defend and rationalize what they were doing; the validity of their activities was immanent in the idea of art itself. Here, however, this idea was under attack: Could it be that the very idea of art had somehow outlived its day? Was it no longer possible to dedicate one's life to the creation of objects destined for aesthetic contemplation only? Was the creation of art an activity so hopelessly separated from life as it was known and lived, by everyday people, that most would have difficulty contemplating it anyway?

Let us return for a moment to the most successful woman artist of the group, Leah Tormey, for the sake of exploring further how she herself had elected to think of this situation. At one time, you may recall, Leah had become convinced that art was "superfluous and useless," and that artists were "not wanted particularly." She had nevertheless managed through the years to comfort herself with the fact that some artists at least were not "alienated workers," like many other people were. Moreover, she had said, to avow the superfluousness and uselessness of art was to admit defeat; it was to capitulate to those who had made it so. And this she refused to do. But why was it that so many experienced feelings of "impotence" in relation to what they were doing? There were at least three interrelated answers to be offered. The first, she had said, was that avant-garde thinking was pretty much over; it had had its "historical moment," as she put it, and the result was that it was unlikely that contemporary artists could transform society in the way that artists had once imagined possible. The second reason that artists felt impotent and that art itself failed to be genuinely respected, she believed, was that art "does not have utilitarian value." As indicated by Fred Woyzek, it was difficult for some to live with the fact that what they were doing had no purpose other than giving a few select people something to look at, probably during their leisure time. Third, the contemporary artist – like a whole lot of other people besides – couldn't help but be riddled and plagued by doubt: about the validity of one's art, about the validity of one's existence as an artist, and about the validity of the world of culture more generally.

It was easy, Leah had suggested, not only to think doubtful thoughts but to *be* doubtful; it was a part of the late 20th-century condition. But it was also easy, she noted, to give more "credibility" to doubt than one ought to, to get sucked into it and let it paralyze you. With this in mind, there was but one suitable response, and that, in effect, was to try to doubt doubt itself, to resist it, through creating works of art that in their very presence would show that they had a compelling and defensible reason to exist. She herself had learned to do exactly this in recent years, and while this "method," so to speak, surely wasn't foolproof, it did manage keep at bay some of those feelings that had so diminished the space of her creativity. In the end, therefore, she seemed to say, the only way out of this doubtful abyss was through art itself, authentic art, that gave voice to what still deserved to be called real.

Chapter 6

The conditions of creativity

In this chapter, I shall briefly review the major findings of the previous four chapters and then try to outline some of the requisite conditions, both psychological and social, within which what I have been calling the space of creativity may be enlarged. This task is a difficult one; again, it is easier to identify pathologies than health, and easier to suggest what *ought* to be, in the best of worlds, than what *can* be, in the one in which we happen to live. I am nevertheless convinced that the attempt to bring to light the various pathologies we have encountered will be of service both in expanding our own consciousness of the dynamics of contemporary artistic activity and in imagining how things might change for the better.

Two points of qualification are in order before beginning. The first is that although we are able to identify what might arguably be deemed *necessary* conditions of artistic creativity, at least for a significant portion of the community of visual artists, we are not on that account able to offer *sufficient* ones. Because we will try to remain as close as possible to the information at hand in the course of working reconstructively from negative to positive conditions of artistic creativity, we shall only be able to speak of the latter as they are implicated in the former. Other groups of artists, from other art schools in other parts of the country (not to mention the world), may have encountered different problems than the ones articulated here, problems that might lead to a different picture altogether. In addition, of course, more information might have been acquired from the present group itself, information that would have helped refine and articulate further the requisite conditions of artistic creativity. The point, in any case, is that it will only be possible to proceed with our reconstructive efforts on the basis of what has been said here, by this particular group of aspiring artists, in line with the specific questions asked of them.

The second qualification is that the conditions of creativity to be enumerated, necessary though they may be here and now, are not on that account to be deemed so for all times and all places. As we noted at the beginning of this book, both creativity and its conditions are socioculturally constituted, deriving their nature from the specific worlds in which they emerge: As the latter change, so too does the former. It could therefore be that at some point in the future we will see entirely different forms of creativity and entirely different conditions giving rise to them. Indeed, it could be that these forms and conditions are changing right now, at this moment. But this should not detract from the relevance of our conclusions. For however "local" these conclusions might be, they can nonetheless be brought to bear upon the future. Indeed, it is in the service of imagining what this future might look like that this project has been undertaken.

DEFYING THE MYSTIQUE OF ART AND ARTIST

Within the sphere of person-related – or, as I put it earlier, *persona*-related – problems in the process of artistic creation, it seemed that for many of the individuals considered, the fashioning of their selves in relation to their art was carried out with a definite product in mind: Many wanted to become *Artists*, like the ones they had heard about, whose personalities and canvases loomed in their minds like a magical vision. There was more at stake for them, we saw, than simply doing art; they were interested in becoming specific kinds of people, art-ful people, the sooner the better. This air of nervous desire, this frequent wish for instantaneous personal and artistic self-actualization, proved to be difficult for many to endure. Things happened too quickly for many of them, so quickly that they came to feel that they could not deliver. While others were painting or sculpting feverishly, putting together their seemingly polished portfolios, the people to whom I am referring here were somehow shrinking, the prospects for their futures appearing dim. It was if by trying to create art and trying to be artists they were laying themselves on the line in such a risky way that there was little choice but to cower and retreat; they did not have the confidence to believe that they could ever fully actualize the images with which they were operating. They might have seen themselves as too average, too dull and unexceptional, in relation to the bright lights they saw all around them.

What is most important to notice here are the interrelated problems of impatience, which derived in part from these individuals' expectations that they were quickly to become mature, fully formed artists, and doubt, which derived from the conviction that they would not be able to meet these expectations and that the course of their lives could all too easily become a gradual but inevitable descent into artistic nothingness. There were some who stated that they didn't know how to be artists yet, and it was therefore difficult to envision a future filled with real achievements. The only evidence that they might have been exceptional may have issued from family members and the like; and while this may have been enough to lead them to art school, it may have come to strike them as somewhat hollow.

Others sketched out a different scenario altogether. They too were impatient, wishing to launch themselves immediately into the exotic world of art and artists. Rather than retreating from the challenge at hand, however, they embraced it, confidently assured that they had the stuff to make things happen. Indeed, a few of them did make things happen, at least temporarily; they were the overnight successes that continue to feed the American imagination. But the problem was that, by and large, they still were not developed enough, as artists or as people, to assimilate fully the reality of their new situations. Their narcissism and grandiosity, it seemed, could rarely hold up under the massive strain of the real, and the result was that

253

they could be sent sprawling backward, to a place where they were forced to rethink the extent of their own power. We can think of this phenomenon as a kind of conceit, wrought out of an illusory and sometimes arrogant conviction that one was wholly ready to encounter the world of art head-on; and we can trace its origin to many of the same issues operative in the emergence of doubt. While there were some who retreated backward, daunted by the prospect of an all too unexceptional future, others raced forward, in hot pursuit of the various prizes that had seemed to be there for the asking, this energetic two-way traffic apparently being regulated by the same basic set of signals. It should be reiterated that neither the images these individuals held in their minds nor their motivations for variously retreating backward or racing forward were strictly unitary ones. Those who elected to continue, we saw, may have been as much enchanted by the possibility of their own bohemian dereliction and marginality as they were of hobnobbing with the beautiful people at some chic get-together in SoHo or the Hamptons. For both of these "goals," in any case – which were often recollected as being equally perverse – the notion of exceptionality looms large: the former in the direction of romantic degradation and solitude, the latter in the direction of romantic decadence and sociability.

Art and the process of becoming an artist were intensely important for many of these individuals, particularly early on; it was all that many of them lived for. For some, this importance served them well. They were so committed to realizing their dreams that any and all obstacles in their way could be tossed aside; whatever it took for them to get where they wanted to go, that is what they would do. It was also clear, however, that things could become too important as well, too large, too single-minded, the result being that some of them became staggered by their own momentum and suddenly found the need to screech to a halt. There is a sense in which these sorts of people, as painful as their experiences may have been, were more fortunate than some of the others in that they managed to muster the wherewithal to catch themselves in the act of their own reckless projects. They had the option at that point of either slowing down and trying to do some art or leaving art altogether. Some of the less fortunate, on the other hand, may have never quite arrived at this realization, and they may still be living in sorrow for the artists they never became.

The point here, it should be emphasized, is not that art ought to have been *un*important to these people; like any other serious pursuit, it needed to be something to which they were wholly committed. What I am suggesting instead is that their commitment often seemed to go beyond art itself and began veering into its various trappings and traps. In this respect, we might say that art could become, if not too important, then too *magical*. This magic, which we can think of in terms of the substitution of the unreal for the real, often became identified as such. In the face of their own alienation from what they were doing and who they had become, a number of artists finally became aware of their own dissemblance. Less severely, they might have become aware that the mythicized images they held of art and artist were illusory, serving to take them away from their true concerns. Once they were able to do this, perhaps they would be able to get on with their work in a less mystified way. For others, however, there may have been little left after becoming aware of the magical duplicity of their ways. These people realized that their motives may have been duplicitous to begin with, that they had actually been seeking something other than the creation of art itself.

Bringing together the ideas of impatience and doubt, along with conceit and magic, we can begin to understand how distanced many of these individuals were from their art. In seeking to become artists before their time, and in variously fleeing from or embracing the challenge before them in line with their self-perceived artistic capacities, many were left sadly unable to differentiate the images they possessed from the realities they were. Most centrally, then, it seems that the mystique of art and artist often pervaded the process of artistic creation itself in such a way as to render it deeply alienating. Some, again, became palpably aware of this alienation in the course of their activities; others did not. Either way, their own creative activities often suffered.

One of the requisite conditions of artistic creativity may therefore be the capacity to *defy* the mystique of art and artist, at least in its more destructive forms. One of the ways this might be accomplished is by artists abiding by what might be called "developmental realism": For aspiring artists to become fully engaged in the process of artistic creation, they need to have in their possession some recognition of their developmental status as artists, some sense that they are in all likelihood neither the hopeless causes they may feel they are nor finished products, happily ready to have it all. Again, those who were plagued early on by doubt, particularly about what they did or did not "have" as artists, could not help but be wary about their futures and could not help but bring this wariness to the process of creating their art. This was no ordinary challenge they were facing; it was a quite extraordinary one in their eyes, and, operating frequently with essentially nativistic theories about what creativity was, it was unclear whether they were up to it. None of what is being said here is to imply, of course, that these artists were equally talented. Nor, further, is it meant to imply that some artists' lack of conviction in their own artistic potential was not well founded; some of them had undoubtedly reached a quite veridical appraisal of their own worth and were probably fortunate to reach the conclusions they did. It is nonetheless clear, however, that many of these individuals' artistic potential had been cut short by the unrealistic images and goals with which they were operating: Unable to exist in the grand shadows of those they "knew" to be superior, their own projects could only be deemed finite. Some of them therefore stopped before ever having truly started, their most basic presumption being that they were artistically inept rather than immature. Had they been more developmentally realistic, they might have been able to move forward with their art with a surer sense that the endeavor was worthwhile.

Those plagued by conceit, on other hand, who felt that their main challenge was simply to release the inherent potential they believed they had, could easily be defeated by their own developmental hastiness. Thinking that their natural gifts would allow them to join the ranks of the great and that it was merely a matter of time before this would happen, these people's most basic presumption was that they were already mature artists. For them, once more, fame and fortune seemed to be there for the asking; success was just around the corner. The problem, however, was that it was further away than they knew. They too found it difficult to be developmentally realistic.

In each of these scenarios, energy was taken away from the creation of art. If the future appears to be virtually closed due to one's ostensibly meager gifts, then it is impossible for creativity to proceed optimally. Likewise, if the future appears wide open, such that development is understood to be a mere matter of playing out what is already there, inchoate, the same is true once again; creativity, in this latter case, is cut short precisely by imagining that one's greatness is a foregone conclusion. What we can say, therefore, is that alongside some measure of *conviction*, there must also be a measure of *humility*, to serve as a kind of counterbalance, a kind of check on the possibility of conviction turning into conceit and grandiosity.

Aspiring artists also need to understand the fact that there *is* no creativity per se apart from the demands – the quite changeable demands – of the domain of art itself. There is an interesting implication here: Not only must *psychologists* acknowledge the sociocultural constitution of creativity but so must *artists themselves*. That is, they need to understand that natural gifts alone, relevant though they may be, do not creativity make. Two points deserve to be emphasized in this context. First, even though one may perceive oneself to be less gifted than other artists given the criteria of artistic excellence that exist in the domain at a particular time, the fact that these criteria can and indeed do often *change* may be a useful one to keep in mind: One's ostensibly meager gifts now can occasionally become appreciably greater later on, as there emerges a greater degree of congruence between one's talents and the demands of the domain. Conversely, even though one may perceive oneself to be more gifted than other artists, given extant criteria, there again remains the possibility that changes in the domain will render one's gifts essentially obsolete. This was why

257

even the best-known artists in the group remained anxious and uncertain about their futures.

The second point to be emphasized is that whatever gifts one may or may not have, there are numerous other factors, both intrapersonal and extrapersonal, that enter into the constitution of creativity. And what this means is that one's artistic fate is in no way sealed either at the beginning of one's career or at any other time; just as the attributional structure of the domain itself can change, so too can the vast multiplicity of other contributory factors. Being developmentally realistic, therefore, entails significantly more than being able to maintain humble conviction in the face of the future. It also entails some cognizance of the fact that artistic creativity and development, rather than being natural, inherent processes, are instead inseparably intertwined with social reality, acquiring their very shape in line with its dynamic workings. This cognizance is itself very much in the service of defying the mystique of art and artist, particularly insofar as it is tied to the related myth of natural gifts, happily present in some, sadly absent in others.

A further and still more fundamental way in which the mystique of art and artist may be defied is by artists attempting to keep a vigilance over what might be called true desire. I do not wish to reify this idea by casting it into some pure, unadulterated form; none of our desires are to be seen in this idealized way. Moreover, there is little reason to expect or, for that matter, to encourage artists to forget entirely about all that surrounds the creation of art itself; no one lives without some image, perhaps even a mythical image, of who and what they wish to be. Let me therefore try to clarify this issue by framing it in the following way: Even while there will be hints of true desire in the most flagrant cases of self-deceptive mystification and even while there will be hints of mystification in the most untarnished artistic projects, to the extent that other-than-artistic desires take precedence over artistic desires the resultant creative processes cannot attain their optimal form. More simply, if the desire to be an artist overrides the desire to create art, the creative process itself will have in part become a means to an end other than the creation of art. This in turn implies that the art work itself will have been "devised" on some level, whether consciously or unconsciously; it will have been the product of a calculation, geared to the formation of a specific kind of persona. In short, one further way in which the mystique of art and artist may be defied is, quite simply, by being aware of it and by taking measures to ensure that it does not occlude true desire.

There is, however, another way of thinking about these particular issues, a way that gets us closer to the sociocultural nexus within which the mystique of art and artist is enmeshed. What I mean to say here is that not only must this mystique be defied, through individual artists' own awareness and vigilance; it must be taken apart as well, exploded, such that its very pervasiveness and power become diminished. And the only way this is possible is if the project of becoming an artist and of creating art becomes more "normalized" than it presently is, when it becomes a part of life rather than something outside it (see especially Herbert Read's *To hell with culture* [1963]). The prospects of this happening in the near future actually seem quite dim; paradoxically enough, the diminution of art's importance, in the context of education especially, seems to make it that much more extraordinary and exceptional a pursuit, that much more set apart from the decidedly unartistic lives most people lead. Even as art diminishes in *real* importance, in other words, its *magical* importance may be increasing – to think that there still remain people who dedicate themselves to as utterly impractical a pursuit as art. A bit more constructively, perhaps when art increases in real importance its magical importance will diminish.

In sum, it would appear that the space of creativity can only become enlarged to the extent that the mystique of art and artist – and, perhaps, of the exceptional individual more generally – is both identified and made conscious, where it exists, and taken down to size, by integrating the place of art and artist into the fabric of life itself. Now if this were to happen, it may be that art and artist would lose some of their charm, some of their magical allure, some of their status as antidotes to the banality and mundaneness of this world we inhabit; there would just exist ordinary folks who, among other things, happen to create art. In some ways, this seemed to be what Marx hoped for; because it was problematic for him that some people got to lead lives of creative abandon and others not, it was deemed preferable to distribute the wealth, both literally and figuratively. I am not convinced that Marx's specific "solution" is either desirable or practicable, sympathetic though I am to much of what he has to say about certain pathologies of capitalism itself. Nor am I convinced that there should be a world wholly devoid of exceptional individuals, doing their exceptional things. I am fully convinced, however, that unless this mystique of which we have been speaking is taken down to size – which can only be accomplished when there is a more equitable distribution of possible arenas for artistic activity in particular and creative activity in general – the problems we have been exploring here will continue to emerge.

In a world characterized by a conspicuous dearth of arenas for creative activity, such as our own, becoming an artist and creating art will continue to be constituted as extraordinary and exceptional, which is to say bathed in mystique. This mystique, by being complicitous in the process of artistic creation itself, will contaminate it as a matter of course, preventing artists from having both the conviction and the humility to move forward optimally in their work and alienating them from true desire. In identifying, defying, and, most important, undermining the mystique of art and artist by furthering their integration into the fabric of life itself, therefore, perhaps we will see the space of creativity enlarged. A further qualification is in order. I am not suggesting that the practice of art become a job like any other or that art itself become just another commodity, no more or less grand than the countless other commodities with which we surround ourselves. This process of commodification, we learned, yielded its own share of pathologies. How then do we work our way out of this apparent dilemma? That is, how is it possible to undermine the mystique of art and artist without having both the practice of art and art itself be assimilated still further into this process of commodification? My own conviction is that the mystique of art and artist and the process of commodification, far from being at odds with one another, are in fact mutually defining, as the art world shows all too clearly. And this means that even as this mystique becomes undermined so too will the process of commodification; once art and artist lose their magical importance, they will no longer be able to serve in quite the same commodity fetish-like way. Whether this loss of magical importance would in turn serve to diminish the real importance of art and of artists, I cannot say. My best guess, however, is that the exact opposite would happen: With their magical aura having been shattered through their integration into the fabric of life, the aura that remains will be the one that deserves to remain, the one that signifies and expresses the true value of artistic creativity as a form of creative human labor.

There is no simple way, of course, to effect the integration we are now considering. More comprehensive educational opportunities would certainly be one way, as would the attempt to remove art from the rarefied atmosphere of museums and the like. But it would be difficult to expand the *cultural* space of creativity without a significant shift away from the seemingly ever-increasing emphasis placed upon utilitarian value. Along these lines, it was strange for some to see that however much they themselves might have once been bathed in mystique, it had become difficult, later on, to come up with a suitable rationale for why they dedicated their lives to smearing paint on a canvas; there were so many more *productive* things to be doing. Not only had art lost its magical importance for these people; it had lost its real importance as well, appearing to be little more than a frill, a decorative border on the edge of the adult world. What had seemed so large had become terribly small. We need to imagine how this strange situation might be changed, and soon. The result, otherwise, will be the continued aggrandizement of art and artist to the exclusion of their potentially real value.

MOVING INTO THE COMMUNITY OF OTHERS

Turning to the findings outlined in the chapter on interpersonal problems bearing on the process of artistic creation, we saw that for a number of people art and intimate relationships did not easily mix. They were either too fond of their solitude, too put off by the possibility of caring for someone other than themselves, or, as some admitted, too fearful of the effect of their involvement on their art. By and large, however, the reasons these individuals decided not to commit themselves in any long-term way to others had to do with the perceived demands of the life of the artist.

Right away we return to the theme of art's magical importance. Being an artist was seen by many to be different from all other pursuits, no matter how challenging and involving they might be; it was something that required not only commitment but an unswerving devotion and singleness of purpose. Some of these people had in a sense become their own gods, and they insisted on maintaining a properly ritualistic attitude toward the sacred pursuit they had chosen in order to give their lives a measure of true meaning and value. As with all pursuits of this kind, there was often a noticeable tension between feelings of sacrifice and fulfillment, of being a martyr and being a saint. Either way, their situation would be a difficult one.

For those who decided to take the plunge into intimate relationships, especially marriage, similar issues emerged. For men in particular, many of whom were very much taken with the sacred nature of their endeavors, there was a tendency to ride roughshod over their mates, to use them in whatever way fit their needs. Their wives, of course, likely knew what they were marrying into, and may have even desired their mates for their strength of purpose and their relentless devotion to their noble goals. They may not, however, have known the price they would ultimately have to pay. As for these men themselves, unless they were so ruthless and narcissistic that they were unaware of what was going on around them, they often found the underside of their devotion staring them in the face. It was difficult to believe that they couldn't have known, some of them admitted humbly, that even in the midst of fulfilling themselves others were being forsaken. It was therefore not unusual for them to be left with guilt over what they had and had not been and done. If things had gotten bad enough, there might have been anger too, at themselves, arising out of what they came to see as the callousness of their transgressions and their oblivion through it all. Finally, there might also have been the feeling that their single-mindedness had backfired. Not only could their guilt and anger intrude on the process of creating itself, but they might have wound up preventing themselves from receiving the support and care they so desired. In short, many of these men became their own – and others' – worst enemies.

Many of the women in the group also saw art to be a sacred pursuit, one that required an unusual amount of energy and devotion. They, however, often found themselves unable to gather the same degree of single-minded verve as the men. Among other reasons, their husbands were often busily involved in their own pursuits, which might have taken precedence because they were often the primary breadwinners. Moreover, several of these women's husbands had too much manly pride, it seemed, to see their mates individuate; it was seen as an affront to their stature and their power. It is not terribly surprising, therefore, to learn that there was some reluctance on the part of these threatening women to rock the boat: better to keep the peace. But there was more happening than fear or anger or retribution from their husbands. These women themselves had their own images to uphold, their own conceptions of what a woman was and what a woman did, if she was a "good" one; there were certain responsibilities, they often believed, that simply could not be reconciled with the life of the artist, at least as they knew it. Indeed, often coupled with their husbands' attempts to prevent their own individuation, as women and as artists, were the attempts of these women themselves. If the men we have discussed often assumed the role of intrepid hero, living their lives with a vengeance, the women often assumed the role of the cautious and acquiescent victim, living their lives in and for others.

We can see the mystique of the artist at work in the present context as well. Many of these women wanted to do art, they believed, but there was too much holding them back. Again, art was a different kind of occupation than others and it needed to be treated with deference and respect, as did artists themselves. The result was that the entire project of becoming an artist proved to be too big and daunting for many of them, and their own lingering doubt, fear, and insecurity would often pave the way toward their own shame, for having capitulated and missed out; there was too much risk involved in something as powerful and as magical as art. So it was that the space of creativity could not only become diminished but brought to a vanishing point. There could be the sense that their work was forever destined to be without any yield at all.

The story was much the same in regard to family-related matters, the only difference being that upon having a family it seemed to become that much more difficult for women to pursue their art. This is not to say, of course, that men were unaffected by having a family; they certainly were, particularly in relation to financial matters. But for women, the change was often much more severe, much more of a sudden break in their lives. Most of them, it should be reiterated, would never have dreamed of giving up this part of their lives; raising a family was often extremely rewarding. It also meant, however, that their art would have to be placed still farther to the side, becoming that much more unreachable. And the reality of this sacrifice, rewarding families or not, often continued to haunt them, even when the objective circumstances may have been over and done with. Assuming the role of the artist when one was younger was difficult in its own right. Assuming it later on in life, even with one's nest empty, was not much easier. Some of them felt that it was too late to begin anew.

We also saw place and community to be salient factors in relation to the space of creativity. In a very basic sense, the primary problems that these individuals confronted in this context may be described in terms of isolation and inundation. As concerns the first of these problems, those who found themselves out of the mainstream of art, geographically, may have suffered not only the loss of community but the loss of certain kinds of art; each region, they suggested, had its own range of appropriate artistic modes, and it was necessary that they keep this in mind when it came time to go public. Unless they were willing to be complete mavericks, certain "accommodations" would have to be made. Those who fell victim to inundation, meanwhile, seemed on the whole to fare worse. This is because the art community, particularly in major urban centers, seemed to be filled with too many people in dire straits – financially, psychologically, and spiritually – to really work *as* a community. There were too many ulterior motives, some complained, too many calculated moves, and, more fundamentally, too much career-oriented egocentricity and selfishness for environments like these to be conducive to creativity. At an extreme, the entire situation could become sordid and ugly, such that everything and everyone always seemed edgy and strange, somehow essentially at odds with themselves and the world. Others, we saw, simply became bored with the art community, with its cheap mystique and, again, the single-mindedness of its inhabitants, which led them to become less "fully human" than many others. The artists in her community were exceptional, all right, one particularly bitter woman had said, but only because their range of interests was so lamentably small and their human concerns so tragically stunted.

Not everyone was this critical of the art community, of course. Some succeeded in finding a relatively secure and hospitable niche within which they could get some support and do their art. But the art community, as an informal agglomeration of like-minded others, was rarely discussed in positive terms. More often, it was discussed in terms of anxiety and uncertainty, of how fragile so many people's lives were. And even if they were to rise up from the depths and gain a measure of comfort and solace, there could still remain the fear that it could all be taken away with a mere clap of the hands of those who controlled their fate: Reminders were everywhere. Many were nothing short of shocked at the harsh realities they had found themselves living and were eager to find a new way.

Several of the conditions of creativity already considered are easily applied to the sphere of interpersonal relations, particularly insofar as they involve the need to be vigilant over the potentially harmful effects of the mystique of art and artist. By focusing specifically on the issue of gender, however, we may be able to further clarify some issues. A number of men in the group, as we have learned, had become so thoroughly trans-fixed by their desire to become successful artists that they fell into a predominantly instrumentalist mode of relating to oth-ers, including their wives and families. Notice the irony here: However expressive their yearnings might have been, indeed however much these yearnings themselves may have been tied to the desire to oppose instrumentalist thinking, many of them succumbed to exactly this. In speaking, for instance, of how some of them had used others, how they had employed them as actors and actresses in their own personal theaters, it had become painfully clear how crudely self-indulgent some of their motives had been. Now this very self-indulgence, of course, may have been construed by certain people as a neces-sary condition of creativity, particularly early on in their careers, when they were convinced that there was nowhere else to look but straight ahead, undaunted, into the future. Often enough, however, the results of their actions proved them wrong.

We need to be cautious in framing this particular issue. It goes without saying that the singleness of purpose for which artists are often noted remains valid on some level; creating art can be a consuming pursuit, and it would be foolish to suggest that it ought to be otherwise. In addition, the fact that there were some artists in the group whose singleness of purpose seemed to enhance both their creativity and their success belies the notion that it ought necessarily to be countered. For some people, therefore, the claim offered by one man – that you can either have great art or a great life, but not both – may be true, at least in the case of those who are hell-bent on realizing their artistic dreams. For those, on the other hand, who had elected to see if art and life could be brought together in some fashion, the story was a bit different.

In trying to extract a positive condition of creativity with these ideas in mind, I shall simply suggest that as a general rule artists would do well to couple their devotion to the muse with a measure of care for the others in their midst. This does not mean that all artists should get married, have children, and be

utterly devoted to their families. Nor does it mean that explicitly formulated social concerns must inform their art. What
it does mean is that in those cases where others enter into the
equation, they will have not only to be "reckoned with," instru-
mentally, but also to be accorded the attention they deserve.
Otherwise, the process of artistic creation may fold nar-
cissistically back on itself. There is a further implication as well,
and it is one that is of much more fundamental import. And
that is, alongside the requisite concerns for both oneself and
one's art there generally need to exist other-related concerns –
taken very broadly – for artistic creativity to proceed optimally.
Creativity must be infused with *care*, which derives in significant part from one's own relatedness to others and to the
world.

Women in the group often fell prey to the opposite syndrome
than the men. Unsure, perhaps, about both their own artistic
and personal capacities, their decision was often to forgo the
instrumental and to embrace the expressive, which in this context meant that they would live their lives more for others than
for themselves. Many of them were thus neither in the position
to create, as artists, nor to develop, as persons, to the degree
they wished they could. What was required in order to expand
the space of their own creativity and development, therefore,
was some measure of *self-worth*. This condition, like many of
the others, is easy to talk about but difficult to put into practice.
Indeed, self-worth, some of these women themselves might
have suggested, was not the main problem; having too many
responsibilities was. Lessen the responsibilities, they might
suggest further, and the space of creativity would undoubtedly
expand. There is surely some truth to this. My sense, however,
is that the problems cut deeper. For implied in the very feelings
of shame and self-betrayal that many of these women experienced is the idea that self-worth, rather than being something
that would emerge freely once their various burdens were removed, was something that had to be *earned*. Some of them
therefore spoke of having to prove themselves, to others as well
as to themselves; they needed to show that they were more
than dutiful wives and mothers. What they also needed to do,

more generally, was learn how to accord themelves the care and the respect they had often lavished upon others: Without some sense that what they were doing was valid and justified and real, the process of creating art would be irreparably harmed.

I shall not pretend to offer any simple solutions to the problem we have been considering; it goes to the very core of gender relations in our society. Certain art-specific dimensions of this problem may nevertheless be worth highlighting. However much they might have felt entitled to become artists, formally speaking, many of the women in the present group still believed that it would be an uphill battle, the main reason being that there still existed a quite definite masculinist ethos to the entire project (see, e.g., Broude & Garrard, 1982; Lippard, 1984; Nochlin, 1973; Parker & Pollock, 1987; Pollock, 1988). It may be that this situation has changed somewhat during the intervening years, given the rise of the women's movement. Back then, however, when women were just beginning to enter the ranks of what had been predominantly male activities, including art, it was no easy task to forge ahead without feeling belittled or reduced. As for those who elected to marry and have families, moreover, there was the further, more troubling perception that they were merely dabbling, that they were somehow trying, with their newly won "freedom" in hand, to make a statement, precisely about their own self-worth. Many of these women had to work that much harder, therefore, to prove that they were the real thing. This itself might have curtailed their creative activities. What also might have curtailed these activities was the supposition that they had to adopt the aforementioned masculinist ethos in order to become artists: Since it was either all or nothing, and since there were a whole lot of other things to do, many opted for the latter.

In light of what has been said here regarding the issue of self-worth, it follows that in addition to identifying, defying, and undermining the mystique of art and artist, there must exist the recognition that one's legitimacy as an artist and as a person need not be defined in terms that exclude others from their province. More generally, there is the need to believe that there are other ways of being an artist and of being a person than the highly individualized one that many – men especially – tend to employ. This is not to say, of course, that the project of artistic individuation is unimportant; neither men nor women can exclude themselves from the province of their own care without harming their creative activities in the process. Creativity, like human existence itself, needs to reconcile self and other and to establish a suitable balance between them. This much is a truism by now. What is not a truism, however, is the idea that there exist – or that there *should* exist – multiple paths toward becoming an artist. Some of these paths, insofar as they emerge in tandem with the mystique of art and artist, will no doubt remain highly individualized, serving, for better and for worse, to remove people from the mundaneness of everyday life; they will be exceptional paths, which will continue to affirm many of our notions of what artists have to be and do to reach their creative potential. Other paths, however, may be rather less individualized and will seek, once more, to integrate art and life, to show their possible compatibility. We need not privilege one over the other; they each have their place. But we do need to imagine ways in which some of the those paths that have suffered from being deemed illegitimate can be made more legitimate than they have been.

These issues also found their way into our consideration of place and community. Those who had found themselves isolated, we observed, were often either stripped of artistic reference points or alienated by the ones that existed; many of them seemed to want the company of more or less like-minded others. As for those who found themselves in the very heart of the art community, the problems could be more troubling still. I used the word inundation in this context, the idea being that these artists were somehow prevented from being alone enough to create as they wish; they were flooded with the strange and frequently ugly goings-on of the art world to such an extent that it could be difficult for them to return to their studios without feeling compromised, even defiled. Following what was just said, therefore, it would appear that herein lies another instance of the need for maintaining a suitable balance between self and other, between too little community and too much. Yet this rendition of the problems does not seem quite right. Perhaps it is justifiable to speak of there being too little community in the case of those who had found themselves isolated; they were unconnected, unanchored, and were thus condemned to create in what they might have experienced as a kind of vacuum or void. But can there ever be too *much* community? My own inclination is to say no, there cannot. Just as there can never be too much freedom – if freedom is understood in both *positive* and *negative* ways (that is, as freedom *to* and freedom *from*, respectively) – there can never be too much community either: If community is understood to be a "good," and if, as the saying goes, you can't get enough of a good thing, then it makes little sense to speak of artists being inundated by community per se; it is a contradiction in terms.

How then shall we try to understand the problems reported as we try to reconstruct more optimal conditions? What many of these artists came to realize was that they were not really members of a community at all, save in the most cursory sense: Even though people may have been living and working in the same place, there was little evidence that they were doing so *together*, in concert with one another. More often, it appeared, there was simply a collection, a mass, of fundamentally separated and isolated individuals, sometimes coming together to compare notes or to gather some much-needed solace, but usually staying quite apart (see, in this context, Bellah et al., 1985, for their discussion of "lifestyle enclaves"). Indeed, there was the sense that much of what went on around them actually served to counter and retard the possibility of community, the sense that this world they had come to inhabit was a kind of anticommunity, designed to prevent actively the formation of ties that truly bind. There was thus talk, once again, of using people and of being used, and of doing whatever was necessary in this competitive and often hostile environment for people to advance their own artistic projects and careers.

Along with care, therefore, the idea of *affiliation* becomes important in this context. As was the case with some of those discussed earlier, there might sometimes have been such a dogged and singular devotion to art and its various trappings that these people's very humanity seemed to atrophy along the way. Some of them knew it too, and it was hard to believe that a pursuit that had at one time seemed so very noble and pure should have become so thoroughly tarnished. Sadly enough, these artists too often felt unconnected and unanchored. The difference, however, was that their own anxious solitude had become magnified that much further through the presence of others whose plights were all too similar to their own.

Without going so far as to claim that artists need to belong to a well-defined collectivity in order to reach their optimal creative powers, it does seem fair to say that they cannot easily do so without some sense of affiliative belonging, some sense of true membership, in something larger than themselves. Now I say "cannot easily" here rather than "cannot" for a fairly simple and obvious reason: There are no doubt plenty of artists who go it essentially alone and do just fine; even if there are but a few like-minded others with whom to share some ideas, it seems clear enough that affiliation, in the sense that we are considering it here, is not to be regarded as a necessary condition of creativity. More concretely still, there is little reason to suggest that one *must* be a member of some art community in order to create optimally; there remains enough distance between what goes on inside the studio and what goes on outside it to render this claim suspect. It is no less obvious, however, that had some of these people become members of a community, bound through their own affiliation with one another, their own creative activities might have suffered less than they did.

Here again we must ask: How exactly is community to be brought about? In part, we saw, it can be brought about through exclusion: There was one story of women artists and another of black artists, for instance, who, having grown tired both of being banished to the margins of the art world and of going it essentially alone, had decided to band together in opposition for the sake of solidarity and strength. It is true, of course, that these communities remained on the margins of the art world, but there was at least a sense of mutuality and mission, a sense that they were indeed in it together. There were

271

also some who were less marginal who seemed to hold to much the same point of view, even if they had not quite put their principles into practice: Given the way that artists were treated by dealers especially and given as well that many of them had acquiesced to this treatment by becoming willing pawns in their dealers' crude games, there was the need, they believed, for artists to mount a front, to realize their own potential collective power. Without artists, after all, dealers would have nothing. In short, then, one of the ways in which communities might be formed and community itself brought about is through opposition and resistance to power, through "just saying no," as the phrase goes, to those who appear to control their fates.

As important as this opposition and resistance may be, however, there remains one glaring fact that looms large for many artists. And that is, as things have stood in recent years and as they stand presently, dealers and the like often *do* control artists' fates; they *do* relegate artists to the status of pawns in their respective games; and, perhaps most significantly, they *do* have lots of other artists waiting in the wings as replacements in the event that too many malcontents are unhappy with the way things are going. It hardly comes as a great surprise that the art world should seem to consist more of monads than of a community of people bound together by care and shared ideas: One false move, as several indicated, and a steadily evolving career can quickly become a memory. Nor is it a great surprise that the ethos of artistic "individualism" (the terminology of which we will question in greater detail later on) remains as pervasive as it is, its shortcomings notwithstanding. For it is precisely individuals, who concentrate single-mindedly on their own steady artistic evolution, who seem to fare best vis-à-vis the demands of the art world.

What we see, in short, is that there is no disentangling the problematic nature of the art community from either the mystique of art and artist or the highly individualized nature of the path to success. Perhaps more important, we also see that there is no disentangling any of these from the productive and consumptive demands of the field of art itself, ruled as it is in significant part by the power of capital. For the time being, then, let me suggest that the attainment of community, founded in and through affiliation rather than competition for scarce resources, is contingent on the restructuring of the field. Marx is again relevant here: Alongside self-alienation, he argued, there would also emerge alienation from others, in line with the competitive demands of the market; people could easily become pitted not only against the owners of capital, but against each other, the overriding assumption being that another's gain could not help but become one's own loss. This is surely one of the reasons why our own system, for all of its problems, is as resilient as it is: The very reality of people being pitted against one another is what keeps the wheels of production moving and, in turn, what prevents communities bound by affiliation from emerging as readily as they might otherwise.

BEYOND ALIENATED LABOR

The issues became more complex still when we moved on to consider the place of capital itself in the process of artistic creation. Teaching, you may recall, was the most prevalent means of earning a living for those in the present group. Interested in having the time to do their art, which a traditional nine-to-five job might not permit, and in remaining close to art, vocationally, many believed that teaching was the most sensible thing to do. What they did not realize, however, was that it was an extremely demanding and draining job. Moreover, it could be experienced as more problematic than other, less art-related jobs because however close to art itself it might have been, it might also have felt hopelessly far away in terms of what actually could be done; teaching was not the same as doing, and it could be experienced as a kind of tease. The job did not pay well either, particularly in the case of those teaching below the college level.

Teaching college, however, had its own share of burdens, not the least of which included the need for keeping up production. Exceptional though artists may have been in the eyes of their colleagues, it in no way excused them from the usual re-

273

sponsibilities; artists, like everyone else, had to maintain a steady stream of work – a research program, as we referred to it – in order to retain both respect and an ongoing paycheck. There was thus no waiting for the muse; the directives often came from without, and they had to be met squarely. It was not unusual to find that some works were indeed "produced" – which is to say devised as a means to the end of one's continued status as a member in good standing in the college community – rather than created: Demands had to be met. One final point about teaching should be noted. This is that teaching art, though it had been seen by a number of people as being a sacred occupation in its own right, seemed to have become progressively more secular and profane. Fewer students, some said, were taking art seriously and fewer students were coming their way; there were apparently too many more worthwhile and productive things to be doing. Some faculty and administrators appeared to feel this way as well. What is striking here is that the possible demise of art seems to have been considered not only by vanguard painters in New York, but by high school teachers, out in some lonely suburb or in the country's heartland. They too were concerned that art might be on its last legs.

The practice of commercial art was also seen by many to be a sensible pursuit. It was another way, they thought, of remaining close to artistic materials, close to the process of making things, and, if they were lucky, close to art itself. They, like teachers, were aware that there would be external demands – after all, they were laborers, working for a business – but they often felt that, given the variety of available options, this one was pretty good. Some in fact believed that they had a distinct advantage over teachers, in that they would be doing something rather than merely talking about it.

Many of those who elected to go the commercial route, however, did not fully realize how taboo their vocational "solution" was. Teachers, even if they were producing work as calculatedly as commercial artists, were at least doing this because they were forced to, because it was part of the territory. In the case of commercial artists, though, the reigning belief was that they could have been, and should have been, doing something different. Although many of them continued to do some fine art in addition to their commercial art, they might have gradually come to feel that everything they did, whether in the office or the studio, was somehow tainted and poisoned. In opposition to those who prayed to the God of art, these people had engaged in an unforgivable act of sacrilege, of ritual desecration, and they had to pay the price.

Some continued to enjoy their work, even if guiltily, and could still believe that there was sufficient compensation in what they did to make it justifiable. But there remained some serious problems. Foremost among these was the fact that they were often not the ones in control of their work; either they executed the work, in which case someone else would be responsible for its conception, or they conceived the work, in which case someone else would be responsible for its execution, the result being that their own place in fashioning the object would be partial and incomplete. In addition, however similar these objects were to fine art objects, they were nonetheless imbued with an entirely different kind of being; they were functional, a means to the end of creating capital. Because many of these individuals still retained magical ideas of what art and artists were all about – or, stated another way, because they were largely unaware of how similar fine artists' problems could be to their own – they could become filled with frustration, resentment, and envy, alongside their pervasive sense of guilt. Although they did hope to return at some point in the future, it was hardly surprising that some of them left their fine art studios and shut the door, tight.

Hustling was also taboo. Despite the fact that so many people had visions of grandeur and were willing to fight their way to the top, there was apparently the need to be subtle about their aspirations. Success was not something to be overtly orchestrated; it had to just happen, on the basis of one's art alone. Those who believed this strictly, of course, were often the ones who failed miserably and were bitter about how much hustling had in fact to be done. They might also have been bitter about their schooling at the Art Institute, which, with its stern rejection of the commercial dimension of art, had prevented them from learning what it actually took to succeed. It was almost as if the people there were in collusion with those who knew better, as if they had perpetuated the myth of the pure fine artist who might one day be discovered in order to separate out the aware from the unaware.

The truth is, no one talked about having been discovered. This does not mean, of course, that their work didn't enter into how they were appraised, only that in addition to their work they had to want success and to show that they wanted it. It is not surprising, therefore, that the most successful artists in the group explicitly discussed tactics they had employed, from early on in their careers, in order to get their work – and themselves – known. Nor is it surprising that those who were shut out of success often came to feel that talent was irrelevant. Once they saw who was making it and who was not, they felt they knew what the requisite conditions for success were. There may even be some truth to this idea. In some instances, unusual skill in hustling may not only be a necessary condition for success but a sufficient one; because modern art objects themselves are frequently so vaguely defined, there may emerge the suspicion that what is actually there in the art itself is indeed beside the point. But this is too easy and too cynical a way out of the problems at hand. Furthermore, there is no strong evidence for this conclusion; as a general rule, the art itself seems to matter. That hustling – or at least being "art worldly," we might say – is a necessary condition for artistic recognition and success seems, nevertheless, to be beyond dispute.

We must be cautious here in determining who or what is responsible for this. We have heard accusations, for instance, that suggest that artists themselves may be responsible, that some of them possess certain "traits," perhaps, that are especially conducive to hustling. There is surely some truth to this too. Those who hustle obviously have the ability; if they didn't, they couldn't have gotten where they have. At the same time, the evidence we have been considering points to the fact that these traits were adopted by artists largely as a function of their quite veridical perception of what the art world required. And

276

far from being purely "presentational," in the sense of being adopted strictly as a means to the end of getting somewhere, they were at least as often protective in nature. Recall in this context how dangerous some believed the business of art to be, how being art worldly could have meant little more than keeping one's mouth shut in the face of injustice or fending off the various vultures, swooping in for their kill. There was no choice but to be art worldly, it seemed, unless one was content to stay at home or stay local; by all indications, it was forced upon these artists by their very circumstances. Interestingly enough, this process of becoming art worldly might have served a useful purpose in some ways: Encountering the reality of the art world face-to-face could itself lead to demystification, such that the magical importance of doing art and becoming an artist became identified for what it was.

Early on especially, there was often an insatiable desire to be known and seen; it was extremely difficult to wait patiently for things to happen. Although some were unquestionably content with social recognition alone, in the form of simply showing their work and sharing it with others, it might also have been the case for others that the most visible sign that they were on the rise was in the money they received. As noted earlier, I do not mean to say that these people were doing art strictly *for* the sake of recognition or money, only that that these concerns inevitably seemed to creep into their various paths to affirmation or disaffirmation. These concerns also entered into their creative processes themselves. Those, for instance, who might have retreated from the mystique of the artist or the material realities of the art world may have felt that they were left empty-handed; there were no tangible signs that what they were doing was good or worthwhile. Those who embraced these, on the other hand, may have gotten so caught up in the desire to be somebody special and to have others know it that the process of creation may unwittingly have become transformed into a means rather than an end in itself. Many therefore arrived at the realization that they had been producing art objects, as it was put earlier, rather than creating them. Their work – not to mention their existence more generally – simply

277

could not be affirmed by themselves alone; it had to come from elsewhere, the unintended consequence being that they had become engaged in what can only be called alienated labor. This situation may not have changed much, even after one realized what had been happening; many remained very much dependent on others for both their artistic consolidation and their self-consolidation. The only difference was that they knew it and could deal with it, where before it might have taken them unawares.

This again testifies well to the coercive forces through which many of these individuals had been living and trying to do their art. For what they came to see, as we just observed, was that these very forces had apparently rendered them essentially unconscious for a spell, leading them to mistake what they had been doing for authentic, unalienated artistic creation. Indeed, it was precisely through their own process of coming to consciousness, whether via their own subjective alienation from their activities or the progressively massive reality of the field of art itself, that led them to the conviction that their motives had not been wholly their own. Again, realizations of this sort did not necessarily make the process of artistic creation more rewarding or enjoyable; coercive forces still remained. What these realizations did do, however, was make the process less opaque, such that they were finally free to decide what sorts of "accommodations" they were willing to make. This movement of coming to consciousness, which I referred to as desocialization, may have left people with little reason to do art once their true motives were revealed or, more positively, a real reason to do art, namely, to create. In this respect, it should be noted, the process was not unlike what happened for some when they identified the mystique of art and artist. While this phenomenon of desocialization was liberating in some ways, it might also have been accompanied by an uncomfortable awareness of the realities they had been confronting, and would continue to confront as time wore on: Despite the measure of freedom some of these artists had acquired through their own burgeoning sense of the ways in which they and their art had been determined, there was no getting around the fact that the works they created were indeed commodities and thus subject to the demands of the market.

This was no great problem for some. As one man in particular had indicated, there was no reason to expect the situation to be other than it was and no reason to whine about it; art was a business, plain and simple, and it was people's romantic illusions that it was something else that disappointed them so. They would be better off, he essentially said, treating it as a job rather than some magical calling; only then would they be able to purge themselves of the guilt and resentful anger they felt. One had to grin and bear it, he added, by entering the situation unabashedly and milking it for all it was worth. This way, he believed, the space of creativity could gradually be made to expand. Most others, however, were not nearly so upbeat about either the business end of art or the possibility of expanding the space of their creativity through subtly manipulating the system. For one, the creative process itself would inevitably remain subject to a kind of calculus if one operated in this way; it would occur in conjunction with, and as a function of, the "moves" one was willing to make and the risks one was willing to take. Some people, you recall, had grown tired of exactly this. Once there was the desire to take the work out of the confines of one's own studio, one former artist had said, the authenticity of the process seemed immediately to evaporate. The work became other than what it was; it became an entry into an equation and thus was irreparably tainted. There could be no accommodation for this man, therefore, no matter how minimal it might be; the price was simply too great. A further reason for others not being quite so upbeat was that even if accommodations were in fact made, it was unclear whether the space of creativity would expand in turn. As some suggested, it was only power that could do this in any truly significant way; and power, it was added, was largely a function of the capital one controlled. No one in the group controlled quite enough to be able to call his or her own artistic shots.

We have before us a very complicated situation. We could of course make it less complicated by arguing that these artists got what they paid for. Along these lines, some might wish to adopt the grin-and-bear-it thesis: Art is a business and if artists don't like it, then that's too bad; there is no reason why they should have it easier than anyone else, and they should stop their whining and get to work. As concerns federal subsidies and the like, this argument might continue, this is nothing short of absurd and wasteful; there is no reason why artists should be able to escape the laws of the market, particularly when taxpayers are footing the bill and when so much of what they do is utterly useless. We seem to be moving in this very direction right now. Others, from a somewhat less cold point of view, might wish to say that the *real* artist would have no concerns at all about what goes on outside the studio. He or she would simply create, from the heart and soul, and let the chips fall where they may. Some artists were able to do this and urged others to do the same, the best mode of resistance to the stern demands of the market and to utilitarian thinking more generally being to insist on remaining an unalienated worker, whatever the cost. From this perspective, then, artists themselves must take some responsibility into their own hands, by refusing to acquiesce to the prevailing world view, with its ugly, rationalized way of dealing with things; they must retain their radical edge by remaining true to themselves and their art.

In some ways, I find myself sympathetic to this latter perspective. There *are* artists, some of whom are in this very group, who had apparently managed to be true to themselves and their art above all else. They were willing to forsake the present "definition" of success, as one woman put it, even if it meant less fame and fortune, which it undoubtedly would. She, it should be noted, had a steady job at a prestigious university, which perhaps allowed her to be a bit more casual about this situation than some others, but the principle at hand nonetheless holds: Creativity will proceed optimally to the extent that one's motives are (predominantly) intrinsic rather than extrinsic; and this can only be accomplished to the extent that one is willing and able to resist the allure of capital and to forsake its various trappings.

The teachers and commercial artists we have discussed may be instructive in this context. Indeed, it might be suggested that they each provide limited cases of phenomena that are of fundamental importance for the process of artistic creation more generally. With reference to the first group, I am thinking especially of the fact that some of its members were in effect forced to produce works of art, even specific kinds of art in some instances ("relevant art research"), in order to comply with the demands of the academic institution of which they were a part. The results were predictable enough: Creative work does not mix well with production quotas, as both artists and nonartists alike well know. Again, this does not mean that work produced in order to meet these demands cannot be creative, for it surely can; a good artist working on demand will probably still be more creative than a bad one with all the freedom in the world. Moreover, it does not mean that artists working in this manner are necessarily less psychologically connected than they would be otherwise; external demands may even serve as a useful prod for some people, particularly for the chronically lazy or the fearfully uncommitted. They can help ensure that artists will on occasion externalize their passions and thereby prevent themselves from being crushed by their own weight.

These allowances notwithstanding, there is a certain sense in which art created in order to meet specific demands outside itself must inevitably be depleted. Following Marx once more, the idea is that, whether or not the artist is subjectively alienated in this situation, the relationship between subject and object is, objectively, distorted. To place the matter on the ontological rather than the psychological plane, the "being" of the artist cannot be fully expressed in an object that is "produced for" if the "for" in question has no intrinsic connection to the work itself and is contingent more on others' interests than one's own. Along these lines, we might note, the desires of the patron are generally to be distinguished from those of the academic administrator or the (primarily business-minded) dealer. For the first, there will likely exist a communicative relationship based on the (artistic) value of the work, but not, however, for the second.

The condition to which we are referring may be thought of in terms of *ownership*, which in this context should be taken to refer to an autonomously generated, self-possessed mode of artistic action. I realize that, given some of my more critical comments on market-related problems, ownership might seem like an odd term to use. To the extent that the owners of one's art (broadly conceived) are other than the artist, however, what emerges is precisely the aforementioned situation of "producing for." Ownership, therefore, rather than referring here to the possession of one's work as commodity, refers instead to the exact opposite: The reasons of the artist must be fundamentally his or her own for the process of artistic creation to proceed optimally. Let me hasten to emphasize that ownership, in the manner presently being considered, is thoroughly compatible with responsibility to others; by no means am I suggesting that artists must be faithful *only* to themselves or that they ought not to care about the destiny of their work. As I shall go on to suggest, in fact, it would appear that artists do indeed need to be faithful to something other than themselves, something that transcends the confines of their own immediate sphere of experience. But this is not to be equated with strictly external requirements of the sort that lead to producing for another.

A related condition of artistic creativity presents itself in conjunction with some of the issues discussed by commercial artists. Their most serious complaint, it seemed, had to do with the fact that their jobs often required that they work on the conception end or the execution end of their specific projects; rarely were they in control of both. So it was that, with the echoes of fine art still in their minds, they could become uncomfortable and alienated; and this, despite the fact that they probably knew from the start that the division of labor required it. Alongside the idea of ownership, therefore, we also see the importance of what might simply be called creative *wholeness* or continuity: As a general rule, the artist must own the entirety of the process, not just a part of it; otherwise creativity itself will have become divided and fragmented. There are some exceptions to this rule. Some artists, who may not have either the time or the inclination to carry out all of their own ideas, may leave the execution part to others without there emerging problems. Others, perhaps critical of the very notion of originality, may, for artistic reasons, elect to carry out ideas that others have conceived. In both of these cases, however, the partial nature of the process, rather than being dictated by another, has arisen out of a choice made on the part of the artist, thereby preserving, in principle at least, this condition of wholeness. Exceptions aside, if conception wholly precedes execution, there will ordinarily be a measure of discontinuity in the process, the fissioning of what is ideally a whole activity into two distinct parts. Some artists spoke of the difficulty of repeating themselves in this context, of having to reexecute ideas they had already conceived some time ago for the sake of maintaining production as well as their own continuous identities. What makes this difficulty so much more pronounced in the case of commercial art, of course, is not only that conception may precede execution but that different people may be responsible for each. This necessarily spells loss: in the first case of an end, in the second case of a beginning. The conceivers and the executors both exist in the form of halves, not wholes, and "creation" thus becomes less a continuous process than a two-part task.

Moving further into the arena of fine art, we shall turn first to the problem of hustling and try to determine what positive conditions may be implicated in it. As suggested earlier, there may be the temptation to see this problem as separable from the process of artistic creation. In certain respects, it is; it seems perfectly reasonable, for instance, to assume that someone who is an "excellent" hustler can also be an excellent artist. But a problem still remains in the extent to which there is any transfer at all from the self-objectification that is (necessarily) a part of hustling to one's own existence as an artist and as a person, whether in the studio or outside it. This implies that, although it may be possible to "resume" this existence after having been out on the streets pounding the pavement, it would appear to be a difficult thing to do. Individuals, unless they are wholly "situation-specific," are variously formed and deformed out of their practices in the world; they cannot simply abandon what they were at one moment and move on to be something entirely different. The point, then, is this: The process of artistic creation can only proceed in a fully connected way if there is a fully human subject doing the creating. I mean this not only in the sense of being able to be subjectively involved in one's work, which even the slickest of hustlers surely can, but in the sense of being an "undehumanized" subject: a person with a significant measure of control over his or her own destiny, as an artist and as a human being. Without going so far as to claim that artists must therefore be content to simply let the chips fall where they may, as we put it earlier, it would nonetheless seem imperative that they keep a watchful eye over their own entre-preneurial desires. Otherwise, their part-time hustling ac-tivities could become an all too integral part of their very existence, sapping them of just that humanness on which the process of artistic creation relies.

Of more central concern than hustling is the more pervasive way in which the social and material demands of the art world could infiltrate this process. This problem gets us back to sever-al of the conditions already enumerated, especially true desire and ownership. For what we learned was that many of these artists had themselves been producing for, as I have called it, without their being fully conscious of the fact. The problem in-volves much more than mere influence. It would be both overly idealistic and wrong to suggest that artists should be able to carry out their activities utterly free and unfettered, and it would perpetuate exactly that ex nihilo conception of creativity that I have already cast into question. There is no getting away from the world, nor should there be. The problem is instead one of *control*, over oneself and one's work, which is exactly what some of these people, for a time at any rate, did not have. What is meant here by control? Not unlike what was said in our consideration of true desire, control may be said to involve a *true* – rather than a false – consciousness of the very activities in which one is engaged.

Needless to say perhaps, true consciousness, as I am discuss-ing it here, is not to be equated with wholly transparent con-sciousness, as if artists should be able to know, through and through, why they are doing what they are; this would not only be to ignore the possible unconscious and preconscious roots of at least certain forms of creativity but to diminish the possible articulative function of artistic activity itself. In speaking of true consciousness, therefore, I in no way wish to exclude other-than-conscious influences on one's art. In a certain sense, in fact, true consciousness in this context refers less to consciousness per se, taken as a discrete form of subjectivity, than it does to the relationship between inner and outer determinants of the creative process, a relationship that is sometimes rendered problematic by virtue of artists mistaking the latter for the former. More simply: If false consciousness in the present context refers to the unwitting appropriation of artistic directives that are other than one's own, the attainment of true consciousness refers to the disappropriation of these directives, such that one comes to understand what might previously have been opaque and occluded, namely one's very motives to create.

"Alienation," Marx writes in the *Economic and philosophic manuscripts of 1844* (1964, p. 151), "is apparent not only in the fact that *my* means of life belong to *someone else*, that *my* desires are the unattainable possession of *someone else*, but that everything" – including, in some cases, the process of artistic creation – "is *something different* from itself, that my activity is *something else*, and finally . . . that *an inhuman power* rules over everything." Only when this "inhuman power" is able to be identified as such, therefore, can the artist begin to move from false to true consciousness and thus to a more optimal situation for creating works of art. In sum, then, true consciousness entails having reasons for doing one's art that are not only manifestly one's own, as they often were, but truly one's own, as they often were not.

Now, the need for attaining ownership, artistic wholeness, and true consciousness is itself contingent on there existing social and material forces that prevent these from fully emerging. Stated another way, to the extent that these forces remain in operation, artists will need to identify and defy them. Indeed, I hope that some of the findings related here will be in the service of this: If artists can be made more aware of those forces that can take them unawares, perhaps they will be able to expand the space of their own creativity beyond where they would have otherwise. As we have also noted, there exists the need not only to identify and defy forces of the sort we have been considering, but to undermine them wherever possible so that this need itself becomes diminished. But how is this possible? That is, how, aside from identifying and defying those forces that lead to alienated artistic labor, can artists move beyond it, into unalienated labor? Firm determination and resolve are obviously necessary, as was suggested earlier; among other things, freedom entails the capacity to say no, to take a stand in the face of that which would determine one's fate. There are at least two fundamental reasons, however, for why determination and resolve, though necessary, are not sufficient to right the matters in question. The first is that they rely on an awareness of these matters, which, again, some may not possess. The second, and more important reason, is of course that enduring changes in the "proximal" conditions of creativity require structural changes in those "distal" social and material conditions through which they emerge. Let us therefore reframe our questions as follows: How can the social and material conditions of creativity be transformed in the direction of providing more optimal psychological conditions in which to create?

From a strict Marxian point of view, there is but one way: the overhaul of the field. This is unlikely, for reasons that are no doubt obvious enough. Less severely, there could be increased funding from both the public and private sectors, which might allow artists to be less beholden to and dependent upon the ups and downs of the market. Given the recent climate (and government), with its conservatively based disillusionment with much of contemporary art (which seemed to reach a kind of fever pitch during the Mapplethorpe controversy), this too seems unlikely, at least in the near future. There could also be grass-roots movements formed by artists themselves, geared toward humanizing the field, making it more fit for habitation. Some of these are already in place, and even though their effects may not ultimately serve to make as large a dent in the power structure as some might wish, they cannot help but be of some value in transforming the status quo. Are there any other practices, any other concrete modes of action, that can work toward effecting this transformation? My own inclination, which, admittedly, resides largely on the principle of *hope* – in the capacities of human beings both to become conscious of their historical existence and to transform their worlds creatively – is to say yes, there are. And what I am referring to here are those practices, those concrete modes of action in and on the world, that can be subsumed under the rubric of art itself, which has the potential to at once indict the status quo and, through this indictment, point the way toward a better future. It is only fitting, then, to conclude this work by looking once more at some of art's own pathologies and seeing if there is anything to be learned from them.

ARTISTIC CREATIVITY AND SOCIOCULTURAL TRANSFORMATION

It is but a short step from the field-related problems we have just been considering to problems in the domain of art itself. If at the beginning of their careers especially many people fell victim to producing their art rather than creating it, later on in their careers, after waking from their artistic slumbers, they might have become victims once more, albeit of a different sort. Their own desocialization, despite perhaps having given them the requisite measure of psychic transparency to create more freely and optimally, did not necessarily provide them any further artistic tools. Once they were able to see what had been happening in their work and in their selves, therefore, there still remained the problem of how best to resume. The answer, for some, was in effect to invent an art form, to devise something that was theirs and theirs alone, something with a trademark or, more appropriately, a patent. Given the fact that the world of contemporary art was more or less devoid of tradition – or, put more positively, given its manifestly pluralistic nature – there was the need to establish a visible identity in one's work that could serve the purpose of differentiating one artist from others. There is of course something of an irony here: Invention, of the sort being considered, is not terribly dissimilar from production. Both are carried out with essentially – which is not to say exclusively – extrinsic ends in mind.

We often observed, in fact, that however inventive these artists may have been, and however singular, unique, and differentiated their work may have become, it was often necessary to fall back into the production mode itself. The fact of the matter was, it was very difficult for many to feel that they could make a significant move in their work, which is to say to create something new, without jeopardizing this singular identity they had fashioned; significant moves of this sort, far from being a sign of creativity to the consuming public and to the dealers who wanted to serve them, were instead a sign of creative disunity. There was thus the need to go with what worked, with what the people wanted, with what allowed them to believe that they were witnesses to the emergence of a steadily formed artistic project. Little did they know that this project, despite its possible veneer of organic authenticity, may have been quite calculated, a means to the end of continued marketability. This sitation was not a temporary one either. A number of people believed that this sort of strategy was but a phase: Artists, in order to get their foot in the door, had to make certain compromises in terms of the range of their output; once this happened, they assumed, it would be possible, finally, to become the artists they knew they really could be. To some extent, this did in fact happen. Once some of these artists made a good and trusting gallery connection, there might have been the opportunity to branch out. But this was rare. Instead, they often became locked into their own self-constructed identities and "traditions" and were forced to repeat themselves, sometimes with the slightest variations, in order that their careers not be cast into the pit of anonymity. They did not want to begin over again; the thought of doing so was too painful to bear.

None of this is meant to imply that these people were completely unable to be creative with their art. Some, it should be emphasized, simply refused to go the route of artistic uniformity and were willing to suffer the consequences. Others, even while recognizing the dilemma they were in, found enough room to move within their own body of work that they were able to live comfortably with themselves; sometimes they would get to be creative, sometimes not. The main thing was that they were aware of their circumstances and would deal with them as best they could. Others still, however, seemed virtually paralyzed by this dilemma and were either unsure of how they could begin or, if they had begun, unsure how they could continue. The patent, as I have referred to it, seemed to be necessary; this much most everyone seemed to know. What they also knew was that it could easily become the kiss of creative death.

On top of these more practical problems, there may also have been the much more unsettling feeling, among successful artists especially, that there was something phony about their success and about their art itself, that they were impostors, doing what artists did but only on the surface. Knowing what kinds of tactics had been required for their rise to success and seeing what their art had turned out to be – namely, either a variant of work they might have been doing 20 years ago or the latest postmodern thing, designed fundamentally to destroy whatever idols as might still remain – they may have felt awkward and uncomfortable about the fact that they were reaping the benefits of a thoroughgoing sham of what they believed art and creativity could be. There may have been a kind of mourning, in fact, over what art had apparently lost, such that these artists' memories were haunted by ideas, like the real and the true and the beautiful, that had somehow managed to become obsolete and anachronistic, appropriate at some other time or place but certainly not here, now. It was unclear why it had to be this way.

A number of artists wished that they had been hurled into an entirely different world than this one. In times past, they believed, there was a sense of tradition which provided artists with enough structure, enough of an experiential grounding, an ontological foundation, to allow for real – rather than mock – creativity. To be clear about this, these artists were by no means saying that they yearned for tradition because it would have dictated to them what they ought to do, in the sense of giving them a means to flee from the dizzying freedom before them. Rather, they seemed to be looking for some structure of common assumptions, about art and about the world, that artists might share and that might allow them to feel that they were part of a true community, partaking of a vision that transcended their singular, finite selves.

Not only was much of contemporary art essentially unbound by serviceable rules, and not only had it come to appear to some people as a free-for-all, a competitive and somewhat perverse game of searching futilely for something genuinely new to say; it was symptomatic, some suggested, of the very loss of a sense of the transcendent itself, a sense of something – some reality, some truth, some *God* – that existed beyond the all too mundane, all too earthly, concerns of the world. In addition to their longing for tradition, therefore, there were some who took their longing one step further, expressing sorrow over the fact that Nietzsche may indeed have been right in proclaiming that God is dead. Theology aside for the moment, there is, I want to emphasize, an extremely important message implicit in these longings: However important intrinsic motivation and the like may be in the process of artistic creativity, there were many artists who suggested that an art devoid of some fundamental reason for being *outside* the confines of the self could not help but come up short. Indeed, one of the most central problems for these artists was that they were often sapped of *both* intrinsic motivation, due to the presence of the coercive forces at hand, and what we might call *self-transcendent* motivation, due to the absence of an authentic reason for their art even existing. The result was that many of them were doubly depleted: In place of both intrinsic and self-transcendent motivation were the essentially extrinsic directives of the field and domain of art itself. Even if the art world was as pluralistic as the rhetoric indicated, therefore, it may still have been insufficient to open up the gates of creativity. Stripped of the artistic and ontological grounding through which they might have at least gathered a sense of creative resistance, artists might have found themselves staring into a frightening and saddening void (see Adorno, 1984; Fuller, 1980; Gablik, 1984; Hauser, 1979).

As we observed earlier, in any case, there is reason to believe that the art world was *not* as pluralistic as the rhetoric indicated, that were some definite exclusions being made, based on gender, race, politics, even specific styles of art. It also appeared that these exclusions seemed to cohere in some way – that they came together as a group, signifying some of our own cultural repressions. Rather than going into any great detail about this issue, I want to clarify but one point here. My attempt to call attention to these exclusions and taboos could be construed in libertarian fashion. From this perspective, it might be held that the art world, appearances notwithstanding, had fallen short of embracing true freedom for one and all; even though it had moved in the direction of freedom via pluralism, in other words, it did not go far enough, the result being that those on the margins were left as unfree as ever. There is undoubtedly some validity to this perspective. I want to suggest in addition, however, that these very exclusions and taboos, far from merely embodying the effacement of individual freedom, also embodied the effacement of exactly those self-transcendent motivations referred to earlier. For by and large, it was exactly those who wished to break out of the enclave of strictly personal (and, by extension, "purely artistic") motives and to attend instead to broader concerns – the community of women, the community of African-Americans, the world of nature, whatever – who were banished to the margins. Once again, therefore, even if artists might have been relatively free *from* some of the artistic constraints of times past (which is itself, of course, arguable in the present context), they were not on that account free *to* create what they saw to be meaningful art. The plurality at hand was a highly circumscribed one.

In addition to these specific forms of artistic exclusion, there was also a sense, according to some, in which the goal of meaningful communication was itself excluded. As these people came to realize, in light of the distance that had existed between their own (manifest) artistic desires and the interpretive "capacities" of the general public, they had often managed to seal themselves shut in their own essentially private artistic worlds, their own inability to create genuinely thus finding its correlate in the inability to speak, cogently, to others. Indeed, given that these artists themselves were sometimes unable to understand fully what they were doing in their work, it was hardly a surprise that others fared no better; artists and their audiences could easily become compatriots in their own mutual mystification.

Some of the people in the group, following the notion that there would inevitably be a significant gap between the knowing minority and the unknowing majority, decided that there was little choice but to accept this state of affairs; it was just too tall an order to be able to speak to the people. These were often the same artists, it might be noted, who never quite shook the mystique of art and artist; they remained exceptional, a cut above the masses, which is how it had to be. Others, however, decided to call a halt to this insularity by extending the sphere of their artistic concerns beyond their singular selves. Now on the face of it, as we noted earlier, this might seem like a calculated move in its own right, such that the process of artistic creation would become a means to the end of greater communication; because these artists could not simply wish their way to a broader audience, in other words, something would have to be done, consciously, in order to achieve the desired end, thereby tarnishing the spontaneity of the process itself. What most of these people found, however, was that the kind of change we are considering here, rather than further constricting the space of their own creativity, actually deepened and enlarged it: Now that they were doing their work with others in mind – which, again, is not to say explicitly *for* them – their creative energies seemed to be liberated. The main deterrent, in short, was when there was nobody there but themselves. We must not mistake what happened in this context for the need for extrinsic motivation or some such thing; that is not at all what seemed to be going on. Rather, what these artists showed in yet another way was that an art that failed to transcend the confines of the self was but a pale replica of what art was or could be. In some ways, of course, it could be argued that the intrinsic motivation idea is in fact confirmed in this context, for it was exactly when these people returned to their true, inner motives that the space of communication expanded; intrinsically motivated artistic creation, then, may solve the problem of communication by itself. This perspective is fine, I think, but with one important qualification: Intrinsically motivated artistic creation must include *within* it some form of self-transcendent motivation as well.

"Born again" artists aside for the moment, it was clear how futile some felt contemporary artistic endeavors to be. Not only was it seen to be false in certain important respects, particularly in regard to the mystique in which it continued to be bathed, but as a number of people suggested, there wasn't much being done that was any good. Both art and artist were in the end mute, some complained, and there was little prospect of having their voices restored in the near future: Its meaninglessness and superfluousness ran too deep. Notice that we have come full circle in a sense, the problems we are considering here being bound up once again with profound fear and doubt. This time, however, these emotions are being linked not to the *presence* of art's magic but rather its *absence*. We can only hope that there is some middle ground to be found. Let us explore in more detail the four problems just reviewed, toward the end of reconstructing the more optimal conditions of creativity implied therein.

Returning to the problem of the patent, which was discussed in relation to the progressive pluralization of the domain of art, there had arisen the need for artists to fashion traditions of their own. These self-traditions, it was emphasized, were in large measure wrought out of necessity; the market demanded them. As for the result, several of those highly individuated artistic projects we spoke of earlier had become played out in the form of more or less discrete artistic identities, spinning out variations on set themes. Judging by appearances – that is, on the basis of observing the seemingly steady evolution of artists' work – one might be led to suppose that these projects served as testimony to the much-discussed individualism and freedom extant in both the art world and the wider world: Having left behind the putative shackles of more inclusive traditions, artists, like many others, seemed to be in the midst of charting their own incomparably unique destinies. This, however, would be a mistake. For what their own steady evolution often signified, rather than the primacy of the individual or the realization of freedom, was in a sense their effacement. What was present in many cases was precisely the veneer of the individual, along with the veneer of unalienated artistic creativity and development. And beneath this veneer, they suggested, there was often anxiety and fear, owing to the danger of their losing some of the ground they had managed to gain.

Along the lines being drawn here, it can plausibly be argued that at least a portion of the recent onslaught against individualism (in, for instance, Bellah et al., 1985) may be somewhat misplaced, the idea being that much of what *passes* as individualism may actually be something quite different, something that is itself an artifact of social and material forces geared toward fashioning the illusion of self-determination. We will return to this issue in greater detail shortly. For the time being, what I shall suggest, in light of this illusion, is that one of the conditions of artistic creativity is in fact the possibility of artistic *self-determination*, taken here in the broad sense of an artist's capacity to create works of art that are more fully in line with his or her own interests than someone else's. Without this factor of self-determination, there can not only be repetition, largely for the sake of complying with demand, but a potentially disabling sense of impostorship, a sense of impersonating the very artist one might wish to be.

This is not a plea for infinite freedom or for self-determination wholly devoid of outer influences or for artistic heterogeneity rather than continuity. As concerns continuity, for instance, it is undoubtedly necessary and desirable on some level; there probably ought to be some organic connection between the different works an artist creates. But continuity is not the problem here. The problem is where it comes from, whether it is predominantly internally generated, in line with a real developmental project, or predominantly externally generated, in line with maintaining one's own existence as a marketable artist. What has happened, in short, is that pluralism and its attendant material requirements have led to forms of artistic "individuality" that have themselves been produced rather than created, the result being that some artists have been left with the strange suspicion that their entire career might be an "intellectual construction," a simulacrum of what a more authentic career might be. Appearances notwithstanding, therefore, it was exactly the relative *dearth* of self-determination that was responsible for their plights. Once again, of course, it could be argued that artists themselves were at fault. The Sartrians among us, for instance, might wish to say that they had abdicated both their own freedom and their own responsibility, to themselves and to others, by bending, willfully, to either those in power or to their own ignoble desires. There is undoubtedly some truth to this. But this truth ought not lead us to lose sight of the undeniable force of the productive and consumptive apparatus within which these artists were enmeshed.

Lest this condition of self-determination seem too uncritical an affirmation of individualism itself, it should immediately be noted that alongside laments about the relative dearth of self-determination were laments about the relative dearth of a tradition outside the self, one that might provide the self, as suggested earlier, with a greater measure of creative freedom than had been possible. Far from claiming that artists ought to be left wholly to their own devices, then, the idea was exactly the opposite. Being left to one's own devices, despite appearing to be in the interest of freedom, actually diminished it, by removing the very soil in which it takes root. Notice what is being said here: Self-determination, rather than being antithetical to the maintenance of tradition, is its dialectical counterpart, its very existence being contingent upon there being a meaningful enough foundation upon which to grow. There is a further implication as well, namely, that traditions of the self, particularly insofar as they are tied to market demands, are in a certain sense predicated upon the obliteration of traditions outside the self, the goal being the production of new and improved "goods." This implies, in turn, that artistic pluralism is not only at odds with the maintenance of tradition but actively opposes it.

Now this factor of tradition, it must be reiterated, is not to be associated with the static and unchanging, with hard and fast immovable rules with which artists must comply. Nor is it to be associated with artistic uniformity or singleness of purpose. Nor, finally, is it to be associated with nostalgic yearning for the past or a harking back to the supposedly good old days, when art was real and pure and secure in its moorings. Instead, tradition involves the opportunity for meaningful dialogue and exchange, among different voices, past and present, about the worth and value of the domain in question. "A living tradition," MacIntyre (1981, p. 207) writes, "is an historically extended, socially embodied argument, and an argument precisely in part about the goods which constitute that tradition." And far from being tied to the alleged virtues of the past alone, MacIntyre continues, "an adequate sense of tradition manifests itself in a grasp of those future possibilities which the past has made available to the present."

In addition to the condition of self-determination, therefore, artists must as a general rule experience themselves as active participants in a collective project of one sort or another, one in which there exists the possibility of drawing upon some semblance of a common world, a world that transcends their own singular sphere of life. Needless to say perhaps, the features of this common world need not be appropriated in identical fashion by all members, nor must these features be affirmed rather than negated; there is ample room for difference in the context of a truly *living* tradition. We might even move a bit further in this direction by saying that not only is there ample room for difference in a living tradition but that a living tradition is in a certain sense the *only* vehicle for the emergence of difference itself: Without "identity," we might say, there can be no difference, save in the most cursory and anomic way.

As a correlate of the condition of participating in a living tradition, there is also the aforementioned condition of self-transcendent motivation, which suggests, again, that self-determination must bear within it not only the freedom from external constraints but the freedom to create meaningful works of art. And this, I would hold, is only possible against the backdrop of a more or less definable tradition. Stated another way, artists, in addition to the need for being free to create in accordance with true desire, must also have the opportunity to be responsible and devoted to something larger and more comprehensive than the frequently circumscribed rules of the artistic games they are sometimes forced to play. It was easy to become lost in these rules, some complained, trapped in the specificity of language, and to feel that these rules were ultimately arbitrary and accidental, that they had no real reason for being, that they were in fact ordained by others. Both intrinsic and self-transcendent motivation were thus effaced. Also effaced was any *moral purpose* art might have. This is yet another requisite condition for the artistic creativity to proceed optimally.

Those who fell victim to some of the domain's exclusions, interestingly enough, were often those who had adhered in a thoroughgoing way to both self-transcendent motivations and the notion that art did indeed have a moral purpose to which they were responsible. A number of women, for instance, had become interested in pursuing somewhat more collective concerns, as had some African-American artists (whose under-representation in the present group is telling in its own right). There were some who spoke of incorporating their political or their religious concerns into their art as well. Having perhaps rejected the notion that art's responsibility was only to itself and that an art with a "mission" was inevitably a compromised and impure one, these individuals often decided to forge ahead with their concerns, however antiquated, retrogressive, and unartistic they might have been deemed to be.

It is difficult to make adequate sense of this phenomenon. We could of course simply say that the works these artists created didn't have currency in the art world, either artistic or monetary, and that as a result they were effectively banished. We could also say, as we did earlier, that the pluralistic nature of the art world was a much more limited one than it may have appeared to be. The fact that some artists had elected to continue working representationally, only to find that this was taboo in some quarters, indicates clearly enough that this was so. What this pluralistic art world seemed to demand, was – for lack of a better way of putting it – pluralistic art, that is, art that served to

297

testify to the very freedom and individuality that pluralism was thought to engender. Why, then, the specific nature of the exclusions that had emerged? It could be, I suggest, that those artists whose work embodied not only real freedom and individuality but transformative social and moral concerns were threatening, both to their fellow artists, who might have abandoned these kinds of concerns for the sake of their livelihood, and to those in power, who might have had a vested interest in seeing that things remained largely as they were.

I do not want to take this line of thought too far; among other reasons, there are, arguably, enough "specifically aesthetic" factors responsible for these exclusions (the rise of formalism, an increasing emphasis on the autonomy of the artistic object, and so on) to render it sketchy and incomplete. More generally, issues of this sort can help to remind us that even while social and material factors undoubtedly exert considerable influence in determining what forms of art are and are not legitimized, we ought not to think reductively about how this happens; the domain of art is much more than a mere epiphenomenon of the productive and consumptive apparatus to which we have been referring. It is nonetheless difficult to understand the specificity of the exclusions documented without at least being mindful of other than specifically aesthetic factors.

In any case, in line with a number of the conditions of creativity just enumerated, we have found that artists must be able to create works of art that are not only personally meaningful but socially, culturally, politically, and spiritually significant, works that are concordant with what they consider to be the most pressing and important issues in their lives: as women, as African-Americans, and so on. More simply, they need to be able to feel and to believe, should they so desire, that what they are doing is legitimate and worthwhile, even if it runs counter to the dominant view. And this, as I have already suggested, is only possible in a community with enough sense of tradition that it is able to include others, different others, in the "historically extended, socially embodied argument" referred to earlier. The extent to which this argument was able to be carried out is unclear. Indeed, even though there may have been *manifest* differences aplenty in the art world, the evidence presented here suggests that *real* differences were either suppressed or lost amid the din of the plurality of voices eager to speak their respective pieces.

Now, these individuals whom we have been considering were, as we have said, often interested in speaking not just to themselves or their fellow artists or to those "in the know," but to some larger sphere of others; they were insisting not on a private language, but a public one. It is at this juncture that the issues become clearer still, for correlative with the relative dearth of self-determination, some sense of a living tradition, self-transcendent motivation, and so on was often the dearth of *communication* itself: There was just so much that one whose artistic "individuality" had been devised as a means to the end of one's continued sustenance and perpetuity as an artist could speak to others. What was required for these artists to extend the space of communication, to reach beyond the elite and to speak to those more ordinary folks whose lives deserved a greater measure of artfulness? In a sense, we again come full circle. For what seemed to be required, first and perhaps foremost, was true desire, which for many seemed to hold within it exactly those expressive and communicative possibilities that might have been lost in the shuffle of becoming the artists they had become.

Rather than implying that creativity should be a means to the end of communication or that artists must try to communicate with others as best they can because it is their responsibility to do so, implied instead is the notion that creativity, at least in its more optimal forms, is *itself* inherently communicative; it is about sharing, even giving, something of one's own to others. This is indeed the true meaning, it might be suggested, of having artistic "gifts," a meaning that has apparently become debased over the course of time. There was more than mere guilt at the fact that some of these artists might have shut others out through the years, depriving them of being able to receive these gifts. For some, there was also the feeling that they had been unfaithful to the process of artistic creation itself. Art, they realized, has to be communicatively viable and valuable, and the end of communication, rather than being extrinsic to creativity, was at its very core. It was exactly when these artists came to recollect their true desires and to set them in motion in their art that the expansion of the space of communication became possible.

THE FUTURE OF ARTISTIC CREATIVITY

There is implicit in this scenario I have just related a hope, rooted in the dialectical process of artistic development some of these artists underwent. For these artists themselves, it is important to note, there wasn't much talk of overhauling the field or looking toward a more equitable distribution of resources or even, for that matter, of resisting the powers that be through political action. Instead, they spoke of how they had managed to rediscover the redemptive and emancipatory power of art itself. In this respect, they were able to sow the seeds of their own desocialization and disalienation and, subsequently, move on to create works of art that emerged out of the inseparable duality of freedom and responsibility, art that would necessarily find its way to others and, if all went well, move them to a different appreciation of the world than had previously been possible. What is the hope of which I am speaking? This hope, which is avowedly rooted in a kind of humanism, is that artists themselves, on recognizing and actualizing true desire, will create works of art that are constructively transformative of the world, works that show, through their very existence, that there are other human passions than the crudely instrumental ones that often achieve the upper hand in our lives.

Whether these works of art can significantly transform the field and the domain of art itself, such that conditions more conducive to creativity can eventually emerge, I cannot say. I certainly hope so. They cannot, however, effect this transformation alone, without the help of those more far-reaching structural changes referred to earlier. I would have liked to put more flesh on these changes, in the sense of offering more concrete ways for sociocultural transformation to occur. But I am not quite sure, even after having read and thought about this issue a great deal, what exactly needs to be done to provide a better climate for artists. This is because the variety of problems they have faced and continue to face, far from remaining the sovereign possession of the world of art alone, are in certain important respects *everyone's* problems. I refer especially to the longing for both creative work and community, to the corruption of some of the practices we engage in by the intrusion of demands that are in others' interests rather than our own, and, more generally, to the rationalization of contemporary life itself, which has left us with both a society and a culture that are all too fragile and tenuous and that often do not meet our human needs.

It would be easy enough, following the Marxian line of thinking, to assume that these human needs will one day prevail, that through the dialectical march of history we shall eventually be able to call a halt to some of the corruption and the suffering that surround us. There has been evidence in these pages in support of this idea: Many of the artists with whom we spoke, through their own praxis in the world and their own coming to consciousness about their real interests and desires, did indeed call something of a halt in this manner; they were thus able in some way to effect both their own redemption as well as that of others by recognizing more fully the profound interconnection between the two. There is an important point implicit in this idea. However much the earlier Marx especially adhered to a kind of Romantic humanism, based in significant part on the notions of self-determination and self-realization, he was hardly one to focus on the self alone, to the exclusion of others, which is exactly what distinguishes his own form of socialism from liberalism. As Eagleton (1990, p. 224) puts it, following Marx, "We should foster only those particular powers which allow an individual to realize himself through and in terms of the similar free self-realization of others."

More to the point still, Marx offers us an alternative to that sort of "bad" or "premature" utopianism which "grabs instantly for a future, projecting itself by an act of will or imagina-

301

tion beyond the compromised political structures of the present," and which thus fails to attend adequately "to those forces or faultlines *within* the present which, developed or prised open in particular ways, might induce that condition to surpass itself into a future." There is again a measure of hope involved here, tied to the idea that "oppressive social orders, as a matter of their routine operations, cannot help generating the kinds of forces and desires which can in principle overthrow them," that history itself can be transformed by those most "contaminated" by it: "In a condition in which the powerful run insanely rampant, only the powerless can provide an image of that humanity which must in its turn come to power, and in doing so transfigure the very meaning of that term" (pp. 229–230).

There is an important qualification that must be emphasized in this context. Although Marx was not one to reify human nature, there nonetheless remains the sense that he continued to hold a decidedly positive image of what human beings at least *might* be in a less alienating and alienated world; not only were they capable of realizing their own real interests and desires, but there was the idea that these were potentially good, that they were the key to a better and more just existence. I leave it to you to decide on the validity of this image. My own sense, in any case, is that while the situation we face is far from hopeless, it remains unclear whether we are in fact in the midst of a redemptive march toward the future. It is also unclear, I should add, whether structural transformation of the sort Marx envisioned is the most suitable means of excising some of our present pathologies. Although the social and material base of operations is undoubtedly a major contributor to these pathologies, and certain structural changes would undoubtedly be in the service of moving toward a greater measure of health, we ought not minimize the transformative potential of culture itself, whether in the form of art in particular or in the more general form of human beings gathering themselves together morally toward the end of fashioning a more habitable world.

This is essentially the takeoff point for works like Bellah et al.'s

Habits of the heart (1985), which many deem of singular importance in its brave attempt to chart the terrain of contemporary American life. Without in any way denying the force of Marxian ideas, many of which are implicit in much of what these writers have to say, their concern is indeed largely with the specifically cultural dimension of the problems at hand, particularly as manifested in the troubled relationship between American individualism and the search for community. The basic thesis is a Durkheimian one: What we need most of all is a communitarian revamping of the status quo, which will allegedly lead to a less anomic, fragmented, monadic world than the one we live in. Now those who adhere more to the Marxian line, of course (see, e.g., Jameson, 1988), will have trouble with this perspective, in that it fails to attend adequately to the social and material conditions that give rise to the cultural conflicts and contradictions in question. Moreover, as Jameson, among others, has rightly noted, it has been easy for Bellah et al.'s work to be appropriated by the right wing and used as an indictment of liberalism. It is nonetheless difficult to disagree with much of what these authors argue: We *do* live in an anomic world and there are enough points of departure for transforming this world within the scope of culture itself to recommend, for the most part, the perspective being offered.

As I suggested earlier, however, there are at least two problems with this perspective that are especially pertinent to the substance of the present book. The first is that (some of the uglier strands of contemporary) individualism is understood to be a "cause" of a good share of the ills we face. To be fair about this point, I am not suggesting that these authors are endowing individuals with naturally egoistic motives or some such thing; they are sociologically astute enough to know that the individualism of which they are critical has arisen in history. In addition, given that their mode of analysis is avowedly cultural, we ought not to chide them too much for those modes of analysis they left out. At the same time, it is difficult to escape the conclusion that the specific "brands" of individualism we presently encounter signify, for them, much of what is wrong in the world. Why is this problematic? In a distinct sense, it amounts to blaming the victim, which, of course, is what the right wing often seems fond of; perhaps as a way of exonerating some of those larger institutions that may actually perpetrate some of the crimes in question, the decision is that we may in fact have carried the whole individual freedom idea too far. In the wrong hands, it is but a short step from this point of view to the removal of some of those freedoms that presently exist, which, again, is exactly what the right often seems inclined to do. I do not wish to remove responsibility from the shoulders of individuals; there are lots of irresponsible people running around, and to place upon them the noble status of victim would be wrong. I am simply not convinced, however, that it is the "excesses" of either individualism or freedom that most deserve our critical attention.

Indeed, and again, I am not convinced that there *can* be an excess of either of these. Instead, I suggest that what has often passed as individualism is better understood as mock or pseudo-individualism and that what has often passed as freedom is better understood as a cloak for the very unfreedom it disguises. Bellah and company recognize this on some level: In drawing on the distinction between "freedom from" and "freedom to," which we encountered earlier, they realize that what passes as freedom now, in the present, is actually a bastardization of a far richer, more comprehensive idea. Nevertheless, the enduring antinomies between the individual and the social whole, between individualism and community, and, perhaps most centrally, between freedom and responsibility, continue to be maintained, the basic idea being that the balance at hand must be tipped for any gains to be made.

My own perspective is not only that there *is* no intrinsic antagonism between individualism and community – with individualism in the present context referring broadly to a belief in the inherent dignity, worth, and value of human persons – but that the two are mutually constitutive of one another. Consider what we have learned, in a variety of different ways, throughout this book: It was both the individual *and* community that had suffered, and this suffering, rather than being a function mainly of the excesses of the former – present though they often were – were often a function of those false images and motives and wishes that had occluded the very individuality they had appeared to express. If we are to level the blame for some of our present problems on individualism, therefore, we should at least recognize the caricatured, reified, and distorted forms it has assumed, which in certain important respects run exactly counter to individuals' – and communities' – own best interests. Lasch (1988, p. 180) puts the matter well: "It isn't just that individuals are tempted by unworthy ambitions but that the institutional structures in which these practices are carried out almost unavoidably underwrite and legitimize these ambitions." We are talking, in other words, not about the excesses of individualism but about its corruption, and in particular about "the corruption of practices by institutions," as Lasch succinctly puts it. And it is precisely this corruption that plays itself out in those "communities" artists and others have come to inhabit.

We must therefore think dialectically about these issues, which in the present context means that we must continue to think about the complex interpenetration of self, culture, and society as it pertains to becoming both an artist and an individual. Individuality, like creativity, is itself socioculturally constituted, which implies that its very capacity for being transformed resides, in part, in the various "institutions" of which Lasch and others speak. At the same time, however, individuality and creativity, rather than being mere "effects" or epiphenomena of these institutions, bear within themselves the capacity to transform them in turn. We have seen both of these processes in action here: Even in the midst of recognizing the extent to which their desires and activities had been constituted, even determined, from without, many of the artists with whom we spoke had managed to clear a larger space for their own self-determination and thus their own creativity. This space, moreover, rather than confining them in their own private worlds, often led them out of these worlds, toward others.

Bellah and company are therefore quite right to urge us to move toward a new, higher level of social integration. They are also right to claim that the transformation of economic institutions alone is not sufficient to meet this end; social, cultural, and psychological changes must occur as well. What requires further emphasis, however – and they do suggest this in their conclusion when they insist on the need for work to become more intrinsically interesting and valuable than it often is – is the idea that individual self-realization, which finds its living embodiment in artistic creativity itself, must be affirmed as strenuously as possible. Tolstoy (1924), among others, said as much when he argued that ideal forms of artistic creativity and expression were a vehicle for uniting human beings, for allowing them to share with one another some of those thoughts and feelings they had in common and thus to see that they were part of a larger whole. Whether or not the future of artistic creativity will culminate in this salutary outcome is difficult to say. It is largely up to ourselves to decide.

Let me try to bring some of these ideas together with a few brief closing comments. It should be clear that the conditions that have been enumerated in this chapter may be applied to much more than artistic creativity alone; they may be applied to *human* creativity and, by extension, human development as well. Indeed, to the extent that we speak of creativity in *human* rather than exclusively artistic terms, we may find that the dividing line between art and life is not so hard and fast as we sometimes assume. Yet right now there is such a dividing line. It is exactly in the context of this dividing line, in fact, that we can place the mystique of art and artist, the unabashed desire for exceptionality in what frequently seems an all too unexceptional world, and the terribly high prices that are paid for them, both figuratively and literally. The truth is that the American artist seeking to forge a career over the course of recent years has often stepped into a giant lottery, whether in fright or excitement, only to find that the payoff was often decidedly more meager – psychologically, spiritually, as well as monetarily – than had been expected.

Perhaps there are some who believe that the situation that has been described here is not really a problem at all. It could, for instance, be argued that art is not a part of life, certainly not a necessary part at any rate, and that we are now witnessing the last gasps of a mode of human activity that may be in the process of running its course. Artists, from this point of view, may eventually become extinct in accordance with the demands of "progress," which is apparently pointing us in the direction of more practical matters. But there are also those who are disenchanted with this direction and who see in art the potential for injecting a measure of spirit into a world where life itself is too often lived uncreatively and unfulfillingly, a world where exactly these practical matters seem to take precedence over all else. Again, we have before us a choice: to either let things run their course or to try to devise ways of seeing to it that the space of both artistic creativity in particular and human creativity in general is enlarged. The choice is a moral one, in the sense of being inseparable from what we believe human life ought to be. It is also, I think, a clear one.

Appendix: The Artists Project

The present inquiry is but a small portion of an ongoing longitudinal study of aspiring artists who attended the School of the Art Institute of Chicago during the mid-1960s. The study, which began in 1963 under the direction of Professors Getzels and Csikszentmihalyi at the University of Chicago, was at the outset largely experimental in nature, the primary purpose being to find out how various cognitive abilities, perceptual abilities, personality characteristics, and so on were related to the creation of works of art (see Getzels & Csikszentmihalyi, 1966, 1969, 1975, 1976). Dealing with those schooled as fine artists as well as those schooled as advertising artists, industrial artists, and art educators, this earlier work provided valuable insights into creativity. Most centrally, what Getzels and Csikszentmihalyi learned was that at the very core of the creative process was not problem *solving*, as many previous studies had maintained, but problem *finding:* Those with a discovery orientation toward their work, rather than an already established idea of what they would do, generally produced works of art that were judged by experts to be better than the rest. Moreover, upon entering the world of art, it was these same individuals who seemed to gain the most recognition.

What they also found, however, was that there was much more to becoming a successful artist (not to mention a consistently creative one) than a problem-finding orientation. With these individuals out of school only a few years, it was already becoming clear that certain kinds of people would fare better than others, those who were more gregarious, those who could withstand the pressures the art world brought to bear upon them. But there were also a number of other things to be taken into consideration, things that indeed seemed largely out of the control of the artist. No matter how gregarious one was, no matter how forward moving, it was still possible to be stopped dead in one's tracks by the forces at work. The scope of the project had to be expanded.

Another study was therefore carried out. In 1980, some 250 out of an original group of 281 people were located, of which 208 completed questionnaires dealing with basic issues related to their lives and work, over a span of nearly 20 years, both in and out of art (see Csikszentmihalyi, Getzels, & Kahn, 1984). On the basis of this information, many of the questions remaining from the first study could be addressed, particularly the more objectively based questions having to do with the relationship between those variables studied in 1963 and certain concrete outcomes in the 1980s, such as who had remained in art, how successful they had become, and how much they earned.

To gain a more comprehensive picture of those issues that were less easily addressed in the questionnaire format, a smaller group capable of providing the kind of information we desired was interviewed. Of the 208 individuals from whom questionnaires were received, 64 were selected, primarily on the basis of their involvement with fine art, whether in the past or the present, their proximity to Chicago or other places that were fairly accessible (particularly New York), and their willingness to talk with us.

My own portion of this project deals with 54 of the 64 people who were interviewed, my choices being made mainly on the basis of the first of the aforementioned criteria, their involvement with fine art at some point or other during the preceding 20 years of their lives. I deal with some of these people extensively, via comprehensive case histories; others, whose stories are less informative for the present purposes, more anecdotally. Of these 54, 28 are men and 26 are women, their ages (as of 1986, when an initial rendition of the present work, done as a doctoral dissertation, was completed) ranging from 42 to 69, for an average of 48 (47 for men, 50 for women). Forty-four (23 men, 21 women) had been fine art majors in art school, the remainder consisting mostly of advertising art majors. Fifty (28 men, 22 women) received their bachelors degree from the School of the Art Institute of Chicago, and 25 (16 men, 9 women) went on to do graduate work, some in Chicago and some elsewhere. Forty-six (24 men, 22 women) had been married at some point in their lives, 32 (16 men, 16 women) had remained married as of 1986 (with 18, 9 men and 9 women, having been divorced at some point), and 38 (20 men, 18 women) were the parents of at least one child. They were living in Chicago and vicinity (14 men, 17 women), New York and vicinity (5 men, 3 women), the rest being scattered anywhere from the American Southwest to Canada.

In terms of what they have been doing in recent years, the most frequently selected vocation was teaching. Of the 54 individuals studied, 38 (21 men, 17 women) had been teachers (with 20 of these, 12 men and 8 women, at the college level), while, tellingly perhaps, 19 (9 men and 10 women, with 5 and 8 respectively at the college level) have remained as teachers. There was no close second vocationally. There were advertising artists, industrial artists, business people, construction workers, and homemakers, but none of these vocations approached teaching in numbers. As is evident, though, these numbers are strikingly on the wane.

As for these individuals' level of involvement in fine art, 50 (27 men, 23 women) have been either very or moderately active in the creation of art at some time after art school, with 4 leaving immediately and 36 (18 men, 18 women) remaining active through 1986, whether through continuation or, in several cases, return. Of the 50 – and I should avow that there is surely some arbitrariness to decisions of this sort – 31 (22 men, 9 women) have been very active, having been engaged on an ongoing basis in the creation of art, while the rest have been moderately so, having been engaged less often or less intensively than the rest. Of the 36 who remained active, 21 (14 men, 7 women) were very active and the rest, again, just moderately so. Of those who have decided to leave fine art completely and have yet to return, there were 15 (9 men, 6 women). The majority of these people, it might be noted, expressed a desire to return to fine art in some way or other; very few saw themselves as having stopped their involvement in fine art for good.

Finally, and by way of presenting some idea of what the nature of their professional involvement has been, 41 (24 men, 17 women) have been either very or moderately active at some time after art school in showing and trying to sell their work (with 16 men and 5 women having been very active, the rest moderately), while 27 (14 men, 13 women) remained so (with 10 men and 3 women being very active, the rest moderately). Once again, there is some arbitrariness to these categorical decisions. Because in my estimation raw numbers of shows, for instance, could be misleading if taken as an index of serious involvement, I used my own best judgment as to how the group could most sensibly be differentiated. What is most important in any case is that we get some sense of what generally has happened over these years, of the basic directions in which the numbers point.

The interviews upon which the present work is largely based were conducted (in these individuals' homes or, wherever possible, their studios) between 1982 and 1984 by members of the research team, including myself. They were in-depth, semi-structured interviews lasting from 1 to over 6 hours, with most being between 2 and 3. With this in mind, I do not offer "clinical"-type interpretations, which require a great deal more time and personal contact. Nor do I provide detailed exegetical insights into these individuals' artwork; these too cannot be derived over the course of a few hours, no matter how intensive and involved the dialogue may be. I did have access to other sources of information about these individuals and their work (ranging from previous interviews to reviews of shows) and in many instances I made use of these, primarily as a means of either fashioning an interpretive context for the interview information or fleshing out details relevant to my own concerns. I deal, however, only with those issues that can properly and justifiably be addressed on the basis of the materials gathered.

With respect to the format of the interview, there were eight different versions, constructed mainly in line with personal and familial status (single, married, divorced, etc.). In terms of major differences, however, just two of these need to be described: one for those who remained in art, in whatever fashion, and one for those who did not. Given that it was sometimes difficult to decide exactly what these individuals' statuses were – for instance, some who professed that they had left art actually wound up doing more of it than others who professed to have remained – there was a fair amount of shifting between these two versions. As a general rule, in fact, we considered it to be of little consequence which specific version of the interview was used or whether questions were asked as they had originally been written or which order of questions was followed; the main thing was to cover, as thoroughly as possible, the topics of interest.

Each of the two versions of the interview began by asking for a historical sketch of what these people had been doing since art school. As appropriate, they were also asked what they had wanted to do upon leaving, what they actually did, what kinds of jobs they had had, what their family history had been, and what they were doing at the time. This was often the lengthiest portion of the interview; if additional information was provided at this initial stage, questions that would ordinarily have been asked later would be omitted, the most important thing again being that the main topics of interest were covered.

For those who remained involved in art, they were next asked to provide a historical sketch of their art itself, including information related to what kinds of work they had done, changes in style and content, as well as their ideas about art and what it ought to be or do and how this might have changed through the years. Then, after some further questions dealing with their present level of artistic activity, they were asked to describe the genesis of a work they had recently completed. Important here in addition were their ideas about how the work originated, what it was they were trying to do in it, who it was for, and what kinds of effects they hoped it would have on their intended audience. These last two areas were also asked about historically, the aim being to learn still more about the course of their involvement in specifically art-related matters.

They were then asked to describe what they were aiming for in their work more generally, if anything; what kinds of rewards there were, both intrinsic and extrinsic, in being an artist, if any; the process of trying to establish themselves in the art community; and finally, their own personal thoughts on what artistic success was all about and how they believed themselves to have fared in relation to it. Basically, then, the interview progressed from seeking information related to their careers and their art to information related to their present activities, after which time we moved back again to the history of their involvement with the field of art.

Those who had left art were asked to describe what their involvement with art had been and what kinds of work they had created, along with what they had gotten out of it, and why, ultimately, they had chosen to leave. After this, further questions were asked about how, since that time, they had experienced this decision, about whether there were regrets; about what sort of place art occupied in their lives presently, whether they expected or wanted this to change; and about what they had been doing since their decision to leave art and how they felt about it.

After this first section of the interview, both artists and non-artists were asked to go into greater detail about their personal and familial histories, especially as these had both affected and been affected by their respective artistic activities. Of particular concern were difficulties or dilemmas they had encountered in trying to reconcile this more personal side of their lives – for instance, the decision to marry or have children or to remain single – with the desires and demands that were part of what it meant to be an artist. They were also asked about friends, about their physical and psychological health, as well as about their ideas on such topics as art and religion, art and psychotherapy, the role of the artist in society, and the kind of advice they might be inclined to give to those just beginning in art.

The portions of the interview I have attended to most are those that deal most comprehensively with the history of these

313

individuals' various involvement or lack of involvement with art and their concomitant problems. Some of these problems were integrated into the interview schedule ahead of time. Because being an artist and being a parent, for instance, might well be at odds, some questions were explicitly problem-oriented. As noted earlier, however, the portion of the interview that asked about art itself was not formulated explicitly with an eye toward problems. Consequently, rather than asking specifically about problems having to do with selling art, for example, questions were more open-ended and thus more conducive to being answered in these individuals' own categories instead of ours. Once more, it is that much more striking that there was so much to be said about these problems.

References

Adams, H. (1978). *Art of the sixties.* Oxford: Phaidon Press.

Adler, J. E. (1979). *Artists in offices.* New Brunswick, NJ: Transaction Books.

Adorno, T. W. (1984). *Prisms.* Cambridge, MA: MIT Press.

Amabile, T. M. (1979). Effects of external evaluation on artistic creativity. *Journal of Personality and Social Psychology, 37,* 221–233.

Amabile, T. M. (1982). Children's artistic creativity: Detrimental effects of competition in field setting. *Personality and Social Psychology Bulletin, 8,* 573–578.

Amabile, T. M. (1983). *The social psychology of creativity.* New York: Springer-Verlag.

Beardsley, M. C. (1966). *Aesthetics: From classical Greece to the present.* Birmingham: University of Alabama Press.

Becker, H. S. (1982). *Art worlds.* Berkeley: University of California Press.

Bellah, R. N. (1987). The quest for the self: Individualism, morality, politics. In P. Rabinow & W. M. Sullivan (Eds.), *Interpretive social science: A second look.* Berkeley: University of California Press.

Bellah, R. N., Madsen, R., Sullivan, W. M., Swidler, A., & Tipton, S. M. (1985). *Habits of the heart.* Berkeley: University of California Press.

Berger, J. (1972). *Ways of seeing.* London: Penguin Books.

Berger, P., & Luckmann, T. (1967). *The social construction of reality.* Garden City, NY: Anchor.

Bertaux, D. (Ed.). (1981). *Biography and society.* Beverly Hills, CA: Sage.

Broude, N. & Garrard, M. D. (Eds.). (1982). *Feminism and art history.* New York: Harper & Row.

Butler, C. (1980). *After the wake: An essay on the contemporary avant-garde.* Oxford: Clarendon Press.

315

References

Canaday, J. (1969). *Culture gulch.* New York: Farrar, Straus, & Giroux.
Cheatwood, D. (1982). The private muse in the public world. In K. V. Mulcahy & C. R. Swaim (Eds.), *Public policy and the arts.* Boulder, CO: Westview Press.
Cork, R. (1979). *The social role of art.* London: Gordon Fraser.
Csikszentmihalyi, M. (1988). Society, culture, and person: A systems view of creativity. In R. J. Sternberg (Ed.), *The nature of creativity.* Cambridge: Cambridge University Press.
Csikszentmihalyi, M., Getzels, J. W., & Kahn, S. P. (1984). *Talent and achievement.* Chicago: Report to the Spencer and MacArthur Foundations.
Csikszentmihalyi, M., & Robinson, R. R. (1986). Culture, time, and the development of talent. In R. J. Sternberg & J. E. Davidson (Eds.), *Conceptions of giftedness.* Cambridge: Cambridge University Press.
Danto, A. C. (1981). *The transfiguration of the commonplace.* Cambridge, MA: Harvard University Press.
Davis, D. (1988). The billion dollar picture? *Art in Ameria, 7.*
Dickie, G. (1974). *Art and the aesthetic: An institutional analysis.* Ithaca, NY: Cornell University Press.
Durkheim, E. (1951). *Suicide.* New York: Free Press.
Eagleton, T. (1990). *The Ideology of the aesthetic.* Oxford: Basil Blackwell.
Elkoff, M. (1970). The American painter as a blue chip. In M. C. Albrecht, J. H. Barnett, & M. Griff (Eds.), *The sociology of art and literature.* New York: Praeger.
Feldman, D. H. (1988). Creativity: Dreams, insights, and transformations. In R. J. Sternberg (Ed.), *The nature of creativity.* Cambridge: Cambridge University Press.
Feldman, D. H., with A. C. Benjamin. (1986). Giftedness as a developmentalist sees it. In R. J. Sternberg & J. E. Davidson (Eds.), *Conceptions of giftedness.* Cambridge: Cambridge University Press.
Foster, H. (1985). *Recodings.* Seattle, WA: Bay Press.
Franklin, Margery B. (1989). A convergence of streams: Dramatic change in the artistic work of Melissa Zink. In Doris B. Wallace & Howard E. Gruber (Eds.), *Creative people at work.* New York: Oxford University Press.
Freeman, M. (1986). *The construction and destruction of young American artists: A critical inquiry into the conditions of artistic creation.* Unpublished doctoral dissertation, University of Chicago.

References

Freeman, M. (1990). Artistic creativity and the meaning of freedom. *Journal of Humanistic Psychology, 30*, 109–125.

Freeman, M. (1993a). What aesthetic development is not: An inquiry into the pathologies of postmodern creation. In M. B. Franklin & B. Kaplan (Eds.), *Development and the arts.* Hillsdale, NJ: Erlbaum.

Freeman, M. (1993b) *Rewriting the self: history, memory, narrative.* London: Routledge.

Fuller, P. (1980). *Beyond the crisis in modern art.* London: Writers and Readers.

Gablik, S. (1984). *Has modernism failed?* New York: Thames and Hudson.

Gadamer, H.-G. (1975). *Truth and method.* New York: Crossroad.

Gadamer, H.-G. (1979). The problem of historical consciousness. In P. Rabinow & W. M. Sullivan (Eds.), *Interpretive social science.* Berkeley: University of California Press.

Gardner, Howard (1988). Creative lives and creative works: A synthetic scientific approach. In Robert J. Sternberg (Ed.), *The nature of creativity.* Cambridge: Cambridge University Press.

Gedo, J. (1983). *Portraits of the artist.* New York: Guilford.

Geertz, C. (1973). *The interpretation of cultures.* New York: Basic.

Getzels, J. W., & Csikszentmihalyi, M. (1966). The study of creativity in future artists: The criterion problem. In O. J. Harvey (Ed.), *Experience, structure, and adaptability.* New York: Springer.

Getzels, J. W., & Csikszentmihalyi, M. (1969). Aesthetic opinion: An empirical study. *Public Opinion Quarterly, 33*, 34–45.

Getzels, J. W., & Csikszentmihalyi, M. (1975). From problem-solving to problem-solving to problem-finding. In I. A. Taylor & J. W. Getzels (Eds.), *Perspectives in creativity.* Chicago: Aldine.

Getzels, J. W., and Csikszentmihalyi, M. (1976). *The creative vision.* New York: John Wiley and Sons.

Gilbert-Rolfe, J. (1981). Art as style/style as art and the problem with that. *Triquarterly, 52*, 206–215.

Gilligan, C. (1982). *In a different voice.* Cambridge, MA: Harvard University Press.

Goodman, N. (1976). *Languages of art.* Indianapolis, IN: Hackett.

Greenberg, C. (1973). Counter-avant-garde. In M. Rader (Ed.), *A modern book of aesthetics.* New York: Holt, Rinehart, and Winston.

Gruber, H. E. (1986). The self-construction of the extraordinary. In R. J. Sternberg & J. E. Davidson (Eds.), *Conceptions of giftedness.* Cambridge: Cambridge University Press.

References

Gruber, H. E. (1989). The evolving systems approach to creative work. In D. B. Wallace & H. E. Gruber (Eds.), *Creative people at work.* New York: Oxford University Press.

Gruber, H. E., & Davis, S. N. (1988). Inching our way up Mount Olympus: The evolving-systems approach to creative thinking. In Robert J. Sternberg (Ed.), *The nature of creativity.* Cambridge: Cambridge University Press.

Habermas, J. (1983). Interpretive social science vs. hermeneuticism. In N. Haan et al. (Eds.), *Social science as moral inquiry.* New York: Columbia University Press.

Harries, K. (1968). *The meaning of modern art.* Evanston, IL: Northwestern University Press.

Hauser, A. (1979). *The sociology of art.* Chicago: University of Chicago Press.

Hennessey, Beth A., & Amabile, T. J. (1988). The conditions of creativity. In R. J. Sternberg (Ed.), *The nature of creativity.* Cambridge: Cambridge University Press.

Herman, J. (1978). The modern artist in modern society. In M. Greenhaugh & V. Megaw (Eds.), *Art in society.* New York: St. Martin's Press.

Jameson, F. (1983). Postmodernism and consumer society. In H. Foster (Ed.), *The anti-aesthetic.* Port Townsend, WA: Bay Press.

Jameson, F. (1988). On *Habits of the heart.* In C. H. Reynolds & R. V. Norman (Eds.), *Community in America: The challenge of* Habits of the Heart. Berkeley: University of California Press.

Kostelanetz, R. (1980). *Metamorphosis in the arts.* New York: Assembling Press.

Kramer, H. (1973). *The age of the avant-garde.* London: Secker & Warburg.

Lakoff, G., and Johnson, M. (1980). *Metaphors we live by.* Chicago: University of Chicago Press.

Lasch, C. (1984). *The minimal self.* New York: W. W. Norton.

Lasch, C. (1988). The communitarian critique of liberalism. In C. H. Reynolds & R. V. Norman (Eds.), *Community in America: The challenge of* Habits of the heart. Berkeley: University of California Press.

Lippard, L. (1984). *Get the message? A decade of art for social change.* New York: E. P. Dutton.

MacIntyre, A. (1981). *After virtue.* Notre Dame, IN: University of Notre Dame Press.

Marx, K. (1964). *Economic and philosophic manuscripts of 1844* In E. Fromm, *Marx's concept of man.* New York: Frederick Ungar Publishing.

Marx, K., & Engels, F. (1981). *The German ideology.* New York: International Publishers.

Messer, S. B., Sass, L. A., & Woolfolk, R. L. (Eds.). (1988). *Hermeneutics and psychological theory.* New Brunswick, NJ: Rutgers University Press.

Michels, C. (1983). *How to survive and prosper as an artist.* New York: Holt, Rinehart, and Winston.

Myron, R., and Sundell, A. (1971). *Modern art in America.* New York: Crowell Collier Press.

National Committee for Cultural Resources. (1975). *National report on the arts.* New York.

National Endowment for the Arts (1973). *New dimensions for the arts: 1971–1972.* Washington, DC: Government Printing Office.

National Endowment for the Arts (1982). *Artist employment and unemployment: 1971–1980.* New York: Publishing Center for Cultural Resources.

Nochlin, L. (1973). Why have there have been no great women artists? In E. Baker & T. Hess (Eds.), *Art and sexual politics.* London: Collier Macmillan.

Olney, J. (1972). *Metaphors of self: The meaning of autobiography.* Princeton: Princeton University Press.

Packer, M. J., & Addison, R. B. (Eds.). (1989). *Entering the circle: Hermeneutic investigation in psychology.* Albany, NY: SUNY Press.

Parker, R., & Pollock, G. (Eds.). (1987). *Framing feminism: Art and the women's movement, 1970–1985.* London: Pandora.

Perkins, D. N. (1988). The possibility of invention. In R. J. Sternberg (Ed.), *The nature of creativity.* Cambridge: Cambridge University Press.

Poggioli, R. (1968). *The theory of the avant-garde.* Cambridge, MA: Belknap Press.

Pollock, G. (1988). *Vision and difference: Femininity, feminism, and the histories of art.* London: Routledge.

Rabinow, P., & Sullivan, W. M. (Eds.). (1979). *Interpretive social science: A reader.* Berkeley: University of California Press.

Ratcliff, C. (1988). The marriage of art and money. *Art in America, 7.*

Read, H. (1963). *To hell with culture.* New York: Schocken Books.

Read, H. (1969). *Art and alienation.* New York: Viking Press.

319

Ricoeur, P. (1981). *Hermeneutics and the human sciences.* Cambridge: Cambridge University Press.

Ricoeur, P. (1983). *The rule of metaphor.* Toronto: University of Toronto Press.

Robins, C. (1984). *The pluralist era: American art, 1968–1981.* New York: Harper & Row.

Rosenberg, B., & Fliegel, N. (1965). *The vanguard artist: Portrait and self-portrait.* Chicago: Quadrangle Books.

Rosenberg, H. (1965). The art of Establishment. *Esquire, 63.*

Rosenberg, H. (1972). *The de-definition of art.* New York: Macmillan.

Rothenberg, A. (1979). *The emerging goddess.* Chicago: University of Chicago Press.

Said, E. W. (1983). Opponents, audiences, and constituencies. In H. Foster (Ed.), *The anti-aesthetic.* Port Townsend, WA: Bay Press.

Schutz, A. (1967). *The phenomenology of the social world.* Evanston, IL: Northwestern University Press.

Simpson, C. R. (1981). *SoHo: The artist in the City.* Chicago: University of Chicago Press.

Smagula, H. (1983). *Currents.* Englewood Cliffs, NJ: Prentice-Hall.

Steinberg, L. (1966). Contemporary art and the plight of its public. In G. Battcock (Ed.), *The new art.* New York: E. P. Dutton.

Sternberg, R. J. (Ed.). (1988). *The nature of creativity.* Cambridge: Cambridge University Press.

Tax, M. (1972). Culture is not neutral. Whom does it serve? In L. Baxandall (Ed.), *Radical perspectives in the arts.* Middlesex: Penguin Books.

Toffler, A. (1965). *The culture consumers.* Baltimore: Penguin Books.

Tolstoy, L. (1924). *What is art?* Oxford: Oxford University Press.

Tomkins, C. (1976). *The scene: Reports on post-modern art.* New York: Viking Press.

Vaillant, B. (1977). *Adaptation to life.* Boston: Little Brown.

Vasquez, A. S. (1973). *Art and society.* New York: Monthly Review Press.

Wallace, D. B., & Gruber, H. E. (Eds.). (1989). *Creative people at work.* New York: Oxford University Press.

Weber, M. (1985). *The protestant ethic and the spirit of capitalism.* London: Counterpoint.

Weisberg, Robert W. (1988). Problem solving and creativity. In Robert J. Sternberg (Ed.), *The nature of creativity.* Cambridge: Cambridge University Press.

References

White, H. (1978). *Tropics of discourse.* Baltimore: Johns Hopkins University Press.

Winner, D. (1982). *Invented worlds: The psychology of the arts.* Cambridge, MA: Harvard University Press.

Wraight, R. (1965). *The art game.* New York: Simon and Schuster.

Index

Abstract Expressionism, 5, 38, 111, 173, 179, 209, 218
Adams, H., 186
Addison, R.B., 29
Adler, J.E., 5
Adorno, T.W., 290
advertising, 139–40
affiliation, 270–1
affirmation, 167, 277–8
Africa, 226
alienation
    in art community, 123
    and commercial art, 138–9
    and demands on artists, 72
    and modernity, 230–1, 239–40
    and mystique of art, 255
    ownership as remedy, 281–3, 285
    pervasiveness of, 21, 171
    psychodynamic theory, 16–17, 59
    from social whole, 230–1
    in successful artists, 15
    of viewing public, 240
Amabile, T.J., 3, 12, 15
anomie, 123, 303
anxiety, 180, 294
    and pluralism, 189–90
art (*see also* art world)
    "democratization," 6–7, 145
    lack of cultural relevance, 241–3
    lack of transcendent value, 211

mystique of, 252–61
normative view, 10
priority in present-day society, 245
art community (*see* community)
art dealers
    control of market, 116, 155
    pressure on artists, 20–1, 201–2, 272
art education, 212, 236–7
art market (*see* market)
art school
    market influences, 224–5
    and women, 218–19
art world
    bitterness toward, 114–17
    bourgeois ethic of, 232
    commodification, 7–8, 212
    growth of, 5–6
    hermetic dimension, 226
    hustling in, 275–7
    New York as center, 112
    pluralism, 25, 189
    power structure, 116
"art worldly," 276–7
artist-madman myth, 44–5
artistic development
    and commodification, 7–8
    conditions for, 83–5
    and defiance of art mystique, 256–8
    finiteness, 50–3

323